Fat Talk

Fat Talk

A Feminist Perspective

DENISE MARTZ

McFarland & Company, Inc., Publishers
Jefferson, North Carolina

LIBRARY OF CONGRESS CATALOGUING-IN-PUBLICATION DATA

Names: Martz, Denise, 1967– author.
Title: Fat talk : a feminist perspective / Denise Martz.
Description: Jefferson, North Carolina : McFarland & Company, Inc., Publishers, [2019] | Includes bibliographical references and index.
Identifiers: LCCN 2019012865 | ISBN 9781476673042 (paperback : acid free paper) ∞
Subjects: LCSH: Body image in women. | Self-esteem in women. | Discrimination against overweight women. | Body weight— Public opinion.
Classification: LCC BF697.5.B63 M38 2019 | DDC 306.4/613082—dc23
LC record available at https://lccn.loc.gov/2019012865

BRITISH LIBRARY CATALOGUING DATA ARE AVAILABLE

ISBN (print) 978-1-4766-7304-2
ISBN (ebook) 978-1-4766-3584-2

Front cover images © 2019 Shutterstock

Printed in the United States of America

McFarland & Company, Inc., Publishers
  Box 611, Jefferson, North Carolina 28640
  www.mcfarlandpub.com

To my partner—John Paul Jameson—who shares my passion for science and social justice and encourages me to say what I need to say. He not only tolerated my obsessive writing style, but held my hand along the way.

Acknowledgments

First I would like to thank my parents, Peggy and Ron Martz, who have provided me with unwavering support across my career and in my life. I wish to thank my sons Christian Ludwig and Forrest Ludwig for their enduring love and ability to make me laugh. It has been a pleasure seeing you grow and being your Mom.

I could not have pursued this line of research without the brilliant colleagues who have made collaboration productive and fun: Lisa Curtin, Doris Bazzini, Rose Mary Webb, Amy Galloway, Courtney Rocheleau, Lucinda Payne, and Sandy Gagnon. There have been numerous students who have been willing to choose honors and master's thesis topics on fat talk that allowed me and my colleagues to mentor them while they learned and contributed to this body of research: Amy Barwick, Delvon Blue, Lauren Britton, Jennifer DeStephano, Amanda Driver, Jordan Ellis, Mallory Fiery, Lauren Francis, Christine Mikell, Cassidy Miles, Madison Morsch, Anna Petroff, Courtney Rogers, Crystal Thornhill, Brooke Tompkins, Kate Tucker, and Allison Warren.

During the writing of this book, I would like to thank Dr. Chris Holden for consultation on his expertise in evolutionary psychology. My research assistants offered me immense help with feedback about the readability of this work. I would like to thank Hadley Brochu, Margaret Booth, Katheryn Garwood, Jessica Hoon, Hayley Hughes, Amaka Imoh, Kelsey Lam, Elaine Mansure, Jaxeli Martinez, Tara O'Neil, Katie Rigali, Sophie Pillsbury, KG Smith, Alaina Swick, Natalie Vogel, and Dominic Ysidron for all of their editing advice.

This work has been a labor of love and I would not have been able to accomplish it without all of their wonderful support.

Table of Contents

Preface

Fat talk is defined as a communication exchange with the focus on individuals' physical appearance, especially critical dialogue pertaining to body fat, weight, shape, style, or fitness. This ritualistic form of conversation is common in girls and women. On the surface, this form of discourse may seem innocent and harmless, yet closer feminist analysis suggests that fat talk compromises individuals' self-esteem. Operating much like an addiction, engaging in fat talk brings some women short-term relief or reassurance, but scientific literature suggests this behavior is associated with poor body image, lower self-esteem, and eating disorders when done habitually. Speaking poorly about oneself to others reinforces those critical attitudes about the individual's identity. How will a woman personally rise and achieve equality in a culture that fosters her own fat talk? Feminist theory extends feminist politics into scholarship and aims to help scientists understand and remedy gender inequality in our society. Feminists should be very concerned about fat talk, as this toxic dialogue is a way that women have become their own private enemies.

While fat talk primarily focuses on oneself, another modern adversary for women involves bullying about physical appearance. *Body snarking*—also called fat shaming—is when people say, print, or post public critiques of women's appearance on social media, often anonymously. Snarking women about their appearance, and whether or not they adhere to our culture's gender role expectations, strips many targeted victims of their perceived influence, effectiveness, and power. Snarking is a symptom of a larger form of sexism and misogyny in U.S. culture. How are women, collectively, to rise and achieve social and political equality in a society that supports this nasty form of bullying towards women? From a feminist perspective, people who cut other women down through body snarking are also women's worst enemies. This book will apply feminist theory to extant scientific research to help readers understand women's fat talk and why women are the victims of body snarking. These behaviors are understandable considering human evolution and modern Western culture. However, they are *not* excusable! My goal is to inspire a feminist agenda to reduce both of these toxic forms of communication—our *feminine enemies.*

This book will review and analyze the origins of fat talk and body snarking. Such dialogue taps into a historic dispute between evolutionary psychology/biology and feminist theory scholars (i.e., the classic "nature versus nurture" debate). Although feminist scholars and evolutionary researchers have often disagreed politically over the other's conclusions about extant scholarship on women's issues, I will propose an integrative feminist and scientific analysis of our feminine enemies. Rather than asking if fat talk and body snarking are derived from nature versus nurture, I prefer the question, "How have nature *and* nurture interacted reciprocally across human evolution to arrive at our modern-day culture that reinforces these conversational habits?" Understanding the forces that drive fat talk and body snarking will be key to determining how to formulate personal and social change. I will argue that the scientific evidence, supporting the meta-theory of evolutionary psychology, explains why human beings have evolved to value beauty—especially as an attribute in women. Evolutionary adaptations, such as the human tendency to notice another person's appearance, are products of varied environments across extensive human history. As such, fat talk for many women is commentary about one's own attractiveness or appearance, in attempts to create or manage the impression of others. Body snarking, as an aggressive form of gossip, is a method of feeling better about oneself by cutting others down. As a type of intra-sexual competition, according to evolutionary theory, body snarking reduces the social attractiveness of the target woman. This provides the aggressor with more social dominance and greater access to potential mates. Our feminine enemies function in ways that help people manage their insecurities and feel better about themselves, while damaging self-esteem and maintaining societal misogyny in the long term. Both represent the distasteful aspects of modern-day humanity.

Human evolutionary mechanisms always have environmental context; thus, I will argue that contemporary culture also has tremendous influence on the modern-day obsession with female beauty. Although appearance ideals for women have fluctuated somewhat across documented history, these standards have dependably emphasized physical images that women do *not* look like men, and women's beauty imperatives have consistently symbolized standards that convey female fertility to others. Ideals for men include taller height, more muscularity, and the V-shape broad shoulders and chest indicating male strength. Conversely, ideal beauty for women usually consists of the hourglass design and includes curves that indicate fat deposits in the breasts, hips, buttocks, and thighs, as well as facial features that signal youth and femininity. A feminine aesthetic that clearly signals womanhood and fertility has been key to heterosexual mate selection and effective human reproduction over time. Fertility signaling is especially important considering that humans have concealed ovulation, as opposed to the obvious and dramatic fertile estrous period like the mammals from which we have evolved. Consequently, in contemporary culture, many women's ambition to appear youthful and beautiful is a means to facilitate attention from others, including possible mates.

Humans are wired to notice the physical features of those who surround them, as these are key perceptions for forming impressions of others and for finding mates. Most people are unaware that these evolutionary forces are operating within them today, but evolutionary psychology research confirms their presence. Present-day fat talk and body snarking will be explained as a product of evolutionary forces interacting with contemporary culture as the foundation for why these behaviors exist. In the 1990s Mimi Nichter coined the term "fat talk" to reflect girls' commentary about their body fat in response to the cultural thin ideal for Caucasian girls at the time. In this book, our feminine enemies will be discussed broadly as negative dialogue about oneself or other women in regards to physical appearance—thus extending Nichter's definition beyond critique about body fat specifically. I will present research on how gender, race, and age are predictors for those who do and do not engage in this type of dialogue as a function of their standards about physical appearance. The appearance ideal that dominates American culture is a thin and fit-looking woman who is dressed femininely, if not sexily, with a body type that has sufficient curves to communicate that she is indeed a woman— not a man. Yet popular media oftentimes heralds feminine ideals that grossly exaggerate unique aspects of a feminine body. Prescribed methods of feminine embellishment have evolved over time and across cultures (e.g., historic corsets that thinned waistlines; modern buttock/thigh implants to enhance "booty"), but these ideals are always about enhancing unique feminine features—especially those that convey fertility and heterosexuality. Conversely, dominant historical norms and cultures have rarely heralded beauty ideals for women expressing features associated with masculinity (e.g., facial hair, broad shoulders, very short hairstyles, square waists & hips). Note that these ideals represent preferences for heterosexual men and women because they indicate qualities in mates that would make for the most successful reproduction and propagation of their DNA into the human gene pool. These appearance ideals are often questioned and rejected by contemporary men and women who do not identify as cisgender or who do not identify as heterosexual, as well as others who ascribe to more flexible, fluid, and individualistic appearance options. Modern feminism, which embraces issues of intersectionality, advocates for more flexible equality for any groups experiencing societal oppression. Although evolutionary biology and psychology explain why many critique their own and other women's physical appearance, these sociocultural influences on these habits of dialogue and messaging are not above reproach. Understanding their origins is important for the purpose of explicit personal reflection and strategic activism that helps our society move beyond such gender, racial, and sexual identity stereotypes.

The socialization of exaggerated heterosexual-normative appearance ideals begins in childhood for most girls. This book will review the science on the effects of Barbie dolls as well as exposure to Western idolization of Disney princesses. Present-day media—both traditional forms and social media—affect beauty values, women's body image, and fat talk. After establishing why many individuals engage in fat talk, the research showing its associations with pathology, specifically poor body image, internalization of the cultural thin ideal, and eating disorders will be presented. I assert that fat talk takes on somewhat of an addiction process for those who participate in it habitually. Girls and women fat talk to feel better in the short term, but chronic use of the behavior creates more damage across a lifespan. Fat talk has been documented as harmful for individuals who initiate the conversations. Reminiscent of exposure to second-hand smoke, fat talk it is also damaging for those who have to listen to it. From a feminist stance, fat talk is an unintentional way in which women have become their own worst enemies. How can women achieve equality in this culture when they are bringing themselves down?

Perhaps even more aggressive is the use of body snarking that suppresses targeted women. Similar to the impulse to engage in fat talk, the desire to bully women into subjugation has origins in the meta-theory of evolutionary psychology of intra-sexual mate competition. In modern culture, snarking tends to be directed mostly at women and fits into feminist concerns regarding women's objectification, especially sexual objectification. Social media has created the possibility for internet trolls and bullies to engage in this aggression, often anonymously. Contrariwise, American culture unfortunately embraces fat stigma because most lay individuals believe that obesity is caused by individuals' character flaws, and that obesity is always unhealthy. I will review the fat shaming and fat stigma literature to explain the origins of body snarking, yet I will also clarify that the scientific literature does not support the stereotypes associated with obesity. Both the Fat Acceptance Movement and the Health at Every Size organization are advocacy groups fighting fat stigma and the common cultural stereotypes of obesity in the United States. The traditional medical philosophy, on the other hand, which most Americans include in their stereotypes, posits that overweight and obesity are always unhealthy; thus, large people must lose weight for their psychological and physical health. These two divisive schools of thought about obesity will be reviewed to illustrate this contemporary controversy. A health behavior change approach will be introduced as a way to reconcile this debate. Even if women have not been victims of body snarking personally, this behavior has probably affected them culturally and politically. What was once bullying towards women that took place either face-to-face or within gossip, current media (i.e., internet sites, social media applications, and 24-hour news shows) have allowed this snarking to become public and pervasive. Celebrities who tend to have a frequent presence in the public eye are often targets of trolls who critique their weight, their shape, and their fashion. In addition to being nasty at times, these posts distract attention from what the female celebrities have accomplished in their acting, musical, or comedic careers. An even more pernicious distraction is how reporters have gender stereotyped and snarked women running for public office. Rather than point to their capabilities and views on policies, reporters often focus critically on their appearance, or they focus on their relationships with others. This is an important feminist issue if political candidates, who are much more likely to support gender equality and policy addressing oppression of other marginalized groups, are bullied by media in a manner that sways voters. Body snarking is one of the factors contributing to America's inability to elect political candidates who represent feminist policies and activism.

Fat talk and body snarking have been extremely damaging for a feminist agenda in U.S. culture, and many individuals today are unaware of the pervasiveness of these feminine enemies in our psyches and society. I assert that interdisciplinary study of the forces that support these toxic forms of communication are key to designing interventions for change. The social psychology research from my research lab and others has shown a very interesting disconnect—women *think* other women fat talk as a means of showing humility and bonding with other women, yet they *personally* seem to prefer hearing self-acceptance and confidence from other women. This phenomenon is called pluralistic ignorance by social psychologists, and it describes how unhealthy norms, such as women's tendency to fat talk, are maintained in society. This provides researchers with some optimism for how to attempt to end fat talk in the future. The penultimate chapter will remind us of the feminist adage that the "personal is political" and offer evidence-based interventions such as cognitive behavioral therapy, acceptance and commitment therapy, compassion-focused therapies, and exercise interventions that can assist women in personal change of their self-esteem, body image, and eating disorders in the quest to address personal fat talk and its psychological sequelae. There are some wonderful ways that women can secure a better relationship with their bodies, food, and exercise by breaking free from these unrealistic appearance ideals.

The end of the book will focus on ongoing activism and scientifically-studied community interventions targeting body image issues, eating disorder prevention, and fat talk interventions. I will note that some of these interventions have actually backfired and made things worse once their impact was scientifically evaluated. I will review Operation Beautiful and how it has affected fat talk and women's need to feel attractive. Tri Delta Sorority has held what it calls Fat Talk Free Weeks on their college campuses, and one study has found a positive outcome from this intervention. Finally, I will review how *The Body Project* has been effective in improving young women's self-esteem, body image, and in preventing eating disorders. Members of my research team and I recently attended *The Body Project* peer-leader training program, brought to our campus by our counseling center. Trainees evaluated U.S. appearance ideals and made arguments countering these unhealthy norms. They effectively rehearsed responses to others' fat talk to build communication skills that break free from these habits. A scientific approach is necessary to find effective interventions for women personally or interventions that change American culture in order to empower women as we strive for social and political equality and to overcome our feminine enemies.

This book is meant to be a feminist analysis of how fat talk is associated with feminine objectification and gender stereotyping while using relevant scientific research throughout. It has been written for educational purposes and could be used in psychology, sociology, behavioral biology, linguistics, and women's studies courses. I hope that the narration throughout the book helps bring the reports of our feminine enemies to life in a manner that can be understood by students, scholars, or anyone interested in learning more about this common form of social dialogue. Consequently, there are references to popular culture throughout the book to help make discussion of fat talk and body snarking timely and relevant to readers' daily lives. Note that I have delved more specifically into the research methodology and statistics on the studies directly associated with fat talk for more in-depth instruction on research methodology and inferential statistics. Conversely, ancillary studies will emphasize less of the methodology and simply review and compile their results and meaning. As such, this book is meant to educate students on both interdisciplinary sciences and feminist theory. Throughout the book, I will use the universal term "we" to mean girls and women, "we" as feminists, and at times, "we" as humanity. As a feminist and a scientist, this use of the word "we" emphasizes my personal commitment and investment in advocacy to eliminate our feminine enemies so that we advance gender equality in our culture. This book will integrate research from biology, sociology, communications studies, political science, clinical psychology, community psychology, and feminist theory in a manner that tells a story about why girls and women engage in fat talk and body snarking, as well as how we can act as social activists to end these forces that are disempowering female citizens of our world. Whether they are examined on the individual, interpersonal, or societal level, fat talk and body snarking are indeed feminist issues. As an attendee of the Women's March in Washington, D.C., in January 2017, I was reminded that feminists have some serious problems to address, both on the home front and internationally. Power for change comes in numbers and through the collective optimism that we can make a difference. This book will use known scientific scholarship to help us understand why this problem exists and how we can intentionally break these toxic forms of feminine communication—our feminine enemies.

1

The Evolution of Fat Talk

"We recognize that we are collective agents of history and that history cannot be deleted like web pages."—Angela Davis, American political activist, scholar, author

The following scene eavesdrops on the high school girls featured in Rosalind Wiseman's novel *Mean Girls*.

Having lived in rural Africa with her parents, teenager Cady has joined a new high school. There is a popular clique of young women known as the "Plastics" that Cady is getting to know. While looking in a full-length mirror in Regina's bedroom together...

KAREN: "God my hips are huge!"
GRETCHEN: "Oh please. I hate my calves."
REGINA: "But you guys can wear halters. I've got man shoulders."
CADY: [voiceover of thoughts] I used to think there was just fat and skinny. But apparently there's lots of things that can be wrong on your body.
GRETCHEN: "My hairline is so weird."
REGINA: "My pores are huge."
KAREN: "My nail beds suck."
[They all look to Cady for her response.]
CADY: [Feeling pressure to join in and say something] "I have really bad breath in the mornings."
They respond "Eww!"

Later on in the school cafeteria...

REGINA: "I really want to lose three pounds." [Nobody jumps on the response, until Regina gives them all a dirty look.]
GRETCHEN: [Jolted into realization of her need to reassure] "Oh my God what are you talking about?"
KAREN: "You are so skinny."

These are examples of fat talk from the film *Mean Girls* (2004). These conversations illustrate that fat talk can indeed be critique about actual body fat or it can be defined more broadly as *any type* of derogatory comments about one's appearance. In a later scene, these high school girls also demonstrate that fat talk is intended to elicit support from one's friends or family members. When one girl fat talks, the expectation is that others reassure her that she is *not* fat and then they are supposed to reciprocate with their own appearance critique. As examples of fat talk in an unscripted world, Fortin (2014) made a YouTube clip called "Fat Talk—The Recognized Epidemic," in which she shares clips of what real young women tend to say in fat talk:

"Ugh, I have thunder thighs."
"This shirt makes me look big."
"My face is so fat."

"I wish I could be a little more thinner. Mainly I want to build more muscle. I don't think my body is the size I want to be yet because I'm not confident, not fully confident with how I look yet. So, I'm still working on it."

Fat talk is broadly defined as a communication exchange with the focus on an individual's physical appearance, especially critical dialogue pertaining to body fat, weight, shape, style, or fitness (Martz, Curtin, & Bazzini, 2012). For instance, in the dialogue of the young women featured in the YouTube segment quoted above, they engage in fat talking but there is also a sense that they are conflicted about it. As this book describes, fat talk is understandable considering multiple influences including our culture and our evolutionary background, and yet, fat talk is unfortunate and inexcusable. Women can be their own worst enemies with their fat talk and at times to other women when body snarking or fat shaming others. As this book will show, these feminine enemies are quite harmful. So why do we engage in such behavior? Fat talk, as a normative phenomenon, brings some women short-term reassurance and relief, but results in long-term personal and societal harm. In that regard, fat talk functions somewhat like an addiction. It is a way for women to feel better about feeling bad about their bodies, while simultaneously implying all girls/women feel the same way. Current science—that will be covered in this book—suggests fat talk is associated with depression, poor body image, eating disorders, body shame, social anxiety, and low self-esteem. Further, body snarking is a very powerful way to harm another person and create serious damage for its female victims. Body snarking has targeted female celebrities and female political candidates. Although the societal forces influencing the 2016 presidential election were complex, body snarking and gender role stereotyping may have kept a woman from the U.S. presidency. Fat talk and body snarking reinforce sexism and misogyny in our culture. They are significant contemporary feminist issues.

Fat Talk Has Evolved from Multiple Contexts

Social scientists have long documented how girls and women tend to feel critical about their bodies compared to their male counterparts (Feingold & Mazzella, 1998). Such body image dissatisfaction is understandable— yet unfortunate—and has recently consumed the conversations amongst many women. Based on their research and interviews of Caucasian middle school girls and their mothers, anthropologists Mimi Nichter and Nancy Vuckovic (1994) coined the phrase *fat talk* to describe this ritualized and reciprocated discourse. Fat talk is broadly defined as a communication exchange with the focus on individuals' physical appearance, especially critique pertaining to body fat, weight, shape, style, or fitness (Martz et al., 2012). Fat talk appears to be rather common, especially in certain demographics. Becker, Diedrichs, Jankowski, and Werchan (2013) conducted an international online survey of women throughout the adult age range and found that 81 percent reported engaging in occasional fat talk and 33 percent reported engaging frequently in this behavior. Among predominantly Caucasian college women, up to 93 percent report engaging in fat talk (Salk & Engeln-Maddox, 2011). While inherently feminine in nature, and with sharp gender differences in reported frequency (Martz, Petroff, Curtin, & Bazzini, 2009; Payne, Martz, Tompkins, Petroff, & Farrow, 2010), fat talk is like a compulsive addiction. This is because fat talk can create short-term personal relief, interpersonal intimacy, and may result in reassurance (Salk & Engeln-Maddox, 2011), yet it is also associated with significant negative consequences in the long-term (e.g., depression; Arroyo & Harwood, 2012; Arroyo, Segrin, & Harwood, 2014; Rudiger & Winstead, 2013; Shannon & Mills, 2015). Indeed, from a feminist stance, fat talk is a means by which women become their own worst enemies. It is a symptom of a larger societal problem. Some of women's inability to achieve equality in our culture is the result of covert oppression by others; however, women perpetuate and participate in some subjugation. Fat talk is a way to cut oneself down, and body snarking is an aggressive way to damage other women. We, as women, need to *own* this reality before we can move towards needed change. I have been researching and speaking about fat talk for over a decade now. As soon as my students learn a name for it, they return to me surprised by how often they encounter the phenomenon. Much like invisible airborne pathogens lingering in the dry winter air waiting to give us the flu, fat talk surrounds many of us without our knowledge. We are oblivious to its ability to gnaw away at self-esteem, body image, and our collective feminist energy to conquer more important social and political issues. If you were not aware of fat talk dialogue before— or had no name for what you spoke or heard—I bet your awareness will be growing soon.

Dr. Deborah Tannen (1990) is a sociolinguist who researches gender differences in how women and men in the U.S. speak differently in general. She specializes in what is called *discourse analysis*—messaging which is conveyed in language beyond the actual words (Tannen, 1994). In her book *You Just Don't Understand: Women and Men in Conversation*, she describes many of the motivations and benefits in how girls and women speak to one another. She writes that their "conversations are negotiations for closeness in which people try to seek and give confirmation and support, and to reach consensus" (p. 25). Fat talk can be construed as a type of feminine dialogue. U.S. culture fosters a norm for girls and women to present as humble when they are self-confident.

If women appear to be too confident, then they are considered to be arrogant—or, at worst, bitches. If women deviate too far on the other end of the spectrum past humble, then they are considered to be insecure—or, at worst, mentally ill. Hence, women walk a fine line in how they present themselves to others. There are forces in how women learn to use language that keep them more uniform with one another instead of fostering diversity and individuality (Tannen, 1994).

Fat talk is a means of acknowledging that women do not think their bodies are perfect. Women are humble, noncompetitive, and more interested in building rapport than in making enemies. As Tannen (1990) says, "Girls are expected not to boast about it, or show that they think they are better than others" (p. 44). Girls and women talk to one another in ways that build rapport, relationships, intimacy, and community, whereas boys and men tend to speak competitively in order to create hierarchies of power and status. Much like speaking about the weather in a polite conversational interchange while buying coffee, or similar to the way that some men find the universal male language in sports dialogue, fat talk is a way that women often find common ground. Girls and women in the United States know that females' body image is a sensitive topic and that many of our friends and family members harbor concerns and insecurities. As such, body image is a common feminine agonist. Some believe fat talk helps girls and women feel better by talking about feeling badly about their bodies with one another. If it has been raining for a week and you have grown weary from lack of sunshine and the ability to do anything outside, it is comforting to know that the grocery clerk, whom you do not know personally, is also feeling a bit depressed by the wet weather. Even for strangers, finding common ground helps us feel like we are in this together.

Fat talk is so normative—especially for Caucasian girls and women in the United States—that we know it can help individuals find common ground. Even women who dislike fat talk know that they are supposed to reassure another person who has initiated the dialogue. Tannen (1990) notes for women that "language of conversation is primarily a language of rapport: a way of establishing connections and negotiating relationships. Emphasis is placed on displaying similarities and matching experiences" (p. 77). If an acquaintance complains about weight gain, most women can find something that they dislike about their appearance, even if it is the woman with straight, thin hair wishing she had long, heavy, curly locks, or the woman with wavy hair expressing admiration for the sleek, straight look. That is what is so amusing about Cady's response to her new friends in Rosalind Wiseman and Tina Fey's *Mean Girls*. Cady had been in rural Africa most of her life and now lives in Chicago. Her new friends stand in front of a full-length mirror, each taking turns critiquing their looks. Then Cady thinks, "I used to think there was just fat and skinny. But apparently there's lots of things that can be wrong on your body." She is struggling to understand the nuances and the reciprocity of the fat talk, which is why the line is funny. She responds with the worst thing she can think about herself and mumbles something to her friends about sometimes having really bad breath in the mornings. Just like we can admire the sunshine or complain about the weeklong rain, girls and women *know* how to make conversation about their bodies, faces, and appearance. However, when we discuss the weather with a stranger or people discuss sports with one another, it builds a sense of community *without* harm. Fat talk, on the other hand, may seem innocent enough, but it is insidious for women personally and maintains a cultural sense that they deserve objectification for their appearance. Thus, it *does* create harm because it perpetuates sexism and misogyny. Fat talk is a feminist issue!

Evolutionary Context of Fat Talk

Although fat talk may feel like a contemporary social trend, exploring the origins of this conversational style takes us back to the evolution of human life on earth. The meta-theory of evolutionary biology and psychology is a theoretical and scientific approach to the social and natural sciences that examines how human behavior is a function of natural selection and sexual selection across human ancestry. Evolutionary psychology tends to focus on human psychological structure and behavioral tendencies, whereas evolutionary biology tends to focus on how human anatomy and physiology have evolved. These inherited tendencies can be both adaptive and maladaptive depending on the context. The tendency to engage in fat talk or to body snark others is an evolutionary remnant of humans' value of beauty that can be considered maladaptive in contemporary society. In order to appreciate how evolutionary remnants function in modern day life, I will first highlight some examples of how our behavioral tendencies work for us or against us.

Some of our anatomy, physiology, and behaviors remain very adaptive. For example, the way our opposing thumbs and fingers work in our hands is remarkable compared to most mammals. When I teach about nutrition in class, we talk about how plants with the most pigmentation are the healthiest. Ideally, we are consuming the "rainbow diet" composed of foods with bright pigment such as berries, salmon, and broccoli (Walsh, 2011). Since humans had to forage for nutritious food throughout history, it makes sense that we have evolved to see in color. The ability helped us eat well, survive, and reproduce. Further, human sex drive has evolved in a manner to maximize the chances of reproduction. Humans, compared to other mammals, do not have an obvious estrous cycle or go into "heat." Consequently, women can be sexually receptive at any phase in the menstrual cycle. Also, humans engage in sex for love and for pleasure regardless of a desire to reproduce. This enduring desire for sexual activity has maximized the probability of reproduction across the lifespan for our species.

Conversely, many of these genetic behavioral tendencies that were incredibly adaptive across history can be maladaptive in contemporary society. If you have ever almost been in a car accident, you know how quickly that adrenaline circulates and fuels muscles for energy and movement. If the crash is averted, you sit there shaking with excess energy for quite some time. As I teach my students about stress, I emphasize how this *fight, flight,* or *freeze* response had survival value in a very dangerous, ancient world. Across evolution, humans were hunted by large prey and either fought back, ran away, or froze and played dead in attempts to stay alive when animals were trying to eat them. This lightning-fast physiological response was adaptive to life and therefore allowed humans to reproduce and pass genes that programmed this response into the next generation. If you are ever bothered by someone who is high strung and uptight, you can reflect on the fact that their behavior was caused by the same genes that facilitated human survival. We all have this fight, flight, or freeze response hardwired into our autonomic nervous system. I can think of thousands of times that my brain and my body have experienced one of these responses, but there have been very few times that the response was adaptive in modern life. Once I had to undo a seatbelt and jump off of a runaway mowing tractor as it slid over an embankment on a steep hill in wet grass. The whole act did not seem to require a single thought. I saw the threat and my adrenal glands went into speedy action, giving me the powerful energy to jump off quickly. I lay physically unscathed on my lawn shaking uncontrollably for quite some time, quietly saying a prayer of thanks to still be alive. The tractor fell over the embankment and crashed nose-first onto the pavement. I can testify personally that this very quick fight or flight reaction can be lifesaving. However, these same fight, flight, and freeze responses—which are quick and powerful physical, emotional, and psychological responses—are not very effective with many contemporary stressors, especially when we conjure up imaginary stressful events that have not even occurred in real life. Fretting over an uncomfortable conversation or panicking during a challenging college final exam are some examples when this hardwired anxiety reaction tends to backfire. Thus, evolutionary theory lends explanation for how human bodies look and function and how human brains tend to behave. In modern society, these adaptations have function and dysfunction, and many tend to be contextual.

Fat talk is a way to verbalize in modern-day western culture that women care about physical attractiveness and worry about how they measure up. Signal theory in evolutionary psychology proposes that humans have inherited appearance qualities that communicate information about them to other people. Beauty *signals* or conveys to others that people are healthy, vibrant, and disease-free. The opposite of this would be someone with disease, injury, or deformity. It is challenging to watch somebody who is injured, diseased, or sick—not only because we feel empathy for their pain and suffering, but also because it breeds some sense of fear in us that being close to them could mean we are also in danger. This is why individuals often psychologically blame victims of assault, rather than the sexual perpetrators, in their thoughts and conversations. Known as *blaming the victim*, a classic example would be asking what a woman was wearing or if she had been drinking alcohol after learning that she had been raped. If the human mind can figure out what *she* did wrong, then *we* can make sure that we do not do that same thing and land ourselves in that horrible situation. In reality, it does not matter what this woman was wearing or what she did or did not do. Her clothes did not cause the rape. The perpetrator is to blame. Yet, you hear about this type of questioning and victim blaming frequently. Done rather unconsciously, victim blaming is not intended to harm the victim, even though it often does. It functions to keep the audience psychologically protected. Again, if we can find fault in what the victim did "wrong," we can protect ourselves from doing that "wrong" thing in the future so that we do not fall victim to sexual assault. Thus, some of our instinctive thought habits are twisted because of our evolutionary wiring. In this way our brains often work in a manner more fitting for human history than modern times. Our perception of what we consider to be beautiful works the same way.

Fat talk and body snarking are conversational extensions of how the perception of beauty functions in the 21st century. Beauty conveys many things to others. Beauty can signal youth—meaning that if a man invests in this woman, she will have lots of time to offer him a return on that investment through her reproductive potential. Keep in mind that humans did not always have a life expectancy into the late 70s or early 80s. Youth has been very important throughout evolution because humans once transitioned from youth to old age very quickly. Further, beauty in women signals fertility to men, which has been especially important because human ovulation is concealed, rather than an obvious estrous period of fertility like our mammalian ancestors, the chimpanzees. Relational investment in a young, beautiful woman renders the possibility of some lovely, disease-free children. Beyond reproduction potential, affiliation with beautiful women raises men's social status. While he may not appear to be attractive himself, he may look much better with a beautiful woman by his side. He becomes beautiful-by-proxy. This is why many older, rich, and powerful men find younger, beautiful women, usually fashion models, or other famous women to marry (e.g., Donald & Melania Trump). Those bonds can satisfy evolutionary drives in both the husband and the wife. Beauty in this regard means choice, promise, and power. While some of these preferences are socialized and learned, many of them are hardwired in us so strongly that they begin operating soon after birth. Human infants instinctively prefer attractive faces, and evolutionary theory has explanations as to why. Babies pursue and lock gazes onto human faces to pay close attention to the people who take care of them. Human infants are born excessively dependent on their caretakers, and for a longer period of time than any other mammal. As an example, most do not walk until they are at least one year of age, and they certainly do not begin walking quickly and reliably enough to keep up with the adult pack. Human parents must feed and nurse them, bathe and change them, and carry them around for a long time. This delights the companies that make products like strollers and other baby carriers. I recently heard a story on NPR about a deluxe baby stroller that sells for $1,600! I thought to myself that $1,600 was enough to buy a used car back when I was pushing around my sons in their $30 hammock strollers, and they turned out just fine. The baby industry is making some good money off of the human baby's deep and lengthy dependency needs.

Evolutionary biology and psychology explain why human babies are equipped at finding human faces. Those faces should be able to take care of that little baby's needs whether it is thirst, hunger, a dirty diaper, or time for cuddling and interaction. This desire for faces, particularly for cute and attractive features, explains our love of stuffed animals and dolls. Remember the closet scene from *ET* (Mathison & Spielberg, 1982), when ET was in little Gertie's (i.e., young Drew Barrymore's) closet full of stuffed animals all lined up looking in the same direction? What a cute scene! Attraction to human faces for basic care and survival is one reason why infants lock their gaze on human faces. However, even when presented with pictures of strangers, who are not going to take care of these basic needs, babies still prefer attractive individuals over unattractive individuals. This also has an evolutionary explanation.

Judith Langlois and her team have conducted a series of studies examining human infant preference for attractive faces. The research method that they use is to have photographs previously rated for attractiveness by multiple adults. Adults tend to have strong consensus in what they find to be attractive and unattractive in these pre-rated photos (Langlois et al., 2000). They take the photos rated by adults as being most and least attractive and they show the photos to babies in random order. The researchers then time how long the infants gaze at each photo. A longer gaze indicates the baby's desire to connect and interact and is a sign that the baby sees the face as attractive. And it is logically assumed that three to six-month-old babies have *not* learned cultural biases about beauty and appearance. Langlois, Ritter, Roggman, and Vaughn (1991) conducted three of these studies and were able to show not only that six-month-old infants prefer attractive to unattractive faces, but that they did so regardless of the sex, age, and race of the faces. And these faces are those of strangers. They are not faces of potential caretakers—the people who will likely feed, burp, and cuddle with them. To explain why these infants see attractiveness in diverse faces, we return to another evolutionary mechanism.

Langlois and Roggman (1990) have studied how people tend to find faces that resemble a human prototype to be more attractive than faces with very unique and distinct features. They have digitalized pictures of different faces together and have found that their participants rate the digitalized and averaged faces as more attractive than single photos of individuals voted to be attractive. Also, they found that the level of attractiveness increased as a result of adding more and more photos into this visual human melting pot. They state that evolutionary biologists would say that average is good because the genes of individuals that have been averaged across natural selection are the genes that have maximized survival. Individuals with very unique features could be carrying harmful genetic mutations. Thus, there is security in looking average. Moreover, this beauty standard is detectable by human babies whether they are finding it in men or women, young or old, Caucasian, Hispanic, African American, or Asian. Human evolution occurred all over the world and we *all* carry this beauty ideal in the collective eye of the beholder.

Evolutionary Explanation for Why Beauty Is More Important for Girls and Women

If humans are wired to favor attractive individuals starting in infancy, then why do girls and women feel *more* pressure to be physically attractive than boys and men? Evolutionary biology and psychology help us to understand this phenomenon also. Charles Darwin (1871) proposed that both natural selection and sexual/mate selection are responsible for the evolution of humankind. The genes humans carry have been adaptive across history. They explain how human bodies are made and much of programmed behavior. The genes that were maladaptive lead to death. When dead, there is no repro-duction. If there is no reproduction, there is no passing of those genes into the next generation. Conversely, genes that dictated survival and successful mate attraction and reproduction were the genes that were passed down in the human genome. Human genes dictate what people find to be attractive in others as well as assets within them that are attractive to potential mates.

Sexual mate selection involves the attraction to certain qualities in a partner that bode well for one's self personally and possible future children for both men and women. In this regard, humans pay attention to physical, personality, and behavioral characteristics of others in their mating prefer-ences and choices. While this sounds so clinical and sterile ("I chose my mate because of his strong broad shoulders"), these forces of attraction in hetero-sexuals are alive and well in modern culture. And in contemporary times, most people feel like these perceptions and behaviors just come naturally to them. They are usually unaware of the commanding historic nature of these forces. What we find attractive in who we wish to date and become romantic with generalizes to what we tend to find attractive in friends, family, and even strangers shown in media and advertising. When I give my lectures on body image, fat talk, and eating disorders, my students often get passionately fired up when discussing our culture. I get it. Modern media is rather sexist and condescending to women. It makes me mad, too, and you will hear more about my opinion and the science about this in the body snarking chapter that follows. What my students often struggle with, however, is the fact that we humans program the media. I jokingly say to my students when we want to blame the media on all that is wrong in the body image/fat talk world, "I like watching a movie where George Clooney is shirtless and doing strength training with the pull up bar in his doorway." That is entertainment for me, at least … and I bet I am not the only woman with a Clooney crush. The fashion industry, the movie industry, the broader entertainment industry, and commercial advertising clearly know what humans like to view. The influences go both ways. We pick our media and the media reinforces who we are and who we wish to be. This also explains how images in media evolve with other cultural norms. Current media is portraying some idealistic women who are much curvier than previous generations that heralded thin-ner women (e.g., Calista Flockhart as Ally McBeal). In real women, thinness in one part of the body is usually reflected in thinness in other parts. Body fat creating curves in one part is typically associated with body fat and curves elsewhere. Today we have some alternative ideals for women's bodies that are now rather unrealistic in unique ways. As examples, we have the Kardashian sisters and rapper Nicki Minaj, who have some very curvy parts (e.g., breasts & buttocks) but also some very thin body parts such as waist, arms, and face. Most normal women are not shaped like this alternative ideal and may be reaching for cosmetic procedures—like butt implants—to achieve this "big booty" look. Regardless, the parts that women are accentuating continue to be body parts associated with feminine sexuality; thus, again this could be modern-day women's attempt to appear attractive to men for sexual selection. Evolutionary forces are still upon us.

When humans consider whom to date and with whom to form committed romantic relationships, the forces of human perception and attraction are clearly operating. This makes some sense in that these are individuals who people pick to look at *a lot* and for a *long time.* Obviously there are many more qualities that individuals find attractive in potential mates. Relationships are not just about two people staring at one another into eternity, but I think you get my point about how powerful physical attraction can be. There is a plethora of research validating these evolutionary remnants in modern-day human behavior. Buss (1989) produced a review paper assessing heterosexual men and women's differences in human mate preferences across 37 *different* cultures and verified that women value in men the qualities considered to be more broadly defined as "resource acquisition"—ambition, security, ability to make money—and men appreciate in women the qualities that could be considered "reproductive capacity," an impression surmised from women's physical appearance. The cross-cultural nature of what men and women tend to find attractive is a testament to the universality of genetic wiring. As a more specific example, Buss and Barnes (1986) surveyed married couples inquiring about their favorite partner qualities out of 76 possible human characteristics. Women chose "considerate," "honest," "dependable," "kind," "understanding," "fond of children," "good earning potential," "ambitious and career-oriented," "good family background," "tall," and "well-liked by others" as the most important traits for men for a longer-term romantic relationship. In fact, the magnitude of gender differences documented across scientific studies concerning the different qualities valued in male versus female mate selection is one of the *most* robust in the psychological literature (Petersen & Hyde, 2010).

Across evolutionary history and continuing in the 21st century, forces of sexual attraction and mate selection have had very different consequences for men and women. Men could copulate and impregnate a female with minimal investment required for raising their biological children. However, the cost of impregnation for a woman usually leads to significant and necessary behavioral, emotional, and financial investment of raising a child into adulthood (or, in modern times, some serious decisions about whether or not to terminate a pregnancy). Thus for men, sex could mean an investment that lasts for a few minutes. For women, sex could be an investment that lasts for 18 or more years. After a very long labor delivering my first son, Christian, I was still awake 24+ hours after labor had begun. It was nighttime and my baby and I were struggling with the latching and nursing. I was exhausted yet feeling like I should be welcoming this time to bond with him. My doctor, who had several children of her own, could detect my dilemma as she checked on me when the nurse offered to take Christian to the nursery to allow me time to sleep. She said to me, "You know he will be rooming with you for the next *18* years!" I needed some sleep before I could ponder that type of commitment. Christian went to the newborn nursery with the nurse, and I welcomed the 18-year commitment *after* I had slept! Mating, indeed, tends to have greater consequences for women. Thus, it makes perfect sense that many women are attracted to men's qualities that will give her a good return on investment for herself in the long haul, especially if the union bears children.

If the investment of partnering and mating has a higher cost for women, it makes sense that we would have evolved in mate selection to desire secure qualities such as resource potential and being "considerate" and "fond of children." This same evolutionary psychological theory explains why modern women in heterosexual relationships tend to be the "gatekeepers" to sexual relations, because the consequences—including possible pregnancy and sexually transmitted disease, as well as concerns about their reputation and emotional well-being—are qualitatively different than the sexual thoughts of men who tend to focus more on sexual desire and being the initiators of sex in heterosexual relationships (Maas, Shearer, Gillen, & Lefkowitz, 2015). Moreover, evolutionary theory explains the endurance of the so-called *double standard*—which is when women tend to be judged negatively for sexual activity, especially multiple sexual partners or casual sex (i.e., "sluts"), while men tend to be favored for the same behaviors (i.e., "studs"; Sprecher, Treger, & Sakaluk, 2013). While seemingly unfair for women from a feminist perspective, Sprecher and colleagues have been tracking this norm in young adults in the U.S. and have found that the double standard did not change between 1990 and 2013. Through a feminist lens, the double standard is certainly *not* fair. I like to see my women's health students become passionate about this topic. Most of them know someone—and sometimes it is themselves—who have been stereotyped and harmed by these norms. Even the recent and controversial Netflix series *Thirteen Reasons Why* featured a young woman by the name of Hannah who had died by suicide and left a series of audiotapes that recorded her motivations for killing herself. This novel and the television series by Jay Asher (2017) depict the extreme harm that can come from "slut shaming." The same romantic incident (and in the series it is even unclear if the original sexual event really happened) is considered heroic and worthy of bragging rights for the young man, whereas it is absolutely devastating for Hannah. Although *Thirteen Reasons Why* was quite controversial in my professional community (and I have some opinions about the series that would be tangential to this book), viewing that episode brought me back emotionally to some of the feelings and events that I had witnessed in high school that now seem foreign to me in adult life. I had forgotten how powerful those experiences and feelings could be. The double standard is indeed *not* fair. Women deserve to enjoy sexual relationships with whomever and with however many partners they choose, just as many men currently do. However, consequences such as unplanned pregnancy, reception of sexually transmitted infections, potential regret, and possible bullying in the form of slut shaming are just some of the real-life possibilities that prevent the abolishment of this double standard. It is no wonder parents often worry about the onset of sexual activity in their daughters a bit more than they do about the same developmental events for their sons.

Women are the typical gatekeepers to sexual activity in heterosexual relationships and they tend to look for security qualities and a man's resource potential, yet mate selection for men tends to focus on other gendered qualities. Buss and Barnes (1986) found that men rated "physically attractive," "good-looking," "good cook," and "frugal" as the most important mate characteristics. For men, having a beautiful woman at their side elevates their social status and translates into physical health, fertility, and the reproductive possibility of healthy and attractive children. They become beautiful-by-proxy. The preference for a "good cook" who is also "frugal" in her spending of resources also sounds like a "win-win" choice for many men too. In his summary of this extensive cross-cultural and evolutionary psychology research, Buss (2008) asserts brazenly, "A woman's physical attractiveness is a cardinal component of women's mate value" (p. 134). Consequently, if attractiveness is of utmost importance to heterosexual mating relationships for men, it makes sense that women's physical appearance would be a priority for many of them in their search to find a romantic relationship.

Fat talk could be a way to signal to others that women embrace this evolutionary value of physical appearance. Nichter and Vuckovic (1994) state, "Girls are taught from an early age that attractiveness is an intrinsic part of pleasing and serving others and, in turn, of securing love" (p. 120). Discussions about physical appearance can focus on a variety of aspects. The woman with straight, thin hair could want the thick, curly locks; the woman with the curly hair could want the straight, sleek look. The taller woman may wish that she were shorter; the short woman may wish that she were taller. Girls and women do comment on other aspects of appearance, so why does much of our body talk focus on *fat*? Evolutionary biology and psychology have some answers to this question also. In the context of an industrialized society in which adults usually gain adipose weight with age (Andres, 1989), women who maintain slenderness into mid-life tend to look younger and hence more fertile than women who have increased in size. Buss (1989) suggests that age provides a powerful cue of a woman's fertility, and age is surmised through her behavioral and physical attributes. More specifically, women's waist-to-hip circumference ratio conveys information about attractiveness, health, and fertility. To calculate this, one would simply take a measure of the smallest part of the waist and place that number, whether in inches or centimeters, above the number reflecting the largest circumference of one's hips. That number is the ratio that we refer to as the waist-to-hip ratio. Normal waist-to-hip circumference ratios for premenopausal Caucasian women range between 0.67 and 0.80 (D.J., Lanska, M.J. Lanksa, Hartz, & Rimm, 1985; Marti et al., 1991). Singh and colleagues reviewed the literature and conducted their own cross-cultural research documenting that regardless of body size as measured by body mass index, participants of varied races rated women with lower waist-to-hip circumference ratios as more attractive than women with higher ones (Singh, Dixson, Jessop, Morgan, & Dixson, 2010). More specifically, Schutzwohl (2006) used a test that was more realistic to everyday life to assess men's perceptions of women's attractiveness based on waist-to-hip circumference ratios and confirmed that men find a measurement of 0.7 to indicate more fertility and the highest level of attractiveness. This means that whether a woman has a small frame in total body size or is quite large in total body size, her waist relative to her hip circumference dimensions are signaling important evolutionary beauty and fertility information.

The expectation for women to accentuate their fertility through their physical aesthetics has been consistently represented in documented art across multiple centuries. Simply search 18th, 19th, 20th, and 21st century "ideal women," and Google will present images of women who varied somewhat in fashion and body types, but who all have figures that express womanhood. They do not look like men in their shape, fashion, hair, or make-up. Further, the tendency for waistlines to be smaller than the bust line and waistlines that are smaller than hips/buttocks remains stable across these centuries. The images, particularly of 18th and 19th century women, emphasize their use of corsets to shrink the waistline and bumps and petticoat layers to accentuate the hips and buttocks. Fashion and fitness trends over time unfailingly exaggerate the unique physical qualities of womanhood (e.g., breasts, hips, waistlines). This documentation presents an ideal example of evolutionary forces interacting with cultural forces over time. Ideal women express their womanliness.

Another reason that heterosexual men tend to view the hourglass feminine body as most fertile and thus more attractive is because larger female waistlines also convey some important evolutionary signaling. If heterosexual men find the waist-to-hip ratio of less than one (or 0.7, to be exact) to be most attractive in women, what does evolutionary biology and psychology say that a ratio *above* 1.0 conveys? This would translate into a woman having a wider waist than her own hips in circumference. Singh and Singh (2011) suggest there are well-documented relationships between a large waist-to-hip ratio and endocrinological disorders, such as polycystic ovary syndrome, which reduce women's fertility. More frequently than signaling disease, however, a large waist-to-hip circumference ratio could indicate pregnancy (i.e., perhaps from another man), which would reduce men's sexual attraction to her (Schutzwohl, 2006). When I was about seven months pregnant with my son Christian, I was out jogging one morning and had the very unpleasant experience of being catcalled by a male driver who had first seen me from behind. (By the way, you don't "run" later in pregnancy. The whole event gets demoted to "jogging.") As this man passed by me jogging on the side of the road, he got a glimpse of my very pregnant and protruding belly that must not have been as visible from behind. The catcalling was uncalled for and quite unpleasant, but the look on his startled face was precious! That man had his very own unexpected evolutionary psychology crisis. I hope the event helped him to learn to be more respectful to women.

Beyond a current pregnancy, a larger waist-to-hip circumference can signal to a new potential mate that this woman already has a child (or children), again from another man who may or may not be responsible for their welfare. Most women find that our bodies shift in very normal ways following the birth of our children. Thickening of the waistline is a classic consequence. In this regard, larger waist sizes signal a greater possibility of current or previous pregnancies, whereas leaner midriffs convey a greater likelihood of being nulliparous and/or pre-motherhood in physical development. While seriously malnourished women or women suffering from the eating disorder anorexia may be rendered infertile—from an evolutionary physical and hormonal adaptation to famine—healthy but leaner women will appear more youthful and hence more fertile compared to larger women. If leanness, especially in the waist-to-hip dimension, shows youth and fertility, then leaner women would have more dating and mate options whether younger or older. In this regard, leanness coincides with feminine power in the dating and mate selection world.

In later chapters I will talk about the construct of *drive-for-thinness*, which is when individuals strive to be lean either by trying to lose weight or through behaviors meant to suppress weight and remain lean. Girls and women often pursue this drive-for-thinness thinking it will magically make them happy, but it usually does not. However, some of this pursuit may stem from evolutionary forces of needing more power and agency in one's life. This hypothesis that women find power in leanness is the converse of fat women being socially stigmatized. It also helps us understand how some women who are absolutely stunning can feel intimidating to others. They may be perceived as powerful. Although it is inexcusable, this may be some of the fuel for body snarking. The latter behavior is a way to aggress upon somebody who feels threatening. It also explains the temptation to engage in body snarking through social media and do so anonymously. It is a safe—but cowardly—way to assault another person.

Women's beauty and fertility signaling determine their social status and power. Buss (2008) found that attractive women had higher standards for their male mates. In fact, he found that the women rated as most attractive, relative to those considered to be less attractive, had significantly higher standards on multiple areas of male characteristics. These domains included signals of good genes (e.g., muscularity), good investment indicators (e.g., good income), good parenting indicators (e.g., a desire for a future including home & children), and good romantic partner indicators (e.g., being loving and emotionally invested). Buss acknowledges that a man who falls high on each of these four indicators—who is also single—is a statistical rarity in the real world. Because men tend to find women's physical attractiveness as a necessity rather than a luxury (Li, Bailey, Kendrick, & Linsemeier, 2002), very attractive women have more choices of available men. They, therefore, have more dating power and relationship value than less attractive women.

Consequently, if fat talk is an attestation that a woman values physical attractiveness in herself, it may also be an impression management technique advertising her high standards for her own appearance in romantic mate selection. Fat talk could indicate ownership and internalization of the cultural thin-ideal female physique and one's personal desire to maintain a youthful and lean physical appearance. In turn, a woman's fat talk (in mild but probably not excessive levels) could be attractive to potential mates in that it conveys her intent to stay leaner and more physically attractive for his benefit. Thus, low levels of fat talk in heterosexual relationships could afford some women more power in that relationship. Morsch, Martz, Miles, and Bazzini (2018) presented three vignettes randomly assigned to 106 men and women on Amazon Mechanical Turk (Mturk). The vignettes all depicted a fictional young married couple named Jessica and Michael. Although Michael's behavior was stable across each of the three stories, Jessica either engaged in a mild level of fat talk, an excessive level of fat talk, or said self-accepting things about her body. Participants were asked to rate the likability of both of them. Michael's likability did not vary across the three study conditions—which was predicted, given that his behavior did not change in each of the stories. However, both male and female participants liked Jessica the most when she said self-accepting things about her body, liked her a bit less when she engaged in a mild level of fat talk, and liked her least when her level of fat talk was portrayed as extreme in the vignette. Therefore, women's excessive fat talk was not attractive to men.

Anecdotally, by surveying students in my classes, I have noted that college women seem to make a connection between high levels of a woman's fat talk and poorer body image and increased self-consciousness. They can also extrapolate how poorer body image likely results in worse sexual functioning for these women. If a woman is not comfortable in her own skin, she is not going to be very comfortable being nude with a sexual partner. Recently, we ran several focus groups with a male research assistant and college men who had been in longer-term, committed, heterosexual relationships. In one of the focus groups, we had a young man speak about his ex-girlfriend, who had told him, "I'm a lights out, shirt left on kind of gal." Wiederman (2012) has documented that poor body image is related to women having decreased sexual satisfaction with partners. Positive body image means a better sex life for women; body image dissatisfaction means a less satisfying sex life for them. My female students—whether they have positive or poor body image— are able to project that a woman who fat talks excessively probably has poor body image, will likely be self-conscious in bed, probably does not experience the same sexual pleasure as women with positive body image do, and may even have sexual dysfunction and struggle to achieve any pleasure or orgasms.

In contrast, in class discussions and in the focus groups that we have run through my research team, college men do *not* seem to be able to forecast the relationships between a woman's fat talk, her body image, and her sexual-comfort level or ability to perform and experience normal sexual pleasure in bed. Our college men who had been in a committed romantic relationship tended to express, naively, that if their girlfriends were having sex with them, then the girlfriends must like it and be enjoying it. I remember some of my young female research assistants just shaking their heads when we listened to these focus group transcripts. Most sexually experienced women know that women sometimes have unfulfilling sex. Similarly, young women see the potential toxicity of fat talk for a woman in a heterosexual relationship for the woman herself, and the potential longer-term consequences for the sexual relationship with her mate. The young men in our focus groups were not anticipating this. Therefore, we ran another study and proposed that excessive levels of fat talk in heterosexual relationships would be a "turn off" for men with more relationship and sexual experience (Miles Martz, Webb, Bazzini, and Morsh, 2018). If she is not comfortable in her own skin, she is likely not going to be very comfortable with him sexually. This is essentially what we found. Using the same vignettes about Michael and Jessica described above (Miles et al., 2018) surveyed 239 heterosexual men and women with long-term relationship experience (i.e., at least 1 year), recruited from Amazon Mechanical Turk. These participants reported perceiving Michael and Jessica as experiencing the least amount of sexual and relationship satisfaction when Jessica engaged in excessive fat talk during their date night. We also hypothesized that participants would perceive the couple as experiencing the most satisfaction when Jessica talked about her body in a self-accepting way. However, participants did not perceive a significant difference in the couple's satisfaction levels when Jessica minimally fat talked and when she engaged in self-accepting body talk. Based on this study, a woman's excessive fat talk may negatively impact relationship and sexual satisfaction, but minimal levels do not seem to have this effect. Participants' perceptions of Jessica's positive body image were also examined and this mapped onto her amount of fat talk; she was perceived as having the greatest level of positive body image when she engaged in self-accepting body talk and perceived as having the least level of positive body image when she engaged in excessive fat talk. Lastly, participants perceived Jessica as having a moderate level of positive body image when she minimally fat talked. Time and experience with romantic relationships with women with positive body image and women with poor body image likely helps older men see the connection between body image and female sexual functioning. Research on the interpersonal consequences of fat talk is in its seminal stages and is ripe for more attention.

The Power of the Beauty Ideal on the Human Psyche

From a feminist standpoint in a culture that objectifies women and demands beauty from them, it would be satisfying to say that beauty should not matter. I want these feminine enemies to end forever. When interviewed about my fat talk research, even I have told reporters that "I wish women would worry less about their bodies—while taking good care of their health through behaviors like stress management, regular exercise and healthful eating—and spend more time learning, helping, educating, leading, solving problems, rising to influence and contributing to society" (Goudarzi, 2007). This sounded respectable when I said it and I wish it were all that simple. Unfortunately, the science suggests it is *not*.

Langlois et al. (2000) conducted an empirical and theoretical review about beauty based on common axioms in contemporary language as an exercise to show the complexity of beauty's power. Since the dawn of humankind's ability to think, write, and create, it appears that human beings have been intoxicated by beauty. Even the philosopher Plato called beauty a "privilege of nature" (Cotton, 2009). Langlois took three popular maxims about beauty and addressed each to see if science supports them or not. The first maxim is "Beauty is in the eye of the beholder," which means that different people have consistently different opinions about what they consider to be beautiful. Scientifically, this would mean that various people who have rated the perceived attractiveness of others would have very little reliability in their combined ratings and would therefore disagree. As an example, some people could find Cynthia to be stunning and others could view Cynthia as homely. Langlois and colleagues reviewed extant studies that had examined just this dynamic. A study referred to as a meta-analysis, which is a compilation of multiple studies investigating the same topic, found that adults reliably agreed on what they considered to be attractive with an average correlation of $r = .90$ (i.e., 0.0 means no association, whereas a 1.0 means perfect congruence as a correlation; $r = .90$ indicates very high agreement among people about what they consider to be beautiful). In studies examining the reliability of children in their ratings of attractiveness, the researchers also found a substantial average correlation of $r = .85$. They then selected studies with raters that crossed ethnicities and found high reliability with $r = .88$ and higher agreement when they evaluated raters cross-culturally with $r = .94$. Thus, humans agree on what they consider to be attractive in people even in other cultures and across ethnicities. Beauty is not simply in the eye of the beholder. My bet is when people say this, they are speaking less to a diversity of beauty opinions and more to the fact that people attract and have relationships with people who matched their own level of physical attractiveness. A person who is moderately attractive would likely be attracted to and able to attract a mate who is also moderately attractive. A moderately attractive person is not likely to find a mate who is stunning in appearance. Therefore, this untrue maxim that beauty is in the eye of the beholder could be a consequence of people's experience with real-life successful mate selection.

The second maxim Langlois et al. (2000) examined was "Never judge a book by its cover." This means that external features, such as physical appearance, should not be considered important. It is the content or what is said inside the book that should be kept paramount. Translated into scientific methodology, this would mean that people do not judge others or form opinions about their physical appearance. This would also mean that they do not treat others differently according to level of physical attractiveness. Langlois and colleagues performed a meta-analysis of all of the studies on adults and all the studies conducted on children that examined this belief. Yet again, their results did not support the maxim. They found that both adults and children *do* form judgments about others' physical appearance and that most effect sizes (which tell us the extent of the relationships and were measured in Cohen's ds) were quite robust. A Cohen's $d = 1.0$ would be one full standard deviation of difference between variables. It is customary in psychology to consider an effect size of 0.8 to be quite large, whereas 0.5 is medium and 0.2 is small. Langlois et al. (2000) found for children that ratings of attractiveness were strongly related to social approval ($d = 1.33$), perceived academic and developmental competence ($d = 1.30$), perception to be better adjusted ($d = .95$), and perception of being more interpersonally competent ($d = .92$). Attractive adults were perceived more positively than unattractive adults on varied dimensions including their occupational competence ($d = .90$), social appeal ($d = .49$), more interpersonally competent ($d = .45$), and better adjusted ($d = .25$). The authors did the same in compiling studies that tested how attractiveness impacted the treatment of others in both adults and in children. Consequently, the meta-analysis failed to support the maxim. For children, it was found that attractiveness versus unattractiveness had an impact on their evaluations of the children's competence ($d = .81$), negative interaction ($d = -.64$), positive interaction ($d = .52$), and a smaller effect for attention and caring ($d = .29$). The results were similar for adults in that attractive adults were treated with more attention ($d = 1.09$), more reward ($d = .68$), more positive interaction ($d = .57$), more positive impression management ($d = .53$), negative interaction ($d = -.42$), and help-giving/cooperation ($d = .36$). According to the present research, there is plenty of evidence that people do judge other humans by their physical appearance. This is evident in some modern-day dating, such as the use of Tinder, where participants swipe right on their device if they wish to meet a person for a date only after they have evaluated their physical appearance.

The third maxim that Langlois et al. (2000) evaluated was "Beauty is only skin deep." This means there would be no relationship between individuals' physical appearance and their behavior or personality. Once again, the science failed to support the maxim. Attractive children, compared to unattractive children, were more popular ($d = .77$), better adjusted ($d = .32$), and displayed more intelligence and performance competence ($d = .39$). Similarly, the studies that examined these relationships in adults found that attractive ones had more occupational success ($d = .76$), were more popular ($d = .65$), had more dating experience ($d = .55$), had more sexual experience ($d = .31$), had better physical health ($d = .39$), had slightly higher self-esteem ($d = .24$), had slightly greater social skills ($d = .20$), had slightly better mental health ($d = .16$), and were slightly more intelligent ($d = .07$). In conclusion, Langlois and colleagues established that these three beauty maxims are myths—the science fails to support *any* of them. In fact, across the scientific evidence, for each maxim the *opposite* is actually true. Evolution appears to have provided the human race with some strong biases in how others are perceived based on their physical appearance. Beauty has a powerful effect on the human psyche.

Consequently, it is not likely that we will be able to ignore the power of beauty on the human mind, nor make its value diminish or disappear in our culture. Our feminine enemies will not just go away. Contextualizing the importance of women's physical appearance in heterosexual partnering and mating helps us to understand why women may fat talk, yet it does not excuse us from thinking more cerebrally about this ritualized style of self-commentary and social interaction. Just because behavioral tendencies have evolutionary explanations does not mean that we must accept them. In fact, we are more likely to surpass these genetic tendencies once we recognize them, clarify our personal values, and then make deliberate change if we wish to do so. Fat talking, as habit, will continue unless individuals recognize their participation in it and understand how destructive the behavior can be for themselves and society. Moreover, we need a feminist agenda fighting to end the body snarking and fat shaming found so commonly on personal and public social media. Our feminine enemies have a very deep origin in the human evolution of our ancestry. They are better contextualized in more recent history of Western cultural norms.

2

The Culture of Fat Talk

"Girls just want to have fun-damental rights."—Women's March sign, 2017

Regardless of our evolutionary wiring, we must contextualize fat talk within contemporary Western culture. Evolutionary biology and psychology explain the foundations for our motivations to engage in fat talk once we understand the realities of why physical appearance is important for most people. In my research lab's first study on fat talk, we learned that women believe that other women will conform and participate in the conversation when other young women were already doing so (Britton, Martz, Bazzini, Curtin, & LeaShomb, 2006). However, that study made popular press under the title "Female 'Fat Talk' Mandatory Study Finds" (Goudarzi, 2007). Finding that fat talk is normative is very different from finding that it is obligatory. I did not use the word "mandatory" when I was interviewed about that study. Fat talk may be expected, but participation is not required. We have many evolutionarily based motivations such as anger, violence, and sexual desires that are socially unacceptable if not downright illegal. It is comforting to know that humans' highly evolved brain has the capability, within the frontal lobe, to override and inhibit those primitive impulses. Our biology and hard wiring need *not* be our behavioral destiny.

Contextualizing fat talk in modern Western society begs for a feminist perspective. How can girls and women achieve equality with boys and men when there are forces objectifying and subjugating us? When girls and women are objectified, they are viewed as sexual objects meant to satisfy the desire of others, thereby draining their psychological and emotional strength and energy, and stealing the political effectiveness to make corrective changes in our regions, states, and nation. Sadly, these forces within our culture begin to operate in our lives from the day most are born. We feel pulled to call newborn baby girls "beautiful," as if that is the most important attribute for her value. Also starting very early in life, in childhood many women are introduced to their idealization of the feminine physique through the iconic Barbie doll. Barbie is sold in 150 countries worldwide (Matel, 2016), and it is estimated that 59 percent of girls in the U.S. own Barbie dolls (Sherman & Zurbriggen, 2014), although Dockterman (2016) reports the number is as high as 92 percent for girls ages 2–12 in the U.S. If you look closely, especially through adult eyes and a feminist lens, Barbie looks a bit freakish. If she were life size, she would be six feet tall. She would have a 39-inch bust, an 18-inch waist, and 33-inch hips (i.e., a waist-to-hip ratio of 0.55; Lind & Brzuzy, 2008). Real women are not shaped quite like that. If Barbie could really speak, my bet is that she would fat talk, annoying all of her plastic friends in the process.

Appalachian State University's counseling center had a life-size Barbie that would travel campus for various outreach interventions. Her waist was so small proportionate to the rest of her body that her cardboard waistline kept bending and breaking. Somebody had to reinforce her spine with a two-by-four block of wood. Barbie obviously had health issues. Barbie's feet are also weird because she stands on her tippy toes so that she needs high heel shoes to remain upright. For the record, she cannot not stand upright—she has to be held. Barbie is rather dependent. High heel shoes—when worn by real women—create a lifting of the butt cheeks and a curvature in the lower back called mammalian lordosis that is viewed as sexual readiness to be mounted in the animal world. Barbie is one over-sexualized looking doll for a nonsexual being. Interestingly, her exaggerated sexual features were designed to objectify her for the pleasure of viewers. She has no nipples and there is no sense that she has other requisite parts such as a clitoris and vagina. I bet Barbie was not happy in bed. But then her boyfriend, Ken, did not have the requisite parts, either. I looked.

Joking aside, this iconic play doll has been shown in research to harm young girls' sense of self. Dittmar, Halliwell, and Ive (2006) compared the effects of Barbie doll images with the effects of a more realistically propor-tioned doll image called Emme on English girls ages five to eight years old. They also had a no-doll control group. Dittmar and colleagues found that body dissatisfaction was highest in the girls randomly assigned to play with Barbie relative to the other study conditions. Further, they found stronger effect sizes for the youngest girls ages 5.5 to 7.5 than older girls ages 7.5–8.5. Thus, there was more body dissatisfaction for the younger girls who played with Barbie versus Emme, compared to the older girls exhibiting the same, but smaller, scientific effect. Anschutz and Engels (2010) studied 117 six to ten-year-old Dutch girls who played with real dolls by randomly assigning them to one of four conditions: Barbie, the Emme doll, a Tyler doll (i.e., also realistic in proportion like Emme), and a Lego-toy control group. Unlike Dittmar et al., they found no effect for exposure to Barbie, nor any interactions with the girls' ages. They interpreted this to mean that physically maneuvering the dolls in their hands could divert the girls' attention away from their body shapes, as they are focused on what they are making the dolls do. On the other hand, pictures tend to draw attention to the doll's physical proportions in those studies that examined the effects of one-time exposure. To follow up on that hypothesis, Rice, Prichard, Tiggeman, and Slater (2016) exposed 160 South Australian girls, ages five to eight years of age, to one of four randomly assigned conditions including three doll groups and one no-doll control group (i.e., "My Little Pony"). All the children heard a storyline about a character called "Lily." The four groups included a print observation, where the participants looked at Barbie in a picture; physical observation, where they looked at her in real life; physical engagement with Barbie, where they got to touch and play with her; and a physical engagement condition with My Little Pony. The physical observation condition featured Barbie posing motionless like one might see pictured on Mattel packaging. In the two physical engagement conditions, the girls got to hold and move the toys and act out the storyline with their toy. That is, they got to simulate real play behavior. The study had three dependent variables: thin-ideal internalization, body esteem, and body dissatisfaction. Exposure to the Barbie resulted in more internalization of the thin-ideal regardless of whether they observed Barbie in a printed image, they observed Barbie in her theatre, or they got to physically play with and act out Lily's scene with Barbie. There were no differences across the four experimental conditions for body esteem or body dissatisfaction. Consequently, the science suggests that Barbie's appearance does create a cultural ideal in the minds of girls who play with her. In this regard, the iconic Barbie is powerful and quite damaging for a feminist agenda. Consequently, she has quite a controversial history

Barbie's tainted history has endured for quite some time. Dockterman (2016), who writes for *Time*, cites that her creator—Ruth Handler—based Barbie's shape on a German doll named Lilli, who was a gag gift meant to be a prostitute to distribute to men at bachelor parties so they could enjoy her large breasts. (I knew those breasts were over-sexualized! And now I have the disturbing image of men passing her around at a party while lightheartedly sexually assaulting parts of a toy made of plastic.) Handler named her Barbie after her daughter Barbara and introduced her at the New York toy fair in 1959. Apparently, Barbie has never been a feminist. Her teen version was sold with a diet book that said simply, "Don't eat." That's a great message to convey to growing girls! A version of Barbie with preprogrammed language would state, "Math class is tough." Hence, we have "don't eat" and "don't learn math" because it's hard. There is *obviously* nothing keeping girls from achieving equality with boys in this childhood message (said sarcastically, of course). A group called the Barbie Liberation Organization praised Barbie for presenting the message that it is more important to be pretty than to be smart.

Since that time, Mattel has attempted to follow the ebb and flow of cultural values. Barbie was introduced as a businesswoman in 1963, an astronaut in 1965, and as a surgeon in 1973. Look out *Grey's Anatomy*! By the 2000s many mothers were voting against Barbie by withholding their pocketbooks. Dockterman (2016) reported that Mattel, in response to market forces criticizing Barbie, launched new dolls on January 28, 2016. She also cites how celebrities such as Christina Hendricks, most famous for her role on Mad Men, singer Beyoncé, and Kim Kardashian West have influenced American ideals. There are three new dolls described as petite, tall, and curvy reflecting various skin tones. They are named BarbieFashionistas and available in retail stores. Indeed, they are different than the original Barbie, but I still do not see them as representing the physical diversity of real women. I am curious if any researchers will study the effects that these new dolls have on young girls and if they are less toxic than the original Barbie. What we do know is that one toy has likely wrought harm on the psyches and body images of girls and women worldwide.

In addition to plastic dolls, young girls also have significant exposure to stories about princesses. This fairytale genre emerged in literature as early as the seventeenth century. Pugh and Aronstein (2012) have edited a collection of essays regarding the history of Walt Disney World and how this organization brought the modern-day princess to life—creating broad appeal in Western culture. As an example, the animated film *Cinderella* was produced in 1950. I have not studied this myself, but I bet most females in the United States culture know the story of Cinderella and remember that she was beautiful. Whenever I think of Cinderella, I can't help but think of the sort of modern day adult film, *Pretty Woman* (Lawton, 1990), which featured actor Richard Gere as a wealthy and attractive gentleman who originally hires actor Julia Roberts as a prostitute. Eventually, they fall in love and he rescues the beautiful woman from a life of sexual slavery and into a fairytale life of status and riches. I am confident that this is a *rare* event for most sex workers. As I write this, that story sounds ridiculous.

Issitt (2016) has written about the controversy concerning our enchantment with princesses. Some believe that the princess archetype merely reflects basic human fantasies that are echoed in romance in modern ages. The fact that these fairy tales have endured speaks somewhat to their psychological appeal. Conversely, others believe that princesses demonstrate multiple harmful archetypes for young girls. They model the damsel in distress who is often dependent on a man to rescue and guide her (as if that is all modern-day women need). As a damsel in distress in our kitchen, I do feel that way sometimes when my handsome partner volunteers to empty the dishwasher. I have been rescued! Although I love to cook and I like clean dishes, I loathe the chore of emptying the dishwasher. I have no idea why. But for the princesses, the princely gestures are much more romantic. Can you imagine the scene where the handsome prince kisses Snow White? He awakens her. She smiles. They lock eyes and kiss again. Then they ride off into the sunset, usually on a white horse, and live happily ever after. As a side effect, princesses also tell us that life really begins at marriage for a woman—suggesting this should be a girl's only goal in life and that somehow life is complete at that point. These fairy tales fail to capture the mundane aspects of real life. They never show the prince and princess both trying to spit their toothpaste into the one bathroom sink after Mr. Prince has just flushed the toilet. I once worked clinically with this sweet older man who loved his wife and their life together very much. He had developed a powerful emotional crush on a younger woman. He came to me for help, as he did not want to act on his feelings. We did a lot of that real life "sharing a bathroom" imagery to break the spell. It is very easy when we are attracted to someone to conjure up all kinds of fantasies about them and make them absolutely *perfect* in our minds. Princesses are perfect. Seriously, have you ever heard a princess fart?! Real humans are not perfect. If you have ever lived with a real human, you know what I mean.

Also damaging in these stories, princesses demonstrate that beauty is paramount in being able to attract that handsome prince. For the prince in Cinderella, rather than dating and getting to know his future bride, he was stuck finding the woman with the "perfect" sized foot. I am no expert on romantic relationships, but I am pretty sure their quality is not a function of foot size. Further, most princess stories display sharp contrasts between women's and men's roles in society. Men are portrayed as having power and privilege, while women's value is a function of their man and their marriage. Again, how can we envision a feminist ideal of gender equality when our princess stories model stark differences in what men and women can and are supposed to do? Many of these values have infiltrated our culture and are displayed in modern weddings. There can be much ado about her lovely dress, hair, and make-up. Little girls often dream about the day that they will be the beautiful bride. Many women take the man's surname so that they no longer have the last name they did when they were raised. And weirdly, when the father gives away the bride (which can be very touching, I'll admit), he is giving his "property" over to another man. As such, it is an example of modern day heteropatriarchy.

Princesses teach us that beauty is clearly the only commodity that girls and women can ever have. Additionally problematic in this is that there is a stereotype that what is *beautiful is good* and what is *ugly is bad*. Princesses cannot be kind, caring, happy, sensitive or exemplify other positive personality characteristics unless they are also beautiful. What a damaging message this can be to girls. Myers (2002) observed that children learn this *beautiful is good* stereotype at a young age. Cinderella and Snow White are beautiful and kind, whereas the witches and evil stepsisters are depicted as ugly and wicked. My colleagues and I led two studies that examined this stereotype directly in Disney films (Bazzini, Curtin, Joslin, Regan, & Martz, 2010). In the first study, we chose twenty-one animated Disney films that had at least three characters with human facial characteristics (e.g., Cinderella, The Little Mermaid, & Sleeping Beauty). Blind to the hypotheses, four undergraduate research assistants were trained to view these films and code these Disney characters on attractiveness, aggressiveness, goodness, intelligence, outcome (i.e., did good or bad things happen to them?), and romantic involvement. Characters were also coded according to if their role in the film was central, secondary, or merely peripheral to the story's plotline. A total of 163 characters were rated in pairs, blind to one another, randomized across the four research assistants. Reliability for these paired coders was high across each of the characteristics that they rated. This means that both the characters' physical attractiveness and the valence of their personality traits are clearly evident in Disney films if reliability emerges easily by the raters. Overall, results found that across the twenty-one films, attractive characters displayed higher intelligence, lower aggressiveness, and greater moral virtue or goodness. Plus, they had more romantic involvement and more positive outcomes in their lives. It is a privilege to be an attractive character in a Disney film. What is beautiful *is* good.

In the second study, we recruited 42 children between the ages of six and twelve who were accompanied by one parent. They watched either a film found to have a high bias on the *beauty is good* depiction (i.e., Cinderella) or a film found to be low in the *beauty is good* bias (i.e., Hunchback of Notre Dame). After the children watched their respective film, they rated how much they liked or did not like the film, and then they were shown two photographs representing children their age. These photos were pre-tested to be deemed as either an attractive child or an unattractive child by college student raters. After viewing the two photographs, the children were prompted to give ratings on four behavioral characteristics (e.g., "How nice would you say this person is?"). Then they were asked which one of these kids they would prefer to have as a friend. Results showed that regardless of which movie they watched, these children rated behavioral characteristics more favorably for the attractive child photo compared to the unattractive child photo. Furthermore, children picked the attractive child to be their friend over the unattractive child regardless of the movie assigned to them. Thus, they held the *beauty is good* stereotype regardless of how this was conveyed or not conveyed in the film they had just watched. Unfortunately, having just viewed *one* Disney movie that does not convey the *beautiful is good* stereotype failed to undo the stereotype in the minds of these children.

The modern Disney film *Frozen* (2013), which has been ranked as the highest grossing animated film to date (IMDb, 2016), has been lauded as "the first feminist fairy-tale" and "the most progressive movie ever" (Lutrell, 2014). I kept hearing about children dressing up as Elsa and Anna, not to mention the famous *Let It Go* song sung by Idina Menzel. Once I watched it, I thought Disney producers improved upon their female characters in terms of their personalities and their behavior. For example, Anna falls in love with Prince Hans. Her protective older sister, Elsa, is worried that Anna is rushing into marriage and so she intervenes. This is good because the Prince turns out to not be a very good guy. At first he was handsome and charming, but then he became mean and controlling. At least Disney did not follow the "beautiful is good" prototype for Prince Hans.

For a so-called "feminist fairytale," however, I was struck by how beautiful these female characters were portrayed, in both their features and their voices. I was also shocked by how lean their bodies were depicted; we certainly do not see those extremely small waist-to-hip dimensions in real-life women. According to my own calculations, their waist-to-hip ratio was about 0.55! I immediately worried about the body image messages that a widely-popular film was conveying to young girls. My assessment of *Frozen* was formed prior to reading an expert's analysis of the film. Rudloff (2016), in response to popular critics suggesting that *Frozen* had such a positive feminist message for its viewers, conducted her own analysis within the context of feminist and postfeminist media studies. She engaged in gender coding of the animated main characters of the film in terms of how they looked, how they were dressed, how they were drawn, and how they behaved. Rudloff argues that Disney failed to improve upon the physical appearance of Anna and Elsa relative to their own past illustrations of princesses. She notes that they both wore long dresses and were adorned with jewelry while the boys and men wore suits and pants. Their tight dresses revealed very slender frame, tiny waists, firm breasts, and slender wrists, legs, and arms. Further, she critiques the heteronormative nature of the binary-gendered characters and romantic pursuits that send the traditional message that those princesses cannot be happy unless they find and woo their prince. Despite the portrayal of Anna as being "agentic, determined and heroic, Anna is also represented as naive, impressionable and emotional—and concerned with how she appears as she expresses her desire to find Mr. Right. In Elsa, the feminist ideals of empowerment, self-realization and liberation are confused with her outward appearance and sexualization, which equates her inner sense of self with a femininity that is located in her body." In response to Lutrell's (2014) description of *Frozen* as "the first feminist fairy-tale," Rudloff (2016) concludes, "Disney still has a long way to go to promote egalitarian and diverse representations of all genders."

Human Role Models

In addition to the established detrimental effects of exposure to certain dolls and animated images on the body image and self-esteem of girls in our culture, these children also have difficulty finding real-life healthy, positive role models. Female role models in popular U.S. media have decreased in body size in recent generations—a trend that corresponds negatively with women's body image (Grogan, Williams, & Conner, 1996; O'Dea, 1995; Stice, Schupak-Neuberg, Shaw, & Stein, 1994). Although the pornographic magazine, *Playboy*, is certainly not marketed for children, it depicts what are considered to be sexually attractive women across fluid intervals of time. One study found that 99 percent of *Playboy* centerfolds and 100 percent of the winners of the Miss America pageants could be classified as underweight and that 29 percent and 17 percent respectively met the body mass index criterion (i.e., < 17.5) for anorexia nervosa (Spitzer, Henderson, & Zivian, 1999) for the *DSM-IV* at that time. Garner, Garfinkel, Schwartz, and Thompson (1980) documented the declining body weights of the Miss America Pageant winners across a 20-year time span between 1959–1978, and Wiseman, Gray, Mosimann, and Ahrens (1992) documented the sharper decline in the body sizes of the winners between 1979 and 1998. Thus, we herald a beauty standard of thinness that is a "genetic anomaly." Imagine if Americans similarly admired polydactyly (a 2 percent phenomenon; McCarroll, 2000) and felt inadequate without that 6th finger to fit into their gloves or for ring adornment! Genetic anomalies are considered beautiful in one direction and freakish in another.

The female role models that we herald in popular media are toxic for women who frequent the media for social comparison. Swami and Szmigielska (2013) asked if the women who work as fashion models are a high-risk group for having body image concerns. They studied 52 professional models with average body mass indices of 18.2 and found a matched control group of 51 non-models with average body mass indices of 24.6. Indeed, they found that the models evidenced more of a drive for thinness and dysfunctional investment in their appearance compared to the controls. There were no differences between these groups on a metric of body discrepancy, social physique anxiety, body satisfaction, and internalization of sociocultural messages of appearance. Thus, when people view these fashion models who are typically underweight, they are viewing them happy, styled, and carefully coiffed. Viewers are not seeing the harsh behavior the models engage in, likely on a daily basis, in their investment to remain ultra-thin.

A meta-analytic study examining how sociocultural factors influence body image found that women's personal internalization of and pressure to achieve the cultural thin-ideal physique were the strongest predictors for their poor body image (Cafri, Yamamiya, Brannick, & Thompson, 2005). Media can be powerful for individuals who personalize what they see. In their cross cultural study, Swami et al. (2010) found that exposure to Western media was related to a beauty ideal representing a thinner woman for both men and women. Further, exposure to our media was associated with poorer body image in women. Becker (2004) studied the effects of an introduction of Western media into Fiji, which prior to that time had not had any access to broadcasting that had been created in the U.S. Their citizens then later adopted the American thin ideal, leading to a greater drive for thinness and eating disorders in their population. In addition to its effects on body image, media also appears to affect fat talk. We have found from our nationally representative *Psychology of Size* dataset that participants who felt media pressure from the movies, television, the fashion industry, magazines, and the weight loss industry to be a different body size (i.e., the majority wanted to be leaner) were also the ones to report feeling the most pressure to fat talk (Driver, Martz, Bazzini, & Gagnon, 2012). Media conveys unrealistic ideals for feminine beauty. If you buy into it—meaning you believe that you should look like what you see—that results in poor body image. The poorer body image results in fat talk, which makes the poor body image seem normative and expected to other women, and thus the cycle of influence for fat talk is maintained.

Cultural forces and norms for women's beauty ideals do fluctuate somewhat; yet, recall that these vacillations consistently represent the feminine hourglass features that denote womanhood. Karazsia, Murnen, and Tylka (2017) conducted a cross-temporal meta-analysis of 253 previously conducted studies on this topic to examine if body dissatisfaction was changing over time as a function of fluctuating sociocultural influences. They sought to determine if shifting influences were associated with women's drive for thinness and men's drive for muscularity. They found the expected sex differences in that women had higher thinness-oriented body-image dissatisfaction compared to men—whereas men had higher muscularity-oriented dissatisfaction compared to women. Across a 31-year time span, they found that thinness-oriented body image dissatisfaction decreased for girls and women, yet there was no change for the boys and men. They found that geographic region (i.e., continental region), a Human Development Index within countries (i.e., a metric for health & standard of living), and women's age had no impact on their thinness-oriented body dissatisfaction. For a 14-year time span of tracking drive for muscularity, they found no difference across time for either sex. Again, they found no effect for geographic region, Human Development Index within countries, or age on their muscularity-oriented body dissatisfaction for both men and women. Karazsia and colleagues hypothesized that this positive change seen in women over these three decades could be a result of body-acceptance activist movements (Bacon & Aphramor, 2014; Sobal & Maurer, 1999; Stice, Rohde, Gau, & Shaw, 2012), more representation of normal-sized women in the media (Owen & Spencer, 2013), and some mothers intentionally trying to buffer sociocultural pressures for their daughters' body image (e.g., refusing to buy her a Barbie; Maor & Cwikel, 2016).

Not only are Americans attracted to the thin ideal, but they tend to share a disdain for larger, fat bodies. The forces work in both directions. The U.S. is, indeed, a nation of corporeal contradictions. In an ironic contrast to our beloved thin ideal is the fact that more and more women have gained weight and diverged further from the ideal. The U.S. is experiencing record high obesity rates (Flegal, Carroll, Ogden, & Johnson, 2002; Ogden et al., 2006) that have increased from 13.4 percent in 1960 to 36.2 percent in 2010 (body mass index [i.e., BMI] > 30 kg/m²), and an additional one-third of people meet overweight criteria (i.e., BMI 25–29.9 kg/m²; Centers for Disease Control [CDC], 2012; Flegal, Carroll, Ogden, & Curtin, 2010). In a comprehensive review of the literature, Puhl and Heuer (2009) document the pervasive stigma targeting obese individuals in a variety of settings including employment, healthcare, educational, interpersonal relationships, and media. Such stigma is even more ubiquitous for women than men. Consequently, this prejudice is another symptom of disease-maintaining misogyny that is preventing equality for women in our society. If you are a fat man, people tend to pay attention to your other qualities such as intelligence or career success. If you are a fat woman, people pay attention to your body. Reflecting on both the distance of the typical woman from an idyllic thin physique and the acknowledgment that such standards are normally unrealistic, some women engage in fat talk as a means of coping with this incongruity. Many people in our society do not have the bodies that they wish they had. Fat talk is a humble way to acknowledge the norm and admit that a woman does not quite measure up to the ideal in brief conversation with others.

United States' culture is quirky. The adage that "you can never be too rich or too thin" (Oxford Dictionary, 2004) simplifies our values in society. Most Americans want to have more money, and many Americans wish to be thinner. The desire for thinness is challenging in a society where most individuals have abundant access to calorie-rich food. Interestingly, the richer people are, the thinner they tend to be. The poorer they are, the larger they tend to be. One's income, or lack thereof, is evident in how Americans tend to eat. One-half of U.S. food expenditures are for meals and snacks that are purchased in restaurants (Grindy, Karaer, & Riehle, 2007). Moreover, "fast food" is served in large quantities, has more energy density (i.e., higher calories; Prentice & Jebb, 2003), and is less costly and thus more affordable to individuals of lower socioeconomic status [SES]. This makes it easier for poorer people to gain weight. Furthermore, Americans appear to be eating away from home more and more frequently. Cawley (2006) and Lin, Guthrie, and Frazao (1999) documented that the proportion of meals consumed away from home between the 1970s and the mid–1990s increased significantly, from 16 percent to 29 percent. Where Americans live also has an effect on what food they consume. I rarely eat fast food, and when I do it is normally because I am traveling and there are no other options. Yet, this research has me reflecting on the fact that my home is at least a 15-minute drive from any fast food restaurants.

Fleischhacker, Evenson, Rodriguez, and Ammerman (2011) conducted a systematic review of studies examining fast food restaurant geographical locations. Seventy-six percent of the studies found that fast food restaurants were much more likely to be located in low-income areas compared to middle- and higher-income areas. Fast food seems normative for our poorest citizens. It makes some sense that if people have had times when they could not afford food, they would want more "bang for the buck"—which translates into more taste, more calories, and more satisfaction when it is affordable. Fast food restaurants advertise taste and satisfaction, not nutrition. In a cross-cultural study between the United States and Sweden pertaining to how fast food was advertised differently in the two countries, Norman, Natarajan, and Sen (2015) found that the Swedish market targeted consumers who wanted a high-quality meal at a decent price. For the U.S. restaurants, advertising tended to target people looking to eat for a cheap price without concern for the quality of the food.

The availability of fast food seems to have had an impact on body sizes. Morgan Spurlock illustrated this using his personal body in the documentary *Supersize Me* (2004). Albeit healthy from the start, Spurlock chose to eat only McDonald's food for a month. Within such a short stint, he experienced weight gain, high serum cholesterol, and problems with his mood and sexual functioning. It took Spurlock *14 months* on a vegan diet to lose all of the weight that he had gained in that *one month*. Spurlock's documentary was a one-person experiment; however, the science suggests fast food consumption is also an unhealthy way to eat. In a systematic review, Rosenheck (2008) found that six out of seven of the prospective cohort studies that have been conducted on these relationships showed that more fast food consumption was associated with more calorie intake and weight gain. Further, six out of ten studies found body sizes were larger (i.e., higher body mass indices) for individuals living in areas with more fast food restaurants. Close, Lytle, and Viera (2016) studied how frequency of fast food meals and frequency of sit-down restaurant meals were associated with total food consumption in a worksite nutrition intervention trial of 388 participants. They divided the groups into tertiles based on their dining-out habits. There was no association between frequenting sit-down restaurants and total food consumption. However, participants who patronized fast food restaurants the most (i.e., highest tertile), had three times the odds for habitual intake of processed meat (OR = 3.0), more consumption of red meat (OR = 2.3), and more consumption of sweet baked goods and candy (OR = 3.5). Beyond demographic factors that influence fast food consumption, this research suggests that taste preferences and other factors may also play a role in people who frequent fast food restaurants. Alviola, Nayga, Thomsen, Danforth, and Smartt (2014) examined how the proximity of fast food restaurants to public elementary and middle schools was associated with children's body sizes. They found that the presence of fast food restaurants and the number of them within one mile of a school was associated with higher childhood obesity prevalence. They observed that many of the school children would habitually walk and consume fast food as an afternoon snack on their way home. Similarly, Currie (2010) found that the presence of fast food restaurants within a tenth of a mile increased obesity rates by at least .81 percent points. Consequently, living in a poorer region is associated with close proximity of fast food restaurants, and proximity of fast food restaurants to home or school is associated with greater weight gain. Individuals living in wealthier neighborhoods have more immunity to this environmental influence of weight gain.

Conversely, in this "you can never be too rich or too thin" culture, Darmon and Drewnowski (2008) conducted a review of studies examining SES and its association with food consumption. They acknowledged that the scientific literature has shown a relationship between more financial wealth and the habitual consumption of higher-quality, nutrient-dense foods for a long time. Further, they were able to deduce two mechanisms for the pattern of food choices between higher versus lower SES consumers: nutrient-dense foods are more costly than energy-dense foods. Secondly, poorer people have greater access to cheaper fast food that is energy-dense. Thus, it is easier for wealthy individuals to stay lean and healthy and it is easier for poor people to eat in a manner that promotes weight gain and poor health. Further, Virudachalam, Long, Harhay, Polsky, and Feudtner (2013) found that individuals in the U.S. from more educated and wealthier households—as compared to less educated, poorer households—cooked more dinners at home each week and therefore consumed healthier meals. Moreover, young adults who knew how to shop and prepare their own food were less likely to rely on fast food and had better nutritional quality than those devoid of practical cooking skills (Larson, Perry, Story, & Neumark-Sztainer, 2006). Hence, children—who are raised in lower SES homes that rely less on home-cooked meals and more on fast food consumption—are less likely to know how to cook healthier meals for themselves as adults. In this regard, the SES of the family that a child is born into tends to set them on a lifelong trajectory of food habits and thus body size. This is why it is easier to stay lean and healthy when people have wealth and it is easier to gain weight and become obese if people are poor.

In conclusion, women in the U.S. are living in an interesting historical dilemma. Weight gain has increased throughout the course of recent history. Stigma directed at individuals who are obese—especially for women—is rampant and pernicious. At the same time, most U.S. citizens have access to an overabundance of food, and these food options bifurcate as a function of SES, with wealthy, more educated individuals cooking more for themselves and able to purchase nutrient-dense foods that are more expensive. Conversely, poorer individuals are consuming more energy-dense fast foods and are more likely to be obese, moving their body sizes much further away from the cultural thin ideal, as well as diverging from a more moderate healthy physique. Hence, in an intricate dance between SES and the size of the female body, fat talk could again be an attestation to others that a woman embraces the cultural thin ideal and worries about weight gain. Accordingly, it is no wonder that fat talk entails voiced concerns about possible weight gain (i.e., getting fat), as well as talk about getting into better shape or losing weight to get thinner.

Social Media Influences on Body Image and Fat Talk

In addition to living in an interesting time in history in a culture that heralds the thin-ideal female physique, while obesity rates are at a record prevalence, we are at a unique point in history as a result of technological advancements. The development of the internet has changed most of our lives. I have relied heavily on my university's library site to pull literature for this book. When I was in graduate school, I had to physically go to the library and pull scientific articles out of these colored books. It was not easy to access scientific or lay information. Access to the internet has certainly impacted how we gather information, communicate with others, and interact in our real-life relationships. Kraut et al. (1998) conducted original research on the effects of acquiring the internet. They provided computers to 93 U.S. households that did not have previously have them and monitored individuals' psychological health over time. After the first year, greater use of the internet was associated with a decline in the extent of participants' social networks, a decrease in the amount of communication with family members, a decline in a sense of social support among the teenagers, and an increase in loneliness and depression. At the time they called this the "internet paradox" because most users were reporting that they were using it to communicate with others.

Yet, it seemed to have an adverse effect on closer, face-to-face, more intimate communication with others. Longitudinal research, including a three-year follow-up on these same participants, suggested that these negative effects diminished, with the exception of its association with stress (Kraut et al., 2002). Perhaps the introductory phase, whereby some individuals become enamored with the internet "surfing" phenomenon, is more maladaptive than how users tend to use the internet after they have had consistent access over time. Three years later, these participants were experiencing a positive sense in their communications use, good social involvement, and good well-being. Not surprisingly, internet use predicted better outcomes for users who were extroverts than for those who were introverts.

Since the creation of global access to the internet, there have been multiple companies that have designed social media sites, such as Facebook, Snapchat, Instagram, and Twitter, for people to share and gain information about family and friends and to follow celebrities. As of April 2017, Instagram had 700 million users and Snapchat had 250 million daily users (Aslam, 2017). Costine (2017) reports that Facebook has two billion monthly users and Twitter has 68 million users (Fiegerman, 2017). People seem to like how the internet has provided them with access to social media sites, and social media is particularly popular among young women (Kimbrough, Guadagno, Muscanell, & Dill, 2013: Muscanell & Guadagno, 2012). Perloff (2014) discusses unique ways that online social media differs from traditional media like television and movies. Modern social media is inherently interactive in that viewers are receiving influences as well as sending information and affecting others. Therefore, viewers are less passive than required in traditional media; they are now iteratively shaping the course of online information. Modern social media is more personal in that individuals can customize what they view according to their own self-interests and bond with others who have similar preferences. I do not think that people who know me well would be at all surprised by what has been shared and posted on my Facebook feed (i.e., sorry for all the pet pictures and political advocacy, folks!). It is like an online fingerprint for most of us. Modern social media also allows for the loading of images, videos, animation, and graphics that lead to a perception of real presence. This sense of virtual reality can have the net effect whereby viewers suspend their beliefs and at times change their attitudes (Barak, 2007; Green et al., 2004). For myself personally, I have found it fascinating how lost in time I can become when on Facebook. At times, I will be playing a recorded show on my TV. My attention drifts to Facebook on my phone. After what seems like a very brief minute, I am amazed by how much I have missed, and then I need to rewind once I emerge from my Facebook fugue. And social media is available to most individuals around the clock. We have become lost in it.

Moreover, the feedback aspect of modern society could amplify normative interpersonal processes when viewers see the number of "likes" they receive or do not receive. My lab conducted a study on college students' responses to Instagram pictures, and one of our more notable findings was that the women with lower self-esteem were the ones reporting that they would take down posts that received no or few likes by others. Further, social media allows individuals to idealize certain people, either because of their appearance, their lifestyles, their humor, or their inspirational words. And some viewers do not realize that they are only seeing the best of that idol because the celebrity—sometimes via her publicist—is very selective in what is posted. Thus, it is easy to think their appearance and their lives are absolutely perfect. Many individuals, especially those lower in self-esteem, are likely to use social media to admire others and strive to be like them. The scariest possibilities offered by social media are the online sites that allow individuals to support the continuation, as opposed to the recovery, of eating disorders. Called pro-anorexia or *pro-ana* as well as pro-bulimia or *pro-mia*, there are approximately 400 of these sites available from which people can choose (Levine & Chapman, 2001). Examples of material found on these sites include a young girl with tape over her mouth that reads, "I won't eat," and a picture of clothed skeletons holding hands while the caption reads, "It's not a diet. It's a lifestyle."

Cobb (2016) describes the site called *Skinny Gossip* and how females must email *SkinnyGurl*, its leader, with their height and weight including a picture photo verifying their leanness before they are allowed access. Those who are viewed as too large are rejected. Much like checking behavior in obsessive compulsive disorder, these women could be looking for reassurance or checking to see if they look okay themselves. Depending on what they find, Slater (2007) would describe it as "mutually reinforcing" relationships that lead to "reinforcing spirals" (p. 284–285) between the viewer and the negative effects of poorer body image and worsened eating disordered behavior over time. Whether researchers are studying these pro-eating disorder sites or even websites considered to be normal and healthy, the dynamics between viewers and these online sites are probably complex and have only recently been studied scientifically. This chapter will now review the research that has examined how social media appears to affect individuals' body image and eating disordered behaviors. Postings, responses, and communication on these topics can be conceptualized as *electronic fat talk*, and it appears that there is a lot of it.

Facebook intensity is defined as one's emotional connection and integration of Facebook use into everyday life. Walker et al. (2015) studied how Facebook intensity was associated with fat talk and disordered eating behavior. They surveyed 128 primarily Caucasian women about their Facebook use in connection to fat talk and eating disordered behaviors. They found that Facebook intensity was associated with more online social comparison of physical appearance, which in turn was related to more disordered eating behavior. *Social comparison* is the tendency to compare oneself and one's worth to others. An upward social comparison would be comparing ourselves to celebrities on the red carpet, whereas downward comparison would be noting how our attire is better than the person ahead of us in the check-out line at the store. Yet for the women low in social comparison in the Walker et al. study, intense Facebook use was not associated with eating disordered behaviors. As a cross-sectional study, Walker and colleagues were unable to determine if the use of Facebook encourages more social comparison for those who would otherwise not engage in this behavior, or if individuals who already tend to engage in social comparison seek out these sites and use them to fuel their disordered eating behaviors.

Fardouly, Diedrichs, Vartanian, and Halliwell (2015) had 112 college women randomly assigned to spend ten minutes browsing either a magazine website, an appearance-neutral website (i.e., did not focus on humans and how they looked), or their own Facebook pages before they completed state measures of body dissatisfaction, mood, and appearance discrepancies that were weight, face, hair, and skin related (i.e., they wanted to see changes in those bodily features). Their participants reported a more negative mood after exposure to their own Facebook page than those exposed to an appearance-neutral website. The women already high in appearance comparison tendencies had the largest reaction to their Facebook pages in terms of wishing for more changes in their face, hair, and skin appearance. It did not affect their perceived weight discrepancy. Thus, the women high in social comparison felt worse about their appearance, except for their weight, after spending ten minutes on Facebook. They also found that exposure to the online magazine website resulted in more weight and shape discrepancy in women, most likely because magazines show leaner, hegemonic depictions of beautiful women. Individuals' Facebook feed did not affect their opinions of their weight, most likely because Facebook, as opposed to women's magazines, represents more normal women in terms of sizes and shapes.

Experimental studies have shown that viewing attractive images of strangers taken from social media (i.e., typically upward social comparison) is harmful to women's body image (Haferkamp & Kramer, 2011; Tiggemann & Zaccardo, 2015). Using ecological momentary assessment methods, Fardouly, Pinkus, and Vartanian (2017) studied 146 college women who were asked to respond to a brief survey at random times for five days. *Ecological momentary assessment* is a research methodology whereby participants usually carry a device that prompts them for responses multiple times a day. An example would be a smartphone app that beeps and asks the participant when was the last time that she engaged in fat talk. The participant enters the data, and it is compiled as study data that is behavioral, or more "real world," than just having a participant complete a survey about herself one time. Fardouly et al.'s participants were assessed on type of social comparisons (i.e., upward, lateral, or downward), plus the context of these appearance comparisons, their mood, diet, and exercise thoughts, and their appearance satisfaction. They found that 71.2 percent of these comparisons were made in person, 11.8 percent were made through social media, 7.6 percent were made through television/movies, 1.5 percent were made through magazines, and 0.7 percent were made through billboard advertisements. The latter two were combined due to their low prevalence and called traditional media exposure. Upward social comparisons were more common than lateral and downward comparisons or online social media and traditional media. In all of these contexts, upward social comparisons were associated with less appearance satisfaction than when no comparisons were made. Comparing ourselves to beautifully-styled and photo-shopped models makes us feel worse about ourselves than if we were not comparing ourselves to others. Not surprisingly, upward social comparisons to social media were associated with less appearance satisfaction than comparisons made to people in real life. The authors noted that images on social media tended to be more idealized than in-person appearances, and the number of "likes" or comments on social media reinforced the fact that others, as well as the viewer, also find this image to be attractive. People tend to post more flattering photos of themselves than unpleasant ones on social media. Social media is not a good reflection of how people look in reality. Therefore, more comparisons to social media, especially to that of models and celebrities, result in poorer body image for the viewer. Fardouly et al. (2017) found that participants' mood fell into a similar pattern as appearance satisfaction. Upward comparison to social media had the most damaging effect on their mood. Similarly, although social comparison across all of these contexts was associated with more thoughts about dieting and exercising, upward comparison through social media showed the most powerful relationship.

Hendrickse, Arpan, Clayton, and Ridgway (2017) recruited 185 college women with Instagram accounts and surveyed them about their photo activities, their appearance-related social comparisons on Instagram, their drive for thinness, their body dissatisfaction, and their intra-sexual competitiveness for mates. The latter is a construct based on Darwinian evolutionary theory whereby women use their appearance to compete with other women to attract men. An example item on the scale was, "I prefer to go out to clubs with female friends who are less attractive than I am." When I first read about this study, that survey item first made me chuckle, and then it made me feel old! My friends and I ride bikes and go out for nice dinners together; the clubbing days have long since disappeared. Hendricks and colleagues found that photo activities were not related with the outcome variables, unless they examined appearance-related social comparison as a mediating variable. Individuals with higher appearance-related social comparison also had more drive for thinness and more body dissatisfaction. Their intra-sexual competitiveness for mates was positively related to their appearance-related social comparisons on Instagram. This suggests that individuals with an intense need to compare their appearance with others could be using Instagram in ways that cause harm to them and perhaps their friendships/relationships.

Kim and Chock (2015) surveyed 119 female and 67 male students from a northeastern university asking them about their drive for thinness or drive for muscularity, their number of Facebook friends, their Facebook use, and what they call Facebook grooming or engagement behaviors (i.e., how often they visit friends' profiles, post comments to their friends' threads, post likes, etc.). While overall Facebook use was not associated with social comparisons and drive for thinness, the amount of social grooming reported by participants was associated with social comparison and their drive for thinness for both sexes. Also, the number of friends was positively associated with social comparison and a greater drive for thinness. Facebook use or social grooming on Facebook was not associated with drive for muscularity for both sexes in this study. A cross-sectional study like this cannot determine causality, but it appears that individuals with a lot of friends and a lot of time grooming or actively engaging with friends on Facebook is associated with appearance concerns for men and women.

A growing concern for me is how some celebrities have become *influencers* or *Instagirls*. When I was younger, I recall commenting to friends how models and influential media tended to herald youth and take young girl models and style them up to look like young, but older sexy women. This was an impossible look to achieve for real adult women who could not apply the same makeup and look like a 14-year-old girl made up to look like an adult. Now I worry that our influential young women are borrowing heavily not only from the makeup and fashion industries, but from plastic and cosmetic surgery industry as well. My sons, who are in their young twenties, suggested that I look up the Jenners and the Kardashians. I have known about these celebrities, but I do not follow any of them on social media. I did, however, work with a young woman struggling with an eating disorder who reported intense admiration for Kendall Jenner and wished to look like her.

Most famous for their starring roles in *Keeping up with the Kardashians*, Kendall Jenner and her younger sister Kylie Jenner have placed a mark on modern culture for many youth and teenagers in the U.S. As an example, Marie Claire (2016) suggested that Kylie Jenner, daughter of Caitlyn Jenner and Kris Kardashian Jenner, had 91.8 million followers on Instagram. *Time* magazine considered her to be in the top 25 "most influential teens" in 2014 and among the top 30 most influential teens in 2015. Further, by April 2017 Kendall Jenner was considered one of the top 15 most followed celebrities on Instagram (Socialblade, 2017). While Kylie Jenner has admitted to acquiring lip fillers to make her lips look older/sexier compared to her teenage shy and innocent look, she has denied accusations about getting breast implants and buttocks and hip implants (Saunders, 2015). Similar accusations have happened to her sister Kendall Jenner about possible lip fillers, rhinoplasty, and perhaps other procedures (Strang, 2014). This article alleges that her mother, Kris Kardashian Jenner, had suggested to her friend when Kendall was nine years old that she was going to need a nose job. I have no idea if these women have used these procedures or not, but securing cosmetic procedures does seem to be a normative aspect of their family culture.

Cobb (2016) conducted an analysis of celebrity worship of Kendall Jenner in pro-anorexia online spaces that are supposed to support *Thinspiration*. Thinspiration or *Thinspo* is thin-ideal media content that can include images or prose intended to inspire weight loss, often in a way that glorifies dangerous eating disordered behaviors. As a younger teen, Kendall Jenner was embraced by the site's followers. Those same followers also cruelly derided Kendall's older half-sisters that were considered to be too voluptuous (i.e., the Kardashians). Kendall was referred to as pretty, delicate, and feminine. However, as Kendall grew, developed, and became curvier herself, the viewers viciously turned on her thinking she was no longer a positive influence on thinspiration. As I was personally viewing pictures of the Jenner sisters, I was struck by one and was surprised by individuals' responses and reports in interviews. These celebrities are likely stalked by paparazzi constantly. Even though their images and followers make them extraordinary money, the media and followers scrutinize them constantly. One of the Jenner sisters felt compelled to say in an interview that she was human and that she has feelings, too—meaning that she is not just a photo or an object that exists for other peoples' viewing. Yet social media can give viewers that message. As a non-follower, my introduction to the phenomenon left me feeling disturbed. These images portray that beauty breeds happiness, but I know that is not true. In my clinical practice, I have worked with lots of individuals who are obsessively pursuing unrealistic standards of beauty; they are absolutely miserable. The effect that these celebrity postings can have on followers can be powerful. I was surprised by the images because they felt foreign to me. I know, however, that individuals who habitually visit these sites can become desensitized to the images so that they appear normative, expected, and, thus, achievable. They can also begin to feel very personal. A phenomenon called *celebrity worship* leads some followers to feel that they have a special connection or relationship with the celebrity because they *see* them day after day. A few studies have found that celebrity worship is associated with negative body image (Malby, Giles, Barber, & McCutcheon, 2005; Swami, Taylor, & Carvaho, 2001). If a celebrity's look seems achievable and even normative, it could make one's personal appearance seem unattractive. I remember sitting with my teenage client viewing an image of Kendall Jenner. Upon inquiry, she really thought this was how the celebrity rolled out of bed and looked each day, 24/7. We spent some time discussing the reality of Kendall's appearance and what likely took makeup, a hairdresser and stylist, a skilled photographer, and perhaps some computer touch-ups to finish the photo. My client's initial impression was a very dangerous way to think about what is being viewed, especially because this can lead to some extreme solutions trying to match this false perception in real life. The one second it took to capture that image on camera probably took millions of seconds to construct. The viewer is only seeing a moment, not the true story of the model's life.

Brown and Tiggemann (2016) studied 138 predominantly Caucasian college students from Australia who were randomly assigned to view either a collection of celebrity images, a set of equally attractive unknown peer images, or a control set of travel images. They completed a survey that asked about their Instagram usage, level of celebrity worship, negative mood and body dissatisfaction, and a social comparison scale. Their participants reported following between 100–200 people on Instagram including an average of five celebrities. Being exposed to celebrity images and to attractive photos of unknown peers resulted in more negative mood and body dissatisfaction compared to if they viewed the travel photos. Social comparison levels within these women mediated both of these effects. Celebrity worship moderated the effect for exposure to celebrity images in real life. Thus, women who reported the most habitual celebrity worship were the ones to have the most negative moods and body dissatisfaction after viewing the celebrity images— making celebrity worship an additional risk factor for poor body image and, perhaps, depression. Brown and Tiggemann suggest that literacy programs that target critical awareness of the impact of media on body image should include information about peer comparisons and especially upward social comparisons of celebrities in popular media including that which is online.

Ghaznavi and Taylor (2015) conducted a content analysis of 300 images from Twitter and 150 images from Pinterest with one half tagged as #thinspiration and the other half tagged as #thinspo. The typical woman featured in these images was bony, scantily clad, and sexually provocative, and the photo often focused on her abdomen or pelvis. Ninety-one percent of the images were characterized as *triggers*, which are intended to motivate viewers to lose weight, with 4 percent coded as *reverse triggers*, which are intended to be repugnant to viewers (e.g., obesity), and 0.7 percent coded as *distractors*, which are intended to distract viewers from hunger or give them appetite fulfillment through images of food. Very few images focused on body self-acceptance (2.3 percent) or healthful eating and not starving oneself (1 percent). In terms of bodily features, the majority of images (80 percent) focused on the pelvis and another 80 percent focused on the abdomen (some visuals featured both). This is consistent with the evolutionary psychological literature illustrating the importance of the lower waist-to-hip ratio as a virtue of fertility for women. Following the most frequent photos that zoomed in on the abdomen and pelvis, 78 percent focused on thighs followed by 47 percent featuring the head and 36 percent featuring the shins. Fifty-seven percent featured an image of a woman partially clad and 75.3 percent were deemed to be sexually suggestive. Analysis of viewers' tags to these images suggested that they were being used for social comparison of their bodies and included text messages about admiration, desire for perfection, images of celebrities, or disgust with fat or weight gain. A comment that was considered to be self-accepting was rare. Images tagged as #thinspo tended to be more sexually suggestive and contained more extreme thinness than those tagged as #thinspiration. The authors were concerned that girls and young women who habitually view these images come to believe that these bodies are normative when, in fact, they are sickly thin. Moreover, it is clear that these sites help girls and women maintain disordered eating behaviors rather than encourage healthy eating and exercise behaviors. Parents of young women may wish to check out what their daughters are viewing on their devices. Who knew we could discover poor self-esteem and an eating disorder on our smartphones?!

In conclusion, cultural influences promoting poor body image, fat talk, and eating disorders are flourishing in popular media. Their effects can be long-term, damaging, and powerful. Developmentally, children in the U.S. are quickly introduced to gender stereotypes including the hegemonic beauty ideal for girls and women. Playing with the iconic Barbie and exposure to Walt Disney's princesses foster unrealistic and even ridiculous expectations about appearance for girls at a very young age. Further, human role models who are popular in contemporary media underwrite the thin ideal in our culture. Lack of physical diversity in all of these role models helps to support the common prejudice of the American disdain for fat and obesity. This is happening, ironically, at a time in our national history when so many individuals are relying on unhealthy fast food and the U.S. obesity prevalence rates are at an all-time high. Fat talk involves conversational tendencies that may help women reconcile how their ideals of feminine size and shape are not who they really are. Finally, this chapter acknowledges that the internet, especially social media, has changed how we are exposed to appearance ideals and how some individuals feed off of social media in maintaining poor body image, fat talk, and disordered eating behaviors. Fat talk is happening in personal conversations and is rampant and public in electronic form on social media. Consequently, both evolutionary biology/psychology and cultural analyses explain why fat talk appears to be widespread in modern history. The next chapter will describe the evolution of scientific research on fat talk that has emerged within the last few decades.

3

When Fat Talk Got a Name

"I am no longer accepting the things I cannot change. I am now changing the things I cannot accept."—Women's March sign, 2017

I grew up in middle class, suburban America. I have heard fat talk all of my life and I understand women's physical appearance standards. After completing my dissertation on eating disorders prevention and realizing that internalization of the cultural thin ideal is a consistent risk factor for developing eating disorders across the scientific literature (Stice, 2002), I turned my research to body image. Although I was trained and currently practice as a clinical health psychologist, my research interests have always been more social psychological in nature. Fat talk is both a personal and interpersonal phenomenon. It interacts reciprocally between how people feel about their bodies, how that is disclosed in words, and then it affects their relationships and the individuals that listen to those words. How individuals respond and reciprocate fat talk impacts them personally at the level of self-esteem and body image.

Body image is defined as "a multifaceted concept that refers to persons' perceptions and attitudes about their own body, particularly but not exclusively its physical appearance" (*Body Image: An International Journal of Research*, 2018). The body image literature is extensive, and historically focused mainly on individuals' personal body image evaluations. I became curious about how these personal feelings seeped into everyday conversations. Much like how my students who learn the definition of fat talk report that they then become acutely aware of how often they hear it in normal conversations, I was keenly aware that I was hearing women talk about their body image with other women, often in a joking manner, but at times in a more serious, intimate manner. Although body image had historically been studied as a *personal* phenomenon, I was finding that body image was a common *interpersonal* phenomenon. Further, as a clinician who treats eating disorders, I found body image concerns disclosed in psychotherapy taking on an extreme and even pitiful quality. Not only do some individuals report critique of their bodies and body parts, they show hatred for them. That hate, at times, destroys lives. Eating disorders—especially anorexia nervosa—are the most deadly psychological disorders (Crow et al., 2009).

My research team was calling fat talk conversations the *social psychology of body image* when my student, Lauren Britton, whose own research found fat talk to be normative and reciprocated by college women, found Mimi Nichter's book, *Fat Talk: What Girls and Their Parents Say about Dieting* (2000). Note that Nichter's term for this form of feminine discourse reflected Caucasian, middle school girls' appearance ideal of thin bodies during that time in American culture. If the ideal is thinness, then the critique is about fat. Nichter's name for fat talk was much more memorable than our "social psychology of body image." Although fat talk can be a critique about weight gain and true body fat, other researchers and I have extended the definition of the term to include broader criticism about one's physical appearance, as well as diet and exercise discussions if they are focused on self-improvement of one's looks. As such, fat talk is appearance critique.

Fat talk got a name in the 1990s. Called the Teen Lifestyle Project, Nichter and Vuckovic (1994) conducted ethnographic interviews of U.S. middle school-aged girls inquiring about their body image, dieting, and smoking behaviors. In response to the open-ended questions "Do you think that a lot of girls your age are concerned about their weight?" and "How do you know that?" Nichter and Vuckovic recorded these girls' responses and looked for patterns. They coined the term *fat talk* to reflect this imperative and ritualized dialogue and noted that fat talk is not always really about seeing oneself as fat. They also proposed that fat talk serves multiple interpersonal functions.

In the first function, Nichter and Vuckovic said fat talk is used to elicit social validation or gain reassurance from friends. As such, fat talk is "a call for positive strokes" (p. 113). For example, if a girl complains about her body by saying, "I feel so fat today," it might be expected that a friend would reassure her and say something like, "No you are not. Shut up. You know I'm fatter than you." Warren, Martz, Curtin, Bazzini, and Gagnon (2013) conducted qualitative research on college men's and women's responses to fat talk in various situations. These participants clearly knew that fat talk from a same-sex friend or even an acquaintance is a fishing attempt to lure positive reassurance from them. These participants also knew that after they reassure the other person, they are supposed to reciprocate with their own critique. This is what was so funny about Cady's response about having bad breath upon awakening in response to her new friends' fat talk in the movie *Mean Girls* (Fey, 2004). Rather than pick a unique flaw to fit in with the group, Cady picked something she thought was negative, but was also totally normal.

Find me a person who does *not* have bad breath in the morning. Cady's life in rural Africa had kept her from learning the nuances of what was expected in fat talk.

The second proposed function of fat talk is using this dialogue to mask other uncomfortable feelings that one cannot express more directly. In this regard, fat talk is a feminine form of powerless language (e.g., Areni & Sparks, 2005; Hosman & Siltanen, 2006; O'Barr, 1982; DeStefano, 2007), where women have been socialized to hint around and obscure their feelings and opinions, rather than state them directly. For this proposed function of fat talk, stating to others that they "feel fat" may be more acceptable than stating their anger at another person or that they are feeling rejected by others. Saying that they feel fat can also be more socially palatable than saying that they feel depressed or anxious. Just like the first function discussed in the paragraph above, using fat talk to express sensitive emotions is also a fishing attempt to elicit support and reassurance in a time of need. Fat talk also assumes that other girls/women will understand what it feels like to feel fat or worry about one's appearance. Consequently, I have been concerned that fat talk is the universal *girl language*, much like how discussing the weather is the universal polite, small-talk language that we use with strangers. The latter is likely an innocuous bonding behavior. However, fat talk does not harbor the same innocence.

The third proposed function of fat talk is to relieve guilt from engaging in behaviors that might facilitate weight gain or are considered "fattening" (Nichter, 2000; Nichter & Vuckovic, 1994). Girls and women seem to understand that women are presumed to be concerned about their physical appearance, and in this case their body weight, at *all* times. Fat talking, in this instance, is used as an excuse to take a break from that mandate. For example, one girl in a buffet line might say to another, "I know, I know, this ice cream sundae will most certainly land on my thighs." Her friend is then supposed to reply with a supportive comment and perhaps derogate her own body: "We *all* love their ice cream. Let's just see if I can fit into my bathing suit after today." In this capacity, the girl apologizes first to her friend concerning a food rule infringement (i.e., we are not supposed to eat ice cream if it can make us fat). Once they have established intent to violate this rule together, then they can relax and enjoy their treats. It is nice to get a break from needing to care about appearance and needing to suppress weight *all* of the time.

The fourth function is meant to create a sense of group identification and affiliation (i.e., the "in-group" vs. the "out-group"; Nichter, 2000; Nichter & Vuckovic, 1994). One's in-group shares values on how important physical appearance is for *us* and how *we* are supposed to dress, how much *we* are supposed to weigh, and how *we* are supposed to behave. The out-group is *them. They* are different from *us* and *they* dress and look differently; *they* have different appearance values. This social psychological creation of in-groups and out-groups functions to improve closeness and gain approval of those who are in the in-group. Here, group solidarity might be served by body snarking or fat shaming the appearance of another woman in the out-group to strengthen feelings of interconnectedness within a social circle of the in-group. This phenomenon was illustrated in a prelude to a popular rap song by Sir Mix-A-Lot in the 1990s called "Baby's Got Back." A group of Caucasian teens offer the following verbal critique of another woman: "Oh, my, God Becky. Look at her butt. It is so big … She's just so Black!" Additional lyrics clarify that Becky and her group are White "valley girl" types, whereas the girl who has the butt that they are mocking is Black and part of rap culture. This illustrates the in-group and the out-group. While body snarking ranges from discourteous to malicious, it may serve to bring women in the in-group closer to one another as they affirm shared attitudes. As such, fat talk may serve the additional aforementioned function that communicates to others personal conscientiousness about physical appearance and attractiveness, and that one internalizes and values the thin-ideal physique that is heralded in popular U.S. media.

Nichter (2000) and Nichter and Vuckovic's (1994) fifth proposed purpose of fat talk is referred to as "social control," which is arguably most related to what social psychology calls impression management. Here girls may feel pressure to state negative things about their bodies to be liked, to fit into a group of friends, and perhaps to avoid social rejection resulting from the perception of being "stuck up" or a bitch. It is not uncommon for women to conform to social norms to elicit approval from others. Even our own research found that college women professed their personal body image esteem in a female dyad, while also conforming to their partner's fat talk or self-accepting talk, or positive body talk verbally (Tucker, Martz, Curtin, & Bazzini, 2007) and in a nonverbal manner conveying sincerity and genuineness (DeStephano, 2007). Therefore, if friends fat talk, women may be unwilling to deviate from such discourse and risk the collective comfort of the group. They may engage in these body-derogating conversations because they believe that a failure to do so might result in social ostracism, or because they think it is just a way to be polite and roll with the group. Further, fat talk is a socially acceptable way to convey to others that women are humble, flawed, and non-intimidating; basically, it's a quick and dirty way to say women are friendly and far from being bitches.

Fat talk is normative, reciprocal (Britton et al., 2006), and common in that as many as 93 percent of college women report that they engage in this type of dialogue (Salk & Engeln-Maddox, 2011). Behavioral psychology suggests that humans engage in behavior with the expectation of reinforcement and disengage from behavior when expecting punishment. Girls and women would not engage in fat talk if they were not rewarded for doing so. Fat talk dialogue is not being discouraged (i.e., punished) interpersonally. Anecdotally, any discussion encouraging women to disengage or punish another's fat talk tends to make us uncomfortable. Imagine this: a friend has just stated, "my Caribbean vacation was wonderful, but I think I gained 10 pounds in just one week." Think about the other friend stating, "You should not disparage your weight to me in public. It is unflattering." My bet is she would instead laugh at the joke, tell her she looks great, complain about her own body, and then continue to ask questions about the tropical vacation. Friends often take the cue to fat talk from another person and then do it themselves. Thus fat talk, because it is so normative, gets rewarded when others reciprocate it. If girls and women are reinforcing fat talk, it maintains the norm in our culture.

Barwick, Bazzini, Martz, Rocheleau, and Curtin (2012) examined if the size of a target woman who was fat talking or engaging in positive body talk had an impact on the perceived likability of her by other women. Sixty-three women who were primarily Caucasian from a public comprehensive university in the Southeast read a vignette of four women studying for a biology exam whose conversations drift into either negative body talk (fat talk) or positive body talk. The target woman is named "Jenny" and participants were presented with a photograph of her. Note that the name Jenny was chosen because Jennifer, nickname Jen or Jenny, was a popular Caucasian baby name 20 years prior to this study. Thus, the college students who served as research participants at the time would be able to relate to the name. Participants were shown one of four photographs of the target woman, two blondes and two brunettes, who were pretested to be equally attractive. One woman of each hair color was pretested to be heavier than the leaner women. Keep in mind that the size of the larger woman was rated as statistically heavier than the leaner woman, but in reality the larger woman appeared full-figured and curvier, but not obese in appearance. With that in mind, it was not terribly surprising that Barwick and colleagues found that the varied sizes of Jenny did not have an impact on her perceived likability. However, they did find some other interesting effects. When Jenny engaged in fat talk, they found her response to be less surprising to them than the more surprising response of positive body talk. Again, this supports the normative nature of fat talk. Further, they found Jenny's response to be more typical and likely when she fat talked than when she engaged in positive body talk. They were more likely to think other women would respond with the fat talk than with the positive body talk, yet they preferred hearing the positive body talk. They gave Jenny better ratings on multiple personality and interpersonal characteristics when she said positive rather than negative things about her body. When Jenny said self-promotional dialogue, compared to when she fat talked, she was deemed to be friendlier, confident, sophisticated, outgoing, mature, assertive, interesting, a leader, polite, and responsible. Thus, our participants seemed to privately admire a woman who resisted the fat talk norm and said positive things about herself.

Corning and Buchianeri (2016) conducted two experiments to investigate women's responses to another woman who either fat talked or said self-accepting things about her appearance. In the first study, 130 college women, who were primarily Caucasian (72.1 percent), were shown eight photos (four thin & four overweight women) of women's bodies that were each accompanied by a body-related statement that either fat talked or made self-affirming statements. As an example of the fat talk statement, it said, "Every time I look in the mirror, I can pick out something about every part of my body that I'd like to change. I can't remember the last time I was happy with the way I looked." An example of the self-affirming statement was, "Other women talk about their weight in numbers, but I look in the mirror, and I like what I see! This is my body, and I'm going to own it" (p. 123). The dependent variable was a genuineness survey item that read, "How much do you believe that she really means the statement that she made about her body?" on a Likert item from 1–"I don't believe at all" to 7–"I completely believe." Results found that regardless of the weight of the women in the photos, participants found the fat talk to be *more* believable than self-affirming statements—probably because they have heard more of the fat talk, as opposed to the positive talk, in real life. In their second study, they recruited 125 college women with the same demographics, but they designed a within-subjects experimental design, rather than a between-subjects design as used in Study #1. *Within-subjects* means that each participant viewed all eight of the photos that were crossed for fat talk or self-affirming talk. Results showed that they found the overweight women who were fat talking to be more believable than the other three conditions: thin women's fat talk, overweight women's self-affirming talk, or thin women's self-affirming talk. There was a trend for finding thin women's fat talk more believable than self-affirming talk. Overweight women's self-affirming statements were found to be more, not less, believable than thin women's self-affirming statements. Corning and Buchianeri (2016) concluded that these women generally find fat talk to be more believable than self-affirming statements from other women. They also tended to believe what overweight women said about their bodies more than what they believed from thin women's statements. This suggests that self-abasing statements, classically the fat talk, may be heard as more authentic than hearing women speak positively and confidently about their bodies. Given the normative nature of fat talk, this has implications for campaigns aimed at reducing fat talk or aimed at improving women's body image.

Corning, Bucchianeri, and Pick (2014) conducted a third study using these thin versus overweight women's photos, again crossed with fat talk versus self-affirming statements, as a separate independent variable. Participants were 139 college women from a mid-size university in the Midwest who were Caucasian (71 percent), Latina (13.6 percent), Asian (8.6 percent), or other (5.8 percent). Again, as a within-subjects design, participants viewed all eight photos and statements in counter-balanced order (i.e., the order was randomized so that all photos had the opportunity to be viewed first, which controls for effects of the order in which they are seen). This time, the dependent variable was a measure of body dissatisfaction. Viewing the noticeably thin woman compared to viewing the overweight women did impact their body dissatisfaction. Unpredictably for the authors, however, their body dissatisfaction was worse when they heard the thin woman fat talk, as well as when they heard her engage in positive body statements. Following these experimental conditions, body dissatisfaction was significantly lower after being exposed to the overweight women engaging in fat talk, and dissatisfaction of participants was lowest after seeing the overweight women making positive statements. Thus, hearing a thin woman fat talk—compared to a larger woman—has more of a deleterious effect on the female audience. However, hearing the thin woman engage in positive body talk also causes harm. All of these experimental situations likely evoke a social comparison process about physical appearance, which may be the most harmful component. In other words, it may not matter what another woman says about her body—drawing attention to her body and how she feels about it encourages another person to do the same with her own body.

Even though women seem to find fat talk to be normative and even more authentic within feminine social circles, there appears to be a time and a place for it to occur. Using a very clever confederate-based lab study, Gapinski, Brownell, and LaFrance (2003) led participants to believe they were completing a study about consumer clothing preferences for a marketing campaign. These women tried on either a swimsuit or a sweater that composed the clothing style independent variable, while a female confederate in an adjacent dressing room either expressed dissatisfaction with her body (fat talk) or expressed dissatisfaction with a non-body related topic (i.e., problems with her computer as a control condition) that was used as the second independent variable. The confederate's dialogue in each of the two conditions was pre-scripted by the experimenters. Participants were led to believe that the woman in the adjacent changing room was also trying on the same type of clothing (swimsuit or sweater). In reality, the confederate was hanging out in whatever clothing she wore as a research assistant that day. Keep in mind, the participant and confederate talked in adjacent stalls, but never saw one another. What the participants had to wear based on experimental condition (i.e., either revealing attire for the swimsuit or unrevealing attire with the bulky sweater), as well as the second independent variable (i.e., if they heard the other woman fat talk versus complain about her computer as a control condition) produced an interaction effect. Although participants trying on a swimsuit reported greater frequency of body concerns than those trying on a sweater, those women who were exposed to fat talk while viewing themselves in a swimsuit in a mirror experienced lower levels of negative emotions compared to women who were exposed to fat talk while in a sweater. The results suggest that women may feel comfortable with fat talk in a situation in which their own bodies are on display—like while in a swimsuit in front of mirrors—but may actually be uncomfortable in circumstances where the context is less body focused, such as while wearing a bulky sweater that hides their own body. These results suggest that women probably have to navigate the nuances of body talk in varying social contexts.

In conclusion, U.S. women live in a culture where fat talk is being reinforced as a bonding experience among girls and women, so we would expect that fat talk would be associated with positive constructs. However, the next chapter will establish how fat talk is associated, in extant research, with many negative constructs and psychopathology. Consequently, I posit that fat talk operates like an addiction. It is done for short-term gain, even though it has hidden longer-term negative consequences. Perhaps Nichter (2000) and Nichter and Vuckovic (1994) were correct in their assertion that fat talk is evident in many young girls in the U.S. who know its normative tradition and how fat talk functions interpersonally. What these young girls may have not learned yet by the age of middle school is how a pattern of fat talking can result in negative outcomes if continued across their development.

4

What Are the Known Consequences of Fat Talk?

"My body. My choice. My right."—Women's March sign, 2017

Research on the phenomenon of fat talk exploded in the mid–2000s and took somewhat of a different focus than Nichter and Vuckovic's (1994) ethnographic approach studying how it functions for middle school girls. Most research since that time has found more of the negative or psychopathological associations of fat talk, as opposed to any beneficial aspects of fat talk for girls, women, and their relationships with themselves and others. Some of the more recent discoveries that fat talk is more harmful than good may be a function of where researchers have directed their focus. That is, researchers have been looking for associations that are bad or pathological more than they have been exploring associations of how fat talk may function for girls and women. Most feminists would hold that fat talk is unfortunate, harmful, and even inexcusable. Yet behaviorism, as a science, knows that people engage in behavior for reinforcement and people fail or stop engaging in behavior when punished. People would not engage in fat talk if they were not getting something beneficial from it. Fat talk—at least in the short-term—offers reward. Along with Nichter and Vuckovic's proposition that fat talk serves functions for middle school girls, I have tried in previous chapters to contextualize fat talk and explain other reasons for its existence and propagation. I would be remiss, however, to exclude the growing body of research linking fat talk with pathology. This chapter will review studies that have found connections between fat talk and other constructs in an attempt to understand the rather complex interactions between this form of conversational style and an individual's psychology, relationships, and broader culture.

Since fat talk vocalizes diverse but themed statements about one's size, shape, body fat, or eating choices and habits, it would make sense to first examine known relationships between it and body image and eating disorders. Ousley, Cordero, and White (2008) found that college women's frequency of fat talk was associated with body image dissatisfaction and eating pathology in students with a diagnosed and ongoing eating disorder, as well as participants without an eating disorder diagnosis. Those participants without an eating disorder reported engaging in fat talk only rarely, never, or doing it on a monthly basis. As would be suspected, students who had an eating disorder reported much more use of fat talk. In fact, they reported engaging in fat talk on at least a daily basis. Not surprisingly, it appears that individuals suffering from eating disorders are more frequent fat talkers. Fat talk may have that addictive coping nature—that is, providing short-term relief, but causing long-term harm—within the other dysfunctional habits of eating disorders.

Mills and Fuller-Tyszkiewicz (2017) conducted a meta-analysis of 35 studies on samples of all female or mostly female samples published between 1990 and 2016. They examined the association of fat talk and key components of body image disturbance. Results suggested that fat talk tends to precede body image problems more so than the reverse influence of poor body image kindling fat talk behavior; however, they also found studies pointing to more of a bidirectional relationship between the two. Sharpe, Naumann, Treasure, and Schmidt (2013) conducted a meta-analysis of 24 cross-sectional studies and found that fat talk and body dissatisfaction shared consistent and small associations ($r = .30$). Recall that a correlation $r = 0.0$ means absolutely no relationship between two things and a correlation $r = 1.0$ means a perfect relationship. As one variable goes up (e.g., body image gets worse), the other variable also goes up (e.g., more fat talking). A negative correlation would mean that as one variable goes up, the other one lessens. For Sharpe et al., there was a prospective relationship between fat talking and changes in body dissatisfaction in the longer term of one year ($r = .14$), but not in studies showing shorter-term consequences of fat talking ($r = .02$). When my lab first started studying fat talk, we were calling it the social psychology of body image. We conceptualized fat talk as poor body image trickling into social conversations. Fat talk and poor body image are clearly linked and future research will wish to further explore the intricacies of this relationship. My bet is that this trickling hypothesis is a part of the dynamic for the person who initiates fat talk. But what does this do to the people who have to hear it? Is hearing fat talk reminiscent of being exposed to someone else's cigarette smoke?

Stice, Maxfield, and Wells (2003) studied just that. They designed an experiment in which 120 women from a large public university participated in their lab and ostensibly interacted with a young woman who they thought was another participant. However, the other participant was really a trained actor called a confederate. There were two trained confederates who alternated in their role and both were considered to be ultra-thin (i.e., body mass indices at 18.2 & 18.6). Participants completed surveys, watched a video, and participated in a three-to-five minute conversation with one another. As an independent variable, the confederate either fat talked and complained about her weight while discussing her rigorous exercise and dieting routines, or alternatively, she served as the control condition where she conversed about neutral topics like her plans for the weekend. Following the conversation, the experimenter returned to the room and had the two women complete post-test surveys. Stice et al. found that exposure to this thin woman's fat talk compared to hearing her discuss neutral topics created more body dissatisfaction in participants. Hearing a thin woman whining about her body when the other woman is larger than her evokes upward social comparison and thoughts like, "If she thinks she is fat, then I must be humungous." The authors conclude that hearing messages that women may not be thin enough has the net effect of making them feel worse about their bodies through social comparison.

Taniguchi and Lee (2012) created mock Facebook sites that featured either an underweight or overweight profile owner who received messages from her peers to either encourage weight loss or discourage weight loss. The profile owner posted her desire to lose weight across all four conditions. Examples of friends' posts that encouraged weight loss read like, "I lost weight after taking an aerobics class last semester. Try it, it might work 4 u," and examples in the discouraging weight loss condition read such as, "Honey, you are adorable just as you are!" and "R u crazy? U look just fine!" The Facebook sites for these two independent variables were randomly assigned to n = 96 U.S. college students from a university in Hawaii (22.5 percent Caucasian, 48.2 percent Asian, 11 percent Hawaiian, 4.4 percent Hispanic/Black, and 13.9 percent interethnic) and n = 103 Japanese college students. After viewing the Facebook site, participants completed surveys that ascertained their body satisfaction and their psychological well-being. Unexpected to these authors, participants' body satisfaction did not vary as a function of the profile owners' underweight or overweight photo depiction regardless of if they were U.S. or Japanese participants. When they viewed friends' messages that encouraged (versus discouraged) weight loss, Japanese women reported lower body satisfaction. Both U.S. and Japanese participants reported higher psychological well-being after reading the weight loss discouragement versus weight loss encouragement messages, regardless of the profile owners' body size. Hearing women encourage other women to lose weight likely makes the viewer think more critically about her own body, thus lowering her appraisal of herself. Alternatively, it seems that women feel better when they hear more positive content about another woman's body. Note, however, that these Facebook profiles were of strangers as opposed to real friends, as most of us view them in the real world. How do women respond to images prompting body talk by our real friends?

Cruwys, Leverington, and Sheldon (2016) designed a clever experiment with real female friendship dyads. Therefore, to participate in the experiment, each woman had to bring a true friend who also agreed to take part. These women participated in a study ostensibly about "communications in social media" where they viewed images and received instant messenger comments from their friend, who was placed in a separate computer cubicle. Using a deception technique, participants were led to believe that they got to randomly draw who was listed as Friend "A" or Friend "B." Yet, participants were always assigned to be "Friend B," who would first receive comments from "Friend A—the confederate," who served the role of an independent variable of 1) fat talk, 2) neutral talk, or 3) positive talk. Thus, both friends in the pairs were privately assigned to be Friend B so that they got to respond a person who they thought was their friend, but the "friend" was actually comments that were pre-determined by the experimenters and themed according to the independent variables listed above. Participants in the fat talk condition, relative to both neutral and positive body talk conditions, reported more body dissatisfaction, thin-ideal internalization, and negative affect, but no differences in their intent to diet. "Hearing" their "friend" fat talk had a negative impact on them immediately. In this same experiment, they coded how much fat talk the friends expressed as a response to what the other friend had ostensibly commented on in the social media platform. They found that the amount each friend fat talked mediated between their hearing it and disordered eating outcomes (i.e., body dissatisfaction, negative affect, thin-ideal internalization, & dieting intentions). Finally, to determine adherence to their friendship group's norms regarding fat talk or body acceptance, all participants completed the Descriptive Norms for Pursuit of Thinness Scale before they were led to the part of the study where they viewed images and instant message chatted with their friend. Based on their responses to this scale, participants were further categorized as having a friendship group norm that was pro-fat talk or that was pro-self-accepting/anti-fat talk.

Cruwys et al. (2016) ran a regression analysis and found a very interesting interaction between their perceived friendship norm and the experimental condition of fat talk, neutral talk, and positive body talk on a friendship rating scale after the social media exercise was completed. For the friendship groups holding anti-fat talking norms, friends were evaluated most positively when they engaged in neutral talk, friends who fat talked were rated most poorly, and those with positive body talk were in between. In an interesting twist for friends holding the pro-fat talk norms, they rated their friends more positively when they fat talked, as well as when they engaged in positive body talk relative to when they were neutral. The authors did not speculate as to why this occurred. Yet, it appears that surveying a person about their friendship norms for fat talk does not predict how they respond when their close friend conforms to this norm. Having to listen to a friend's fat talk tends to be rough on body image, but our social groups' beliefs about fat talk being a good or bad thing also impacts how people perceive these events. More research is needed in this area to better understand the interactions between friendship group norms of fat talk or self-acceptance and perceptions of friends' behavior in varied social situations.

Arroyo and Harwood (2012), who are communication studies experts, framed "fat talk as a dynamic and collaborative process wherein weight issues are negotiated within people" (p.3). More simply, they proposed that fat talk, as interpersonal communication, both reflects and contributes to individuals' personal psychological processes. They studied fat talk longitudinally in two studies. In the first study, fat talk noted during the first survey, referred to as Time #1, predicted more depression and lower body satisfaction being reported at Time #2. Fat talk served to mediate between young women and men's body weight concerns and mental health issues. Study 2 was meant to replicate Study 1 and remedy some of its scientific flaws. Study 2 again examined young women and men — this time across a two-week time span. Students who reported engaging in more fat talk at Time #1 reported more pressure to be thin and more depression after two weeks at Time #2. There was a trend for having heard more fat talk at Time #1 and feeling pressure to be thin after two weeks.

When women fat talk, they appear to be harming or reinforcing the negativity within themselves, but they are also drawing other women into the negative drama dance. From a feminist philosophical stance, fat talk is keeping the speaker down while also harming those that have to listen to it. As this chapter has described, there are forces compelling girls and women to fat talk. This behavior must have some reinforcement or else nobody would participate. Yet, the research studies featured in this chapter suggest that fat talk does more harm than good. Again, I assert that fat talk probably briefly creates a sense of relief knowing that others also feel bad about their bodies. Fat talk may give girls and women short-term gain, while at the same time creating longer-term harm for us and for our society. Using the addiction analogy, girls' and women's fat talk is a symptom of a larger societal disease of sexism and misogyny.

5

Who Are the Fat Talkers?

*"Continue to embrace the things that make you unique even
if it makes others uncomfortable. You are enough. And whenever you're feeling doubt, whenever you want to give up, you
must always remember to choose freedom over fear."*—Janelle
Monae, American singer, songwriter, and actor

Nichter and Vuckovic (1994) and Nichter (2000) studied middle school
Caucasian girls in their seminal ethnographic work on fat talk; their work
suggested that it is a gendered phenomenon. The girls were participating in
fat talk, but it was not something that the boys, who were the focus of other
research, were commenting about amongst themselves. Parker, Nichter, Vuckovic, Sims, and Ritenbaugh (1995) later interviewed African American middle
school girls who denied participating in this behavior while instead adopting
a more personalized, unique, and flexible standard for beauty and fashion: a
style called "She's got it goin' on." To have it "going on," a person makes the
best of her original attributes. She adorns her body with flattering clothing,
wears no make-up, or uses make-up to accentuate her features as opposed to
using it to hide flaws. She styles her hair in various and unique ways. And,
she keeps her nails and toenails creatively polished. It is a very flexible way
to be. Not everyone wants to look like Barbie!

Although negative body talk does occur in men (Engeln, Sladek, &
Waldron, 2013; Sladek, Engeln, & Miller, 2014), fat talk appears to be a
more prevalent experience for girls and women. Our research lab conducted
two of the original studies documenting that girls and women embrace fat
talk more—which is another reason why fat talk is a feminist issue. Many
women are willfully participating in a form of conversation that diminishes
their success, therefore perpetuating a toxic norm. In this way, fat talk is
destructive for girls and women in their social circles. Martz, Petroff, Curtin,
and Bazzini (2009) used a cross-sectional online survey, called the *Psychology
of Size Survey*, of 4000 age- and race-represented adult women and men in

the U.S. Participants were instructed to imagine three scenarios that involved a group of friends/coworkers commenting "about their bodies." The three situations differed only in the valence of the stated body comments and included:

1. negative/fat talk situation (i.e., "My butt is fat")
2. self-accepting (i.e., "I feel okay about my body")
3. positive (i.e., "I really like my body")

Following these scenarios, participants rated 1) the likelihood of hearing this dialogue in their lives (i.e., exposure to this form of body talk) and 2) the amount of pressure they would experience to join in each of the discussions described above. Outcomes were dichotomized into those who reported these "Frequently" and "Very frequently" versus those who reported "Never," "Sometimes," and "Usually." When asked their likelihood of hearing these three scenarios, there were no gender differences in the self-accepting and positive body talk scenarios. However, of the 100 percent total respondents who said they "Frequently" or "Very frequently" heard fat talk, 73.6 percent of them were women, versus 26.4 percent men. Women were hearing a lot more fat talk than men. We found the same effect when we dichotomized the outcome for "How much pressure would you feel to say either negative, self-accepting or positive things about your body in this group?" into "A lot" or "Extreme" versus "None," "Maybe some," or "Some." Again, there were no gender differences for the self-accepting or positive body-talk scenarios. Of the 100 percent who reported "A lot" or "Extreme" pressure to join in fat talk, 71.9 percent were women and 28.1 percent were men. Thus, American women reported being exposed to more fat talk and they also said that they feel more conformity pressure to participate in this type of dialogue compared to men.

Payne, Martz, Tompkins, Petroff, and Farrow (2010) used the same brief scenarios described above to study college students from the United Kingdom and the U.S. and found that women were 4.3 times more likely to report "Frequently" or "Very frequently" hearing fat talk, and 3.9 times more likely to perceive "A lot" or "Extreme" pressure to engage in fat talk than men. Hence, the gendered nature of fat talk may be cross-cultural and not unique to the U.S. Tzoneva, Forney, and Keel (2015) surveyed men and women from ages 17 to 75 in the fourth wave of a longitudinal, epidemiological study that surveyed the health and eating patterns of college student cohorts that began in 1982. The 2012 survey was the first to include an item of fat talk, "How often do your close friends comment on their own weight or eating?" Consistent with the other studies examining gender, they found that women reported more exposure to fat talk than men.

Racial Influences on Fat Talk

Research has shown that fat talk appears to be more of a normative conversational ritual for Caucasian girls and women compared to their African American counterparts. Parker et al. (1995) found that African American middle school girls reported more flexible standards of beauty and less fat talk than Caucasian girls. Thornhill, Curtin, Bazzini, and Martz (2016) surveyed 157 Caucasian women from a Southeastern public university and had them read vignettes of four college students studying for an exam in a conversation that veered into fat talk. The independent variable altered the name of the protagonist, Ava, to be described as Caucasian, African American, or no race specified. Ava was chosen as the name because it was found to be equally popular for Caucasians and African Americans. When participants were not told Ava's race, 97.8 percent assumed she was Caucasian. Fat talk was perceived to be more normative or typical for these women when Ava was described as Caucasian as opposed to African American. Further, the participants stated they would have responded similarly to Ava by engaging in fat talking behavior when she was described to be Caucasian as opposed to African American. Consequently, Caucasian women seemed to understand that fat talking is either normative for themselves and/or they cannot picture African American women doing so. As a limitation in the research methodology, Thornhill et al. (2016) had women simply speculate about race after reading a vignette of women engaging in fat talk. The next study examines how fat talk is viewed based on the actual race of women in focus group conversations.

Webb, Warren-Findlow, Chou, and Adams (2013) conducted focus groups of young college women in an urban public university in the South. Groups were either African American or European American (i.e., Caucasian) and included discussion prompts of their group's and the other group's ideal body size perceptions. Participants completed an ethnically neutral figure rating scale with depictions of women of varying sizes, and then participated in focus groups with women of their same race. African Americans thought that European American's idealized role models were thin and sickly looking and that their use of fat talk contributed to their body image dissatisfaction. European American women stated that their ideal body type was a specific prototype of a "thin yet curvy-athletic body." Although this description is more modern and does not depict Barbie, it reminds me that most Caucasian girls grew up playing with Barbie and that she represented a very restricted ideal of beauty. Living in a university town in rural Appalachia, the demographics in my region are primarily Caucasian. Our diversity is comprised of dramatic variations of SES more so than diversity as a function of race. When my sons started high school, the only one in our county, the style for girls' hair was long and straight. When the short side bangs became the new style, all of sudden it seemed as if they *all* had the new hairstyle. White girls seem to prefer to look like one another, which probably creates a sense of self-acceptance by the in-group. This phenomenon started with Barbie. For their African American participants, however, Webb et al. (2013) found that these women *resisted* a single ideal prototype. Instead, they voiced preference for individualized standards that shaped personal self-acceptance. In more colloquial language, this idea involves making what you have work for you and is expressed in the saying, "She's got it going on." This is consistent with Parker et al.'s (1995) observations from African American middle school girls.

These racial differences in fat talk appear to exist in U.S. adult women who are beyond college age. Fiery, Martz, Webb, and Curtin (2016) used the same U.S. representative, online data set from Martz et al. (2009) and collapsed the self-accepting and positive body talk conditions into one category, which was called "favorable body talk," and the negative body talk/fat talk condition was called "unfavorable body talk." African American women reported the least perceived pressure to participate in unfavorable body talk compared to Caucasian, Hispanic, and Asian women. Further, both African American and Hispanic women reported more experience with favorable forms of body talk compared to their Caucasian counterparts. Hence, these three studies suggest that fat talk is more of a Caucasian girls' and women's norm, whereas African American girls and women are either immune to the normative nature of fat talk or simply form more individualized, thus non-normative, flexible standards for feminine beauty. Not all of the extant research has found this racial difference in fat talk, however. Engeln and Salk (2014) studied 1,008 women from Amazon's Mechanical Turk website and found no differences in Black, White, Latina, and East Asian women on reported fat talk after controlling for age and body size (i.e., Body Mass Index).

How Age Seems to Affect Fat Talk

Research on fat talk has been conducted only in the past few decades. Thus, researchers have not had much time to study the phenomenon developmentally. However, cohort studies suggest that the age of girls and women has some slight prediction of this behavior, with younger women adopting the behavior more so than older women. Engeln and Salk (2014) studied women from a health and beauty website (i.e., Youbeauty.com) in a survey called the "Fat Talk Quiz" and found a very small, negative correlation between age and fat talk ($r = -.08$). In their second survey of women on MTurk, they found no relationship between age and fat talk. Martz et al.

(2009) surveyed women in an online "Health & Wellness" survey by the Segmentation Company, a division of Yankelovich. They found a small, negative correlation (r = -.23) between age and the women's perceived pressure to engage in fat talk. Becker, Diedrichs, Jankowski, and Werchan (2013) conducted an international online survey of women aged 18–87 that were grouped into the following age categories: 18–29, 30–45, 46–60, and 61 plus. They found that mean levels of fat talk per group slowly decreased as the age categories increased. Similarly, Tzoneva, Forney, and Keel (2015) surveyed men and women from ages 17 to 75 with the question, "How often do your close friends comment on their own weight or eating?" There was no association for men between age and fat talk; women, however, showed a small, negative relationship between age and fat talk (r = -.14).

As a demographic indicator of who fat talks, age appears to be only a slight predictor. In the limited research examining age, it seems that younger women experience this conversational dialogue a bit more than older women. Given the nature of these research designs, however, it is challenging to tell if this is a generational effect. That would mean that younger women fat talk a bit more than older women ever did. This would make some sense considering how modern visual media (e.g., television, Instagram) makes it easier to objectify and critique women's appearance than was possible in previous generations. Conversely, this slight negative correlation between age and level of fat talk could be a developmental phenomenon whereby individual women tend to fat talk more when they were younger, but their personal frequency of fat talk then declines as they age. Future research may wish to examine this.

Body Size and Fat Talk

I, as well as other researchers, have asked if fat talk has anything to do with one's actual body size or amount of body fat. Martz et al. (2009) had women self-report their height and weight, which was converted into body mass index and categorized into underweight, normal weight, overweight, and obese. Obese women reported more pressure to participate in fat talk. Overweight participants reported a trend for perceiving more pressure to participate in ongoing fat talk. Note that participants responded to a scenario during which fat talk was *already* present; thus, these larger women may have felt pressure to comment on their own bodies since other people were doing so, but may not have initiated such discussion of their own volition. There were no differences for body sizes, in this same survey, for women's report of being exposed to fat talk. All sizes of women, therefore, reported hearing fat talk in the same frequency.

In their survey of adult men and women with an average age of 35, Tzoneva, Forney, and Keel (2015) found no association between fat talk and body size. Conversely, in their international sample of women Becker et al. (2013) found that those classified as overweight, but not obese as in Martz et al. (2009), engaged in the most fat talk, whereas normal weight women did this the least. These were the only two weight categories to differ significantly. Engeln and Salk (2014) found a very small, positive correlation between body mass index and fat talk (r = .16) using college participants. In their second survey using participants from MTurk, they found a small, positive correlation between body mass index and fat talk (r = .21). Yet, in additional analyses, they found that there was no association between body mass index and fat talk in women who were overweight or obese. However, the relationship sustained in normal weight women, and the underweight women reported the least likelihood of fat talking. Hence, it appears that women of all sizes are exposed to fat talk, but the relationship between body size and women's tendency to engage in fat talk is limited and seems to trend towards larger women engaging in slightly more fat talk.

The Relationship Between Eating Disorders and Fat Talk

Since fat talk is public critique of one's body image to others, it is natural that researchers have explored the relationship between this type of dialogue and eating disorders. Tzoneva et al. (2015) found that both adult men's and women's report of exposure to fat talk was associated with the Revised Restraint Scale's Concern for Dieting subscale, as well as the Eating Disorders Inventory's Drive for Thinness subscale and the Bulimia subscale. While correlations were significant between fat talk and the eating disorder scales for men and women, they were stronger for women (Fat Talk & Revised Restraint Scale, r = .32; & Drive for Thinness r = .31; & Bulimia r = .25) than these same relationships for men (Fat Talk & Revised Restraint Scale r = .19; & Drive for Thinness r = .22; & Bulimia r = .18).

Ousley, Cordero, and White (2008) surveyed 1500 college students at a large public university in the Southwest using a study titled, "The 2002 Weight Management, Eating and Exercise Habits Survey." They received 272 complete surveys (i.e., 18 percent response rate). The sample was 70 percent women, of mean age at 21 years, mean body mass index at 23 (in the normal range), with 72 percent identifying as Caucasian, 14 percent Asian/Pacific Islander, 4 percent Latino, 5 percent as Chicano/Mexican American, with the remainder described as other or Native American or African American. They used a modified version of the Weight Management Questionnaire that captured a diagnosis for Bulimia Nervosa and updated it to capture Eating Disorder, Not Otherwise Specified. The scale does not diagnose Anorexia Nervosa. Participants were divided into an eating disorder diagnosis category ($n = 55$) or a no eating disorder diagnosis category ($n = 219$). Fat talk was measured in a 5-item scale using a 6-point Likert rating that was developed from previous qualitative research at their university. Participants with an eating disorder reported participating in more fat talk "at least daily," than those without an eating disorder diagnosis (i.e., "rarely/never"). The content of fat talk, for both groups, focused mostly on commentary about other's physical appearance more so than personal fears of becoming overweight or out of shape.

The Nature of Fat Talk

Along with demographic characteristics of gender, race, and age, it makes sense that researchers would also study individuals who merely overhear fat talk, compared to individuals who participate in it after someone else has initiated it, or individuals who initiate these conversations themselves. Arroyo and Harwood (2012) assessed listening to fat talk and participating in fat talk and their impact after a two-week time span. They found that participating in fat talk was directly related to perceived pressure to be thin, as well as depression, but merely overhearing fat talk did not relate to feeling the pressure to be thin or feeling depressed. In a more realistic method of determining what fat talk looks like on a day-to-day basis, Jones, Crowther, and Ciesla (2014) surveyed 67 female college students, who were primarily Caucasian (82.4 percent), and asked them to respond to a series of questions on a Palm Central Personal Data Assistant for five days when it sounded an alarm to prompt them to report what they had been doing. This procedure is called *ecological momentary assessment*. It is a clever and more naturalistic way to capture fat talk and its emotional and behavioral consequences than having participants complete surveys recalling their behavior, or simply responding to vignettes depicting artificial behavior. Participants were beeped by their Personal Data Assistant at 25 random times over five days between 8:30am and 11:30pm and had 10 minutes to respond. To protect privacy, safety, and to allow for classroom time, they were permitted to use a "do not disturb" function for up to one hour. After the Personal Data Assistant beeped and signaled them, they were asked, "Since the last alarm, have you engaged in fat talk?" and if so, "How many times have you engaged in fat talk since the last alarm?" Those who reported engaging in fat talk were further prompted to indicate who made the first fat talk comment in that social interaction by selecting from a menu of self, friend, family member, acquaintance, or stranger. Of the 25 random prompts, participants responded on average to sixteen of them.

The majority of participants (96.9 percent) reported at least one episode of fat talk, with an average of almost ten episodes, across the five days. The nature of the responses was coded using qualitative research methods. In reaction to their most salient episode of fat talk, they reported that 34.5 percent of the time they initiated the commentary, whereas 65.5 percent of the time it was started by someone else (i.e., 46 percent friend, 13 percent family member, ~3 percent acquaintance & ~4 percent stranger). Therefore, using real-world data collection, Jones et al. found that these college students were engaging in fat talk on a daily basis, mostly with their friends, and they were usually responding to others' fat talk as opposed to initiating it themselves.

In further analyses, Jones et al. (2014) used multilevel modeling to examine the consequences of these fat talk episodes reported on the Personal Data Assistants. Their most poignant finding was that recent exposure to this type of conversation was related to more negative emotions, body dissatisfaction, body checking behaviors, and more weight control and disordered eating behaviors. By comparing participating in fat talk versus merely overhearing it, they found that body-checking behaviors were associated with actual participation in fat talk. Participants who were higher in reported trait self-objectification had more of a robust association between exposure to fat talk and body dissatisfaction and body checking behaviors. Interestingly, and in partial testament to how women can aim to break out of the normative nature of fat talk (see chapters eight & nine), these participants reported anecdotally that they were surprised by how often they overheard and participated in fat talk. Some noted that this increased awareness and insight would affect their responses in the future. This is the same thing I hear from my students and research assistants after I introduce them to the concept of fat talk. They cannot believe how often they hear it. This makes me wonder if an intervention that simply has participants record their initiation of or exposure to fat talk and the resulting emotions or behaviors would reduce fat talk.

In an additional study documenting the nature of fat talk, Mills and Fuller-Tyszkiewicz (2018) also used ecological momentary assessment with 135 primarily Australian women across a seven-day period who were paged and prompted from an app on their smart phones to record when they engaged in 1) self fat talk, 2) other fat talk (i.e., body snarking), or 3) hearing others' fat talk. In terms of frequency, 71 percent reported engaging in their own fat talk, 70 percent reported engaging in the body snarking of others, and 49 percent reported hearing others fat talk. Women with negative body image reported more fat talk than women with better body image. As a consequence of these experiences, the authors found that self fat talk, but not the other two types, was associated with a negative impact on participants' body satisfaction. Again, using real-world behavioral measures, this study finds that fat talk is frequent and associated with a cycle of poor body image.

To determine what is said when women fat talk, Bardone-Cone, Balk, Lin, Fitzsimmons-Craft, and Goodman (2016) surveyed 441 primarily Caucasian (74 percent) college women from a large Southeastern university about the content of this type of dialogue with their closest friends. Most of the content (89 percent) was about working out, 56 percent was about dieting, some was about making comparisons to various other individuals (22–39 percent), whereas the minority of the content focused on more extreme eating disordered pathology. Fourteen percent discussed binge eating and only three percent talked about purging. The number of fat talk topics was positively associated with weight/shape concerns and level of eating pathology for these women. Therefore, it appears that most fat talk is really dialogue about exercise and workouts, probably focusing on improving one's shape. After that, women focus on their diets and what they eat or body image and social comparisons.

Arroyo and Brunner (2016) surveyed 488 young female and male adults about how exposure to friends' postings on social media affected their fat talk. They found those friends' fitness posts about workouts or inspirational quotes were positively related to participants' report of fat talk. They also found that this relationship was moderated by the personal variables of body surveillance and social comparison. Consequently, participants who already monitor their bodies and make frequent comparisons of their attractiveness to others are the most vulnerable when reading about their friends' same habits. This then leads them to participate in even more fat talk themselves.

Finally, in a study that has explored the nature of women's fat talk, Lin and Soby (2017) surveyed 321 college women on a "College Women's Health Survey" from a co-ed, primarily Caucasian, liberal arts college in the Northeast. Their mean age was 19.3 with a mean body mass index of 23.8. Participants completed the Fat Talk Questionnaire (Royal, MacDonald & Dionne, 2013) as themselves. Then they were asked in a single item, on a 5-item Likert scale, how often they hear their friends complain about the topics they just read on that scale. Using hierarchical regression modeling, while controlling for body mass index, they found that engaging in fat talk was more clearly related to dietary restraint, body dissatisfaction, and drive for thinness. On the other hand, merely hearing the fat talk from friends was not at all related to these constructs. Lin and Soby (2016) used the same data set and added the construct of upward versus downward appearance comparisons in these relationships with fat talk. When individuals compare themselves to others who are more attractive, this is called an *upward appearance comparison.* When individuals compare themselves to others who are less attractive, this is called a *downward comparison.* I have used this with clients, and I jokingly say in my classes when I am covering eating disorders and body image,

> If you are having a rough body image day, you probably do not want to be flipping through women's fashion magazines, or scrolling through certain Instagram or Pinterest sites. You also probably don't want to spend your day in one of our campus gyms where everyone is young and fit. Get off campus; visit the real world. A bad body image day usually gets better after a visit to Walmart.

It is morbid humor, but it explains what researchers know about social comparison for real life. The students seem to get it. It is easier to move into downward comparison when a person interacts with the general public containing normal people. Lin and Soby (2016) found that women who engaged in both upward and downward appearance comparisons were much more likely to have body dissatisfaction, drive for thinness, dietary restraint, and engage in fat talk compared to women who did not engage in either type of social comparison. Further, fat talk was found in those who only engaged in upward comparisons, but not in those who engaged in only downward social comparisons.

Men's Body Talk

Boys and men are not immune to body image concerns. Their insecurities just tend to take a different form than women's concerns. Older men who have gained weight, usually in their waist and abdomen, are more likely to be worried about fat and engage in fat talk. My father used to rub his robust belly and joke that it was proof of how he overcame anorexia. (For the record, the man never suffered from anorexia; he had just gained weight.) Younger men, on the other hand, tend to be more concerned with muscle mass. Pope, Phillips, and Olivardia (2000) have called this the *Adonis complex*, named after mythical Greek god Adonis who was thought to be the epitome of male beauty and virility. Thus, having an Adonis complex would mean a man's attempt to have the perfectly lean and muscular body that fits our cultural ideal. Taken to the extreme, some men become obsessed to the point of having muscle dysmorphia, which is pathological dissatisfaction with what are considered inadequate muscles. This condition can lead to compulsive exercise, low self-esteem, use of protein supplements, and even risky abuse of anabolic steroids (Cafri, Strauss, & Thompson, 2002; McCreary & Sasse, 2000; Olivardia, Pope, Borowiecki, & Cohane, 2004). Cruz Loeza, Martz, and Ballard (2018), in a nationally representative survey of U.S. young men in high schools, found that having a history of being bullied on school property resulted in a 2.4 times greater risk of anabolic steroid use. Having been cyberbullied resulted in a 3.9 times increased likelihood of anabolic steroid misuse. Although we did not have the survey items to test this hypothesis, it is probable that many of these young men had been harassed about their appearance or size, resulting in an Adonis complex and a desire to become bigger and more muscular.

Research on how boys and men express physique concerns with one another is in its infancy. Despite its greater prevalence for girls and women, body image concerns and body talk can be a real issue for some boys and men. I recall hearing male body talk from my own son, Forrest, and his friends. I was driving a bunch of smelly teens back from an away soccer game when they were on the high school soccer team. They were talking about a team player and how great his abdominal muscles were. They all agreed laughingly, "Yeah man he has the greatest abs," "Like a real six-pack," and "I bet he does crunches in his sleep." I had no idea my son even knew what an abdominal muscle was. The conversation was not concerning, though—just interesting because I spent my workdays focusing on girls' and women's fat talk.

Engeln, Sladek, and Waldron (2013) conducted seminal research on men's body talk. In their first study, they surveyed 66 predominantly Caucasian (81 percent) college men from a mid-sized Midwestern university. Seventy-five percent indicated that they could envision a situation in which a male friend was complaining about his body, with 25 percent stating they thought college men did this frequently. Men tended to focus most on overall muscle content, followed by discussion about chest/pectoral muscles, abdominals, and arms, rather than overall body fat. This is similar to the social comparison that happens with women, yet the focus of the comparisons or competition is different. Contextually, these young men's conversations occurred most at the gym or while engaging in sports and athletics, followed by such conversations occurring in various eating situations. Their negative body talk was positively associated with a drive for muscularity, eating disordered behaviors, and the amount of investment in their appearance, but negatively associated with appearance evaluation. Interestingly, Engeln et al.'s men also reported speaking positively about specific body parts, a phenomenon not often expressed by girls and women. In their second study, 90 college men participated in a discussion after viewing an advertisement featuring an attractive, muscular man sitting beside two other college participants who were really confederates (i.e., trained actors). There were three experimental conditions in which both confederates simultaneously engaged in either: 1) fat talk, 2) muscle talk, or 3) neutral or control talk. The dependent variables were the male participants' body dissatisfaction and their appearance state self-esteem. Relative to the control condition, men showed more body dissatisfaction hearing both fat talk and muscle talk. Similarly, men hearing the muscle talk, relative to the control condition, reported lower levels of appearance esteem. Therefore, men's body talk—like women's—is a function of their body image and also impacts them interpersonally.

Chow and Tan (2016) studied 55 friendship pairs of young adult college men from a public university in the Midwest and measured their body mass indices, body dissatisfaction, and negative body talk. They found that these men's own body mass index was positively associated with their own body dissatisfaction, but their own body dissatisfaction was negatively associated with their friend's body mass index. Having a friend with a low body mass index exacerbated the relationship between their own body mass index and their own body dissatisfaction. Yet, engaging in negative body talk appeared to buffer these relationships. When young men with higher body mass indices engaged in more negative body talk, they had lower body dissatisfaction compared to those who engaged in less negative body talk. Again, use of the negative body talk appears to help young men feel better about feeling bad about their bodies if this talk occurs with a close friend.

In an unpublished honors thesis, my former student, Delvon Blue (2012), used the Martz et al. (2009) nationally representative data set of adult men and women. Of the 100 percent of participants who reported frequently hearing fat talk, 28.1 percent of them were men. Of the 100 percent of participants who reported high pressure to engage in fat talk, 26.4 percent of them were men. The fact that the percentages were similar implies that men are not just overhearing women engage in fat talk. The amount that they hear and the amount they feel pressure to participate in body talk are similar. Blue also examined demographic variables of the men who reported high versus low pressure to engage in fat talk; he discovered that single men compared to married men, fully employed men versus retired men, and Asian men versus Caucasian men reported more fat talk. Although he was unable to tell the reasons why single men and those who were fully employed endorsed more pressure to engage in fat talk, it is likely that these are groups of men more concerned about their bodies and physical appearance, perhaps because of dating, than men who are married or in later age and retired. Our data set did not have a demographic variable for sexual orientation or we would have examined that. When we studied if men's race affected fat talk, we found that Asian men reported more fat talk than Caucasian men. This surprised us at first until we delved deeper into extant research on this topic. Some of the previous literature has found Asian men to have poorer body image compared to other ethnicities (Kelly, Cotter, Tanofsky-Kraff, & Mazzeo, 2015), although these relationships are complicated based on subgroups of how Asian is classified (e.g., Korean vs. Chinese; Ricciardelli, McCabe, Williams, & Thompson, 2007; Yates, Edman, & Aruguete, 2004). Latner, Knight, and Illingsworth (2011) found that Asian college men from Hawaii and Australia who had lower body weights also had greater body image dissatisfaction. Thus, Blue and I hypothesized that the more frequent fat talk found in the Asian versus Caucasian men in his sample was likely the result of more "small talk," or desire for muscularity than fat talk, especially because the body sizes of the Asian men as a group were significantly smaller than the Caucasian men when we compared their body mass indices. Finally, we used a novel metric, called relative clothing size, to examine if this predicted their pressure to engage in fat talk. We asked the men their pants size, which is basically the waist circumference for men in U.S. clothing sizes. We also asked them what would be their ideal pants size and made a composite variable on any discrepancies that were named *relative size*. The men who were smaller than their ideal pant size reported more fat talk than men who were the same as their ideal. This was likely capturing muscularity talk over fat talk. Further, the men who were two or more, three or more, and five or more sizes larger than their ideal pant sizes also reported more pressure to engage in fat talk compared to the men who were the same as their ideal pant size. Although we could not tell this from our study, the latter men were probably engaging in fat talk. We concluded that there is a need for a measure of body talk that is more fitting for men compared to the traditional fat talk scales used to measure this construct in girls and women.

Sladek, Engeln, and Miller (2014) did just that. They developed the Male Body Talk Scale, which was shown through factor analysis in an MTurk survey of adult men to contain two factors: muscularity and body fat. The former assesses their concerns with muscularity and being too small (e.g., I want a six-pack; I wish I had bigger biceps). The latter focuses more on concerns with body fat and gaining weight (e.g., I wish I could lose this belly fat; I need to start watching what I eat). They found that the level of men's muscle talk was related to eating disordered thoughts and behaviors, muscle dysmorphia symptoms, upper body dissatisfaction, drive for muscularity, and investment in appearance. Their level of fat talk was also related to upper body dissatisfaction, muscle dysmorphia symptoms, and eating disordered thoughts and behaviors. This shows that the body talk seen in men mirrors classic relationships found in the body image literature for them. They hear and talk about what most concerns them personally and in their social circles, just like the girls and women do. Based on the research examining gender differences, it just appears that women do this more than men—a finding that reflects gender differences within the body image literature.

Another risk factor for men's body talk could be their sexual orientation. Compared to heterosexual men, homosexual men place more importance on their physical attractiveness (Siever, 1994), report more body image dissatisfaction (Morrison, Morrison, & Sager, 2004), and prefer more attractive partners than heterosexual women tend to desire (Brand, Rothblum, & Solomon, 1992). Thus, it would make sense if they also engaged in more negative body talk. Jankowski, Diedrichs, and Halliwell (2014) surveyed online 77 homosexual and 78 heterosexual men from the United Kingdom about their "appearance conversations" (i.e., their name for what we have called fat talk or body talk), body dissatisfaction, appearance orientation (i.e., how invested they are in their looks), and internalization of appearance ideals. They found that appearance conversations, equally split between positive and negative in valence, were common. Examples of a positive comment might look like, "Wow, your arms are huge. I can tell you have been working out." Negative comments could include, "Dude, how's that beer belly coming along?" As hypothesized, homosexual men reported more both positive and negative appearance conversations. Homosexual men also had more appearance orientation and internalization of these ideals compared to the heterosexual men. Further, mediational analyses showed that differences in sexual orientation for both body fat and muscularity dissatisfaction, as well as internalization of the cultural male body ideal, were predicted by the frequency of these appearance conversations. Jankowsi et al. (2014) caution readers that this study could not determine causality between the level of these conversations and the poorer body image in homosexual men, but they speculate that the dynamic is likely bidirectional and mutually reinforcing. Just like fat talk in women signals to others that one's appearance is important and that she can own up conversationally to some of her flaws, these conversations in homosexual men reflect a personal subculture that places more importance on physical attractiveness. This varies from the dominant heterosexual male culture that places priority on men's ability to obtain resources (i.e., see chapter one's review of evolutionary psychology's explanation for what attracts heterosexual women to heterosexual men). Researchers have documented that gay men experience more pressure to look attractive from peers and other people (Hospers & Jansen, 2005; McArdle & Hill, 2009; Yelland & Tiggemann, 2003) and from cultural media compared to heterosexual men (McArdle & Hill, 2009). In this regard, homosexual men, much like girls and women in Western culture, seem to succumb to similar cultural influences that get internalized into their personal body image and are practiced in their everyday conversations.

Family's Influence on Fat Talk and Body Snarking

Gillison, Lorenc, Sleddens, Williams, and Atkinson (2016) conducted a meta-analysis on thirty-eight associative studies addressing concerns in how parents talk with their overweight children. They found that when parents encouraged their children to lose weight and criticized their weight, this was associated with increased dieting, poorer self-perceptions from the children, and more dysfunctional eating, especially for the female children. Conversely, parental encouragement for the children to engage in a healthy lifestyle, without direct mention of weight loss, was associated with better well-being in two of the studies that examined this. Therefore, it appears that parental focus on healthy behaviors for children is better than focusing on their bodies or deliberate focus on weight loss. I would think that it would be even better if the parents are focusing on their own health behaviors and modeling healthy exercise and healthful food choices for their children. In their article "All in the family? Parental roles in the epidemic of childhood obesity," Moore, Wilkie, and Desrochers (2017) studied how family members steer children either towards or away from developing obesity. Further, in a systematic review on the treatment of childhood obesity, Staniford, Breckon, and Copeland (2012) reinforced the need for treatment interventions to include the entire family while focusing on a holistic approach to physical activity and dietary changes.

Neumark-Sztainer et al. (2010) studied 356 adolescent girls, mean age of 15.8, participating in an alternative physical education program called "New Moves" that was developed for sedentary girls at risk of becoming overweight. The group's mean body mass index was 25.8, with 18 percent falling onto the overweight category and 28.2 percent considered obese. They were surveyed on their body dissatisfaction, unhealthy weight control behaviors, binge eating, and multiple items assessing the family's weight-related environment including mother and father's fat talk and dieting, as well as frequency by which they were teased about their weight. Nearly 50 percent of the girls reported their mothers had encouraged them to diet, with two-thirds reporting that their mothers dieted or talked about their weight. Several of the mothers' variables were pertinent to the girls' disordered eating behavior, after the researchers statistically controlled for their body mass index and other sociodemographic variables. Mothers' dieting was associated with more extreme and unhealthy weight control behaviors in their children. Mothers' fat talking was related to unhealthier and extreme weight control behaviors and binge eating in the girls. Further, mothers encouraging their daughters to diet was strongly related to unhealthy and extreme weight control behaviors and binge eating. Fathers' behavior also had an impact on the girls, but to a lesser extent than their mothers' did. Forty percent reported that their fathers dieted, fat talked, or encouraged them to diet. Fathers' fat talk was associated with the girls' extreme weight control behaviors, and fathers encouraging daughters to diet was related to girls' unhealthy weight control behaviors. Neumark-Sztainer and colleagues examined the combined effect of both parents engaging in conversations, but this had no additive effect on the girls' behaviors. Thus, hearing either parent's fat talking, as well as hearing either parent convey indirect messages about weight, were both associated with detrimental behaviors for their daughters. One would think that more direct messages, such as being teased about appearance or body weight, would be even more detrimental.

That is exactly what the researchers found. Neumark-Sztainer et al. (2010) revealed some powerful associations for these girls if family members had teased them about their weight in the past year. Approximately 60 percent of these girls had been teased, and larger girls were teased more often. Weight teasing was related to more body dissatisfaction, more unhealthy and extreme weight control behaviors, and more binge eating. Girls who reported that they were teased habitually had ten times the frequency of binge eating than girls who reported no teasing. Girls who reported that either parent talked "very much" about their weight were three times more likely to engage in extreme weight control behaviors than girls whose parents did not discuss their weight. Girls whose mothers encouraged them to diet were five times more likely to engage in extreme weight control behaviors than mothers who did not discuss dieting. Consequently, parental weight-related conversations, especially teasing their daughters about their weight, were clearly associated with multiple problematic weight control behaviors. The authors emphasized that in *none* of these instances was family weight talk or teasing associated with better outcomes for these girls. Finding similar results with a different sample of families, Lydecker, Riley, and Grilo (2018) found that 76 percent of the parents reported engaging in personal fat talk in front of their children, and 43.6 percent reported that they fat talked about their children. The latter was associated with children's binge eating, secretive eating, over eating and overweight/obesity. Framed more from a positive psychology approach, Webb, Rogers, Etzel, and Padro (2018) surveyed 333 college women from a Southeastern public university. They found that overhearing family fat talk was negatively associated with these young women's body appreciation, mindful eating, as well as appreciation for what their bodies could do (i.e., called "body as process"). Further analyses determined that having an appreciation for what the body can do explained the inverse relationship between hearing family fat talk and their reports of engaging in mindful eating. Therefore, several studies have documented how exposure to family fat talk is associated with unhealthy forms of eating and weight control, as well as inversely related to healthier modes of body image and eating styles.

Chow and Tan (2018) recruited 100 adolescent girls between the ages of 11 and 18 along with their mothers from a Midwestern metropolitan area of the U.S. They used Actor-Partner Independence Modeling to study the effects of fat talk on eating pathology and depressive symptoms both within the girls and their mothers alone, as well as in statistical interactions between them as "actors" and "partners." Level of fat talk and eating pathology were positively related for both girls and mothers within themselves. Participation in fat talk was a more powerful predictor of eating pathology than merely listening to it in these dyads. An interesting interaction effect emerged between the mothers and their daughters. The girls who engaged in more fat talk had more eating pathology when their mothers responded to their daughters' dialogue with more fat talk. In contrast, when mothers failed to reciprocate high levels of fat talk in response to their daughters' high level of fat talk, this was associated with less eating pathology in the daughters. For depressive symptoms, there was a positive relationship between level of fat talk and depression for the adolescent girls, but this relationship did not exist for their mothers. They found a surprising interaction effect when these relationships were studied interpersonally. Girls who engaged in fat talk reported more depressive symptoms when their mothers engaged in lower levels of fat talk. Chow and Tan speculate that more depressive symptoms resulted when girls failed to receive the expected reciprocity in fat talk from their mothers.

Greer, Campione-Barr, and Lindell (2015) examined how body talk impacted siblings. They used Actor-Partner Interdependence Modeling to examine how positive and negative body talk affected themselves ("actor") when they engaged in it, as well as how their sibling's ("partner") disclosures affected them as well. They studied 101 sibling dyads in which at least one sibling was in high school in grades 10–12. They found that the more siblings disclosed positive body-related issues to one another, the more relationship positivity they reported. Similarly, and speaking to greater intimacy and supportiveness in the relationship, the more both boys and girls reported disclosing negatively about their bodies, the more positivity was reported in those relationships. Further, disclosing either positive or negative body image issues to a sibling was also associated with better body esteem, especially for the girls. Yet, these were all associations about these siblings disclosing body talk *to* their brothers or sisters. On the contrary, being on the receiving end and hearing either positive or negative body-related disclosures was associated with lower adolescent body-esteem, especially for girls and younger siblings compared to the boys and older siblings. The authors suggested that being on the receiving end, being a girl, and being younger could place that sibling in a place of social comparison and envy, thus having a negative impact on their body esteem. And they state that hearing the negative talk could prompt them in their own self-consciousness and have a negative impact on their self-esteem. The latter finding deserves more research to better understand its seemingly contradictory outcome. Perhaps being on the receiving end of body talk by a sibling is more of a function of the sibling leaning on you, whereas you are not able to lean on him or her quite as frequently. This could take its toll on generic self-esteem as well as body-esteem, especially if you are younger and less emotionally equipped for such disclosures. Future research will need to parse this out more.

Research suggests that these influences on body image, captured in the previous cross-sectional studies, tend to endure further into the lifespan. Eli, Howell, Fisher, and Nowicka (2014), for an article titled, "Those Comments

Last Forever," interviewed 22 parents and 27 grandparents from 16 low-income families in the Pacific Northwest who had children or grandchildren ages three to five years old. The interviews were transcribed and subjected to a thematic qualitative analysis. Participants responded to the prompt, "Did you think about your weight when you were a child, around 5–8 years of age?" and "At what age, if ever, did you start thinking about your weight?" The two researchers coded content independently with the goal of extracting the following themes: 1) how participants describe the sources or processes that instigated their body weight awareness in childhood or adolescence, and 2) feelings or experiences that participants associated with the emergence of their body weight awareness as youth. Of the 49 participants, 25 of them had become aware of their body weight by adolescence and thus were included in the data set for this study. Of this sample, 68.0 percent met overweight or obesity criteria compared to 54.2 percent of the rest of the sample. *None* of the participants described this emerging awareness of body weight positively and most stated that it evoked negative feelings or experiences. They spoke to how this lowered their self-esteem as a teen, a feeling that often persisted into adulthood. Could it be that the events that cause this body weight self-consciousness change the psychological and behavioral trajectory of some people's lives? These comments appear to be quite powerful. Four of the participants had developed eating disorders. One commented,

> I just remember always feeling I was fat. And being preoccupied with it a lot … that's when I started making myself throw up and not eating [p. 5].

Another said,

> I had a very unhealthy image of what bodies should look like and I would exercise like four or five hours a day and I would limit my food or lie saying I ate [p. 5].

Fourteen of them said it started when others commented about their bodies and most cited parents or peers who did so. One participant related it to female fat talk stating that she was hearing normative discussions at school and that

> you're at an age where all the girls are like, "I'm fat! My thighs are so fat" [p. 4].

From a parent, another commented,

> My mom would point out when I was nine that I would eat too much or that I needed to go exercise [p. 4].

Many of these stories were about being overweight, but not all of them. One cited,

> I was so skinny I was freaky. And my parents and relatives … they all said I was ugly [p. 4].

As a turn of faith, four of the adult participants linked their negative experiences to a deliberate decision to not discuss body weight with their preschool children or grandchildren. I liked hearing about how some of these individuals were trying to break the cycle for the next generation. In conclusion, for many individuals who were teased about their bodies as children, it appears that others' comments sometimes *did* last forever.

Partner's Influence on Body Snarking

Another interpersonal influence of fat talk that has been studied is that of romantic couples. To determine how fat talk affects newly married couples, Bove and Sobal (2011) studied 20 women and 14 men just prior to marriage and then one year later to ascertain their weight relevance, weight comparisons, and weight talk that was most related to fat talk. They classified some of their weight talk into what they called *pragmatic weight talk,* which was a matter-of-fact discussion about their weight and how to maintain it or manage weight gain. As an example, one participant stated, "We were saying it's time to cut back on the sweets." Another category of weight talk, deemed *active reassurance,* focused more on weight from an appearance perspective in a way that was soliciting reassurance, which is one of the classic functions of fat talk. However, Bove and Sobal noted that some of these participants who had body mass indices in the morbidly obese ranges (i.e., 43.9 & 57.0) also reported eliciting reassurance from their spouse, and commentary such as "you look perfect" or "it looks like you have been losing weight" could potentially cause harm to them if the reassurance excuses weight gain when they are already in morbid obesity ranges (i.e., assuming they are not exercising; see chapter six). The authors called another category of weight talk *tacit reassurance,* which was the case when one spouse gained weight and the other spouse failed to bring it up or seemed to not be concerned about it. *Complaining criticism* occurred when the spouse who had gained weight was actively fat talking and critiquing themselves. Finally, the authors categorized *critiquing criticism* as when a partner complained about the other's weight or weight gain. At times this was blatant and occurring on a daily basis, whereas other times it was more subtle—such as a member of the couple casually bringing up a possible gym membership. Although this happened in only three of the women's reports, each stated that this criticism was always poorly received and failed to help motivate them to lose weight. The authors reported interviewing each of their husbands and none of them thought they were using harsh weight talk for their wives; hence, these partners were not always perceiving these conversations the same way. Similarly, in a study of couples wherein one was diagnosed with Type II diabetes and the other was not, Stephens et al. (2013) used end-of-the-day diaries that were collected for 24 consecutive days to ascertain their dietary adherence or non-adherence and whether they perceived their spouse to have offered dietary support or dietary persuasion and pressure. They found that dietary adherence was better the day after they perceived support from their spouse, but there was more non-adherence on days after they felt like their spouse had pressured them. Again, much like Bove and Sobal (2011) found, Stephens et al. (2013) found that stigma and pressure tends to backfire and result in unhealthy behaviors, whereas supportive behavior helps couples be healthier.

In conclusion, much research has been conducted in the last few decades that has documented that a variety of individuals participate in fat talk and body snarking. It does appear to be more common among girls and women, especially Caucasians. It also seems to be clearly linked to individuals with less body image satisfaction who engage in more weight control or eating disordered behaviors. Although men sometimes fat talk, the nature of the conversation tends to focus more on masculinity. Homosexual men seem to engage in body talk more than heterosexual men. Research on men and women's perceptions of the opposite gender's body talk is in its infancy. Weight teasing, as body snarking directed at loved ones, is detrimental for its victims and has been researched in families in the form of parent to child, sibling participation, and in romantic couples. Fat talk is alive and well and tends to touch all demographics. The next chapter will focus on the feminist issue of the harm caused by body snarking in public media.

6

Invasion of Body Snarking
Our Culture, Healthcare, and Feminist Politics

"Equality is the radical notion that we are all human."—Women's March sign, 2017

Just as fat talk may be a way of helping women feel better about feeling bad about their bodies, body snarking may be a means of helping women feel better about their own insecurities, but at the very unfortunate expense of harming others. It is also a modern-day form of spiteful aggression. Put simply, body snarking is bullying. In this regard, we women (and men) can be enemies to our fellow humans and ourselves. Body snarking is a feminist issue, with girls and women being much more likely than boys and men to be the victims of it. Dialogue, print, and press that perpetuate body snarking are part of a larger form of sexism and misogyny in our culture. It was also a strong force in Hillary Rodham Clinton's loss of the 2016 presidential election. Consequently, not only should we target a reduction in women's fat talk, we also need a heightened awareness of how rigid adherence to gender role stereotypes, and the body snarking that results from this, are harming women. Body snarking is defined by Urban Dictionary (2011) as

rudely talk[ing] about a person's body or body parts, whether in private or directly at the person; the snide, often witty comments about other women's bodies, that have become a part of female communication; the practice of dissecting other women's bodies; to make mean or vicious comments about another person's body.

Malone (2011) suggests the phenomenon has been around in the media for a long time, but newer forms of social media, especially where people can post judgments anonymously, have certainly exacerbated the problem. As a form of interpersonal bullying, it is easier to be cruel to others from an electronic device when perpetrators are not identifiable. It is more of an interpersonal challenge to be malicious to others face to face. I have certainly heard about the harm caused by body snarking from clients, friends and their daughters, and from my clinical psychologist colleagues about the clients they see. Later in this chapter, I will discuss how snarking may have cost us the feminist agenda to position a very qualified woman in the Oval Office.

Although body snarking can involve general critique aimed at others such as hair, wardrobe, and make-up, it is an umbrella term that also consists of the more narrowly defined phenomenon of *fat shaming*. Finn (2016) describes fat shaming as the "act of criticizing and harassing overweight people about their weight or eating behavior." As one example, this topic made popular press in 2016 when former Miss Universe winner Alicia Machado disclosed how Donald Trump had shamed her for weight gain following her 1995 and 1996 victories (Coward, 2018). In an interview with *Huffington Post*, she said that he called her "Miss Piggy." Unfortunately, this is not the only public example of Trump objectifying women and snarking about their appearance. Trump's campaign and days spent in the White House have caused a serious blow to feminism. He has done nothing to move girls' and women's causes towards equality. If anything, he has modeled a return to traditional gender roles and patriarchy.

During his summer 2017 visit to Paris, Trump said to Brigitte Macron, France's first lady, that she was "in such good shape—beautiful" (Henley, 2017). The commentary about her body was considered so inappropriate that Reebok, the shoemaker, sent out a tweet of all the situations in which such a comment from a man to a woman would be *inappropriate* (Rooney, 2017). They listed,

> "Are you in an elevator?" No, don't say that. "Are you a world leader greeting the spouse of a head of state?" No, don't say that. "Are you introducing yourself to your future mother-in-law?" No, don't say that. "Are you in line next to a woman ordering your morning coffee?" No, don't say that. "Are you at the gym working out next to a woman?" No, don't say that. Then the only *yes* was "Did you find a forgotten action figure from your youth, unscathed after decades, in your parents' basement?" Then you can say to your action figure, "Wow, you are in such good shape—beautiful"!

Our president finds it perfectly acceptable to objectify women whether they are engaged in a profession focused on their appearance, such as the Miss Universe Pageant, or in a profession, such as a world dignitary, that should have nothing to do with appearance. Whether he is voicing words of critique or words that he likely considers to be flattery, why should we care about what he thinks is beautiful or not? In such commentary, he is attempting to steal women's power by objectifying them and thinking he knows how to put them in their place, whether they are heralded by him or cruelly demeaned.

Women should be valued for their many complex qualities, not just their physical appearance.

Body snarking and fat shaming fit into a larger cultural context of normative intolerance of fat bodies. As fat talk is an expression of personal physical discontent, body snarking is a form of public shaming and a means of interpersonal bullying. Interestingly, in underdeveloped countries where food is sparse, individuals and their families rise in social status by getting fat. It signals to others that they have the money and the means to afford food, unlike most people in that society. Conversely, in developed countries where food tends to be abundant, individuals often demonstrate social status by staying lean. Their thinness can indicate that they have the will power to step away from all of the plentiful food and the discipline for regular exercise or going to the gym. Swami (2015) has recently analyzed this cultural phenomenon and documented that increasing modernization, industrialization, and Westernization influence cultural tendencies to adopt the thin ideal as opposed to adopting more flexible and larger body ideals. The U.S. is the perfect example of a culture that embraced the thin ideal—that is, Americans prefer leaner bodies over larger ones. Further, retaining a thin body ideal as a cultural norm coincides with prejudicial attitudes of fat stigma.

Fat Stigma

McPhail (2009) suggests that people in Western cultures tend to view fatness as abject, abhorrent, ugly, and despicable. Such attitudes lead to pervasive stigma against fat people. Puhl and Heuer (2009) published a comprehensive review of stigma and obesity and found that stereotypes associated with obesity (e.g., lazy, poor willpower) promote discrimination against these individuals in the workplace, education, healthcare, interpersonal relationships, and mass media. Such prejudicial attitudes are found in the U.S. in children as young as three (Cramer & Steinwert, 1998)! Further, Puhl and Heuer (2010) conclude that stigma against obese individuals is pervasive and causes numerous physical and psychological sequelae for their health. Further, they state that weight stigma is ineffectual in reducing the prevalence of obesity and suggest—rather—that it backfires by creating health disparities, harming health, and interfering with more effective interventions. Major, Hunger, Bunyan, and Miller (2014) had 93 women from a public Midwestern university randomly assigned to read either a news article that featured how overweight women are stigmatized in the job market (i.e., "Lose weight or lose your job") or a control article (i.e., "Quit smoking or lose your job"). During an ostensible break in the study after reading the articles, participants were led into a room and placed near a computer. Next to the computer were snacks that included M&Ms, Skittles, and Goldfish crackers. Participants were invited to help themselves to the snacks. These bowls were weighed before and after each participant sat in the waiting room as a dependent variable of how much food was consumed. They found that the women who perceived themselves to be overweight, who also read the article on weight stigma, ended up consuming more calories and feeling less capable of controlling their eating than participants who read the control article about cigarette smoking. This suggests that articles that profess weight stigma can have paradoxical effects on people threatened by those messages.

Puhl and Heuer (2010) suggest this stigma is rarely challenged in our society, despite a significant increase in obesity prevalence in past decades. Andreyeva, Puhl, and Brownell (2008) remind us that the public health implications of this prejudice have been widely ignored. In commentary on the effects of this phenomenon, Tomiyama and Mann (2013) have stated bluntly in their article "If Shaming Reduced Obesity, There Would Be No Fat People," that fat shaming does not help people lose weight.

Rather, obesity prevalence is increasing for many reasons, and consequently the corresponding fat stigma is increasing as well. However, fat shaming is not the antidote for our country's weight gain problem.

In her scholarly book, *What's Wrong with Fat?* Saguy (2013) asks some thought-provoking questions: Is overweight and obesity harmful to health or is this just a normal variation in the human body that presents in different shapes, sizes, and colors from the human genome? If fat is harmless, why does it get so much negative attention in our culture? Or, if fat is truly harmful, can we really help people lose weight to be healthier? She argues that professionals have not been very successful helping obese individuals lose weight and are especially not very effective in helping people maintain their weight after weight loss. Thus, the attempts at weight loss have not had the net effect of improving health. Saguy even describes herself as a person who has benefited from "thin privilege" (p. 25). I can say the same for myself. When I reflect on how powerful fat stigma is in our society, it begs metaphorical questions on what most people consider to be the *solution*—that is, is it to help obese individuals get thin for supposed *health* or is it to fit our privileged and restrictive standards of acceptable bodies? Thus, if White individuals have privilege, should we bleach individuals with darker skin tones, ostensibly to make their lives better? If there is prejudice against homosexuality, should we be trying to make gay and lesbian people straight? Our mindset is that we should be helping fat people to get lean, but the intention creates more harm than good. In their critical review of the scientific literature, Puhl and Heuer (2010) remind us that health professionals have not been very successful at helping obese individuals lose weight, maintain weight loss, and become healthier. This is more of an ambitious idea than a healthcare reality. Meunnig (2008) argues effectively that some of the health consequences associated with obesity are *more* a function of the psychological stress resulting from weight stigma than the actual extra adipose tissue itself. Thus, the social stigma that corresponds with obesity may cause more harm than the physical condition of having a large body.

When I teach my health psychology course, I present to students the two distinct camps of obesity philosophy. My students are familiar with the "healthy weight camp—obesity is harmful, thus we must help obese individuals lose weight to be healthy." However, they are not familiar with the 1) National Association to Advance Fat Acceptance (NAAFA), 2) Association for Size Diversity and Health (ASSAH), or 3) Health at Every Size (HAES) organizations and their shared points of view. This unfamiliarity among college students is—in and of itself—a testament to widespread obesity stigma. Students tend to know only one side of this very complicated controversy. NAAFA, ASSAH, and HAES aim to reclaim the term *fat* proudly as an accurate description of larger bodies (Wann, 1998) and to encourage fat individuals to adopt healthy and compassionate self-care habits. This is the opposite of the messages heard frequently in the media that they should hate themselves and strive to torture themselves until they are lean. After I present the controversy in my class, I share the personal experience of hearing researchers and advocates argue about this, literally, at professional conferences. My students want to know the truth. Who is correct here? Then I point them to how I personally, as a researcher and clinician—as well as other professionals—reconcile these seemingly different views. Rather than focus on weight loss versus weight acceptance, we can focus on behavior, which actually has more scientific support for promoting health than either of these disparate views. In psychology courses, I call it the *behavior dance* because we focus on human behavior, that of the human consumers of healthcare and public health, and the behavior of the human healthcare professionals, throughout the curriculum. If we (the healthcare professionals) focus on helping people (the consumers) engage in healthy exercise, healthful eating, stress management, positive interpersonal relationships, and healthy body image, they will become healthier regardless of their body size, shape, or weight. This approach also helps to empower individuals with a sense of healthy self-control in that behavior change can help them feel better physically, emotionally, and psychologically. And, it is a non-stigmatizing approach. In fact, Wann (1998) has emphasized the importance of reclaiming the word *fat* to be used in positive context for this activism much like the word *nigger* has been reclaimed by African Americans in speech, terms of endearment to one another, and music—particularly rap and hip hop. Wann has been a strong activist in the fat acceptance movement and has encouraged fat individuals to rally the cause and make their bodies and their pride more publicly visible.

Fat individuals deserve just as much respect and unconditional positive regard as lean individuals. And I am not the first professional to feel this way.

How to Remove Body Snarking and Fat Shaming from Our Healthcare System

Ross, Blaie, de Lannoy, Despres, and Lavie (2015) argue that scientists and healthcare professionals need to shift the goal of weight loss for treating obesity as an endpoint to the goal of changing and maintaining physical exercise and healthful nutrition. In review of the literature, they proclaim that our narrow-minded approach to weight loss for obese individuals has not only proven ineffective, but this approach also has iatrogenic, or harmful, effects on the health of these individuals. Health cannot be determined by viewing a person's body size. Although health, or its converse—illness— can be ascertained by diverse measures and metrics, the most simplistic metric for human health is cardiorespiratory fitness. This is the body's ability to pull oxygen into the lungs so that the circulatory system can send it to the cells in all areas of the body through the blood. The cells use the oxygen for maintenance, and muscle cells use it to create movement. A person who runs marathons has amazing cardiorespiratory fitness. On the other hand, a bedridden person who is so weak that she must be transported in a wheelchair has very poor cardiorespiratory fitness. Cardiorespiratory fitness is *not* a function of body size. It is a function of how often a person has moved in exercise or for work. The marathon runner did not start out by running 26 miles at a time; she had to train and increase her mileage gradually in order to run the total 26 miles in one day. The more a person has trained, the more the body responds with increased ability to perform that task. Our cardiorespiratory fitness is the key biological marker of health and it is a function of exercise—not body size.

Barry et al. (2014) conducted a meta-analysis of ten studies that each researched the relationship between cardiorespiratory fitness (i.e., measured by VO_2 max), body weight, and all-cause mortality. They found that compared to normal weight individuals, those who were unfit had *twice* the risk of death regardless of their body sizes, whereas individuals who were overweight/fit and obese/fit had the *same* risk of death as normal-weight individuals. They concluded that the risk of death was, therefore, a function of poor cardiorespiratory fitness, and not a function of large body size. Hence, it is not weight that is the risk; it is the state of being unfit that is dangerous. Obesity is not the problem. Certainly, having a sedentary lifestyle contributes to weight gain, especially if people habitually overconsume calories. Conversely, physically active individuals tend to be leaner and composed of more muscle mass relative to adipose mass. Physical activity not only burns calories during exercise, which helps prevent the storage of extra body fat, but it also enhances muscle mass, which elevates a person's basal metabolic rate. Muscle tissue burns calories at rest; adipose does not. A sedentary lifestyle certainly contributes to obesity, but the former, not the latter, is the real culprit when it comes to health outcomes.

Most Americans do not realize that many lean-looking individuals are sedentary and unfit also. As I profess in my classes, human beings evolved over history to move an extraordinary amount. We had to forage for plant-based foods, chase wildlife to hunt, run away from wildlife trying to eat us, and traverse miles for basic survival. In modern life, it takes little energy to drive and shop at the grocery store. We do not burn much energy by preparing and cooking our food. Pushing the microwave button probably spends ⅛ of a kilocalorie. Yet, our genes are a product of the environment in which we evolved. It was once an environment in which *famine* and *starvation* posed serious threats to our survival and our ability to reproduce. Many more of our ancestors died of starvation than experienced health threats from being overweight. Looking at evolution this way, health issues associated with a sedentary lifestyle and obesity are very modern problems considering the nearly 200,000 years since Homo sapiens walked the earth. And, as warm-blooded creatures, humans must consume a tremendous amount of energy just to stay warm, for their bodily tissues to replicate and maintain, as well as to move. Historic humans who died of starvation were more likely to have acquired lean genes and an absence of "easy weight gain genes." Those that survived, especially during times of famine, were people with thrifty genes that made it easier for their body to store energy in the form of body fat. Those ancestors could survive and reproduce, thus passing these "easy weight gain" genes onto the next generation. Now, position these genetic prototypes into an environment with plentiful, energy-dense foods and physical space that promotes limited movement, and the results are physical bodies that are unfit and often gain body fat, which is simply stored energy. It is no wonder the human race carries multiple genes that make it easier to maintain and gain weight. This was a powerful survival mechanism that explains why humans are still here. Considering the evolutionary and genetic contributions to modern day obesity, it is interesting how powerfully Americans maintain stigmatizing attitudes about overweight and obesity when there are other culprits compromising the health of our citizens. Most Americans are not aware of how critically our behavior affects our health. Instead, the media and politicians tell us that we should only be concerned about access to healthcare as the primary determinant of our health. Yet, in reality, our behavior is paramount! U.S. citizens, healthcare providers, public health officials, and politicians need to redirect attention to the behaviors that are really harming Americans, causing disability and lost productivity, suffering, and premature death.

From a public health standpoint, if we could magically change any one behavior that would have the most influence on preventing morbidity and mortality, we would want to cease human cigarette smoking and other forms of tobacco use. After that, our behavioral targets would include sedentary lifestyles and how people in the U.S. eat (NCHHS, 1988; USDHHS, 2000). Americans are making themselves very sick with their cigarettes. Smoking causes suffering, disability, and premature death, and it is a tremendous financial burden on our healthcare system. Our citizens are the taxpayers who pay for these costs when victims of smoking tap our Medicare or Medicaid systems. Interestingly, in recent politics and attempts to repeal and replace the Patient Protection and Affordable Care Act (i.e., also known as "Obamacare"), we hear *nothing* in the media about the *causes* of rising healthcare costs, such as how Americans' lifestyle behavior is driving up costs, or how capitalistic economics are doing so also. The increase in our healthcare costs is unmistakable. This trend has been occurring for decades, and the U.S. has accelerated our healthcare spending much more than our sister industrialized countries. In 1960, we spent 5 percent of our gross domestic product on healthcare. By 2012, the gross domestic product was up to 16.9 percent, which is double that of other countries (Organization for Economic Cooperation and Development, 2014). Further, between 1960 and 2013, U.S. healthcare costs rose three times higher than our overall rate of inflation (Bureau of Labor Statistics, 2014; Chantrill, 2014). The U.S. spends way too much money on healthcare, and we are very inefficient in how we do so. The World Health Organization (2007) has the U.S. ranked 37th in performance compared to other countries and 72nd in overall health compared to the 191 member nations in the study. Unfortunately, politicians have recently argued that our healthcare is so expensive because we are trying to get everyone insured. They have failed to advertise the multiple and complicated reasons as to why our costs are astronomical. While Congress was pushing a recent attempt to repeal and replace the Patient Protection and Affordable Care Act, Donald Trump said to the press as members of Congress were wrestling with whether or not to pass the reform, "Who knew that healthcare was so complicated?!" I sat there thinking, "I do—I have been teaching how intricate our healthcare problems are, and how attempts to find solutions are even more complicated, for two decades now." We have known that healthcare has been disastrous for a long time. Moreover, there are many scientists who are experts on the topic, who can take all of the complex variables into consideration at once and think long-term as well as short-term, who should be called upon to recommend healthcare reform as our politicians wrestle with this enormous issue for U.S. citizens. I am not in favor of the status quo. However, I do worry that we will make rushed and simplified attempts to fix something complicated based solely on political affiliations without listening to recommendations from scientific experts on how best to proceed. Many of our industrialized sister countries have figured out better models of healthcare.

Kumar, Ghildayal, and Shah (2011) note that the U.S. is the only developed country, other than South Africa, that fails to provide universal healthcare to its citizens; further, the media and our government have ignored the root causes of the rise in costs. We can blame both Democrats and Republicans here. Both parties have not been paying attention to what the science says or to the real economic issues. We have an entire industry in the middle—health insurance—and every industry must profit to stay afloat. Kumar et al. (2011) noted the inefficiencies in the U.S. healthcare system and have studied other countries to identify where we go wrong. They note that countries with government-funded single-payer systems have lower administrative costs, because there is no third-party insurance system in the middle. Single-payer systems tend to offer high quality care and have high consumer satisfaction. However, they ration healthcare so consumers may not get what they demand for immediately. Barack Obama led major reform with the passing of the Patient Protection and Affordable Care Act and made unprecedented history with the law. There was some very thoughtful consideration on how to legislate change within it. With the ultimate goal of getting all U.S. citizens insured, Obama relied on healthcare experts to decide how best to construct laws to move us towards that goal. If you recall, the website used for enrollment was a horrible failure and Obamacare kept the entire third-party payer health insurance industry in the middle with the capitalistic idea that more competition amongst the insurance companies would suppress costs. The U.S. will never be efficient in our cost of healthcare with an entire industry between the healthcare providers and the consumers needing to profit. It is no wonder many of our industrialized sister countries are able to offer cheaper and more efficient healthcare in their socialized-medicine, single-payer systems.

There are forces, some unique to how the U.S. runs healthcare, driving up costs. This list will not be exhaustive, but it will provide readers with some ideas about areas that we need to thoughtfully consider in problem solving this situation. The solution to our healthcare woes is not as simple as our politicians trying to decide if we keep Obamacare or repeal the law. And if we repeal it, are we left to figure out the consequences on our own? Or will our leaders think of an alternative to replace it? Ethically, I think our citizens deserve healthcare just as we deserve public education, just as we deserve our police protection, just as we deserve access to fire fighters if our homes/buildings catch on fire. Why not make healthcare public and universal also? However, until we figure out how to address the root causes of the accelerating expenses—such as the insurance industry in the middle—we will not effectively manage the cost inflation, at least without severely sacrificing the health of individuals in our nation. This is both an ethical dilemma and a fiscal quandary.

United States citizens are in the habit of relying on medications and procedures or surgeries to fix what ails them. Popular media reinforces this custom. The pharmaceutical companies are marketing to consumers and healthcare providers and dominating how we think we should treat disease. There are no checks and balances for their costs. In his book *Profits before people? Ethical Standards and the Marketing of Prescription Drugs* (2006), Weber conducts a careful analysis of the power of "big pharma" and performs ethical analyses on how they are cleverly marketing to consumers and healthcare providers and attempting to maximize their profits. In 2006, the U.S. dominated pharmaceutical purchases in a $637 billon dollar global market (Kumar et al., 2011). Further, U.S. citizens are enamored with our fancy and very expensive medical technology. The cost of this technology gets passed along to consumers. I have been suckered into the technology myself. One of my cats, Monty, came home limping with an obvious injury to his knee. I promptly made a veterinarian appointment and took him in. They recommended a magnetic resonance image (i.e., MRI) of his knee that ended up costing about $330 dollars. I love my cat, so it seemed like the right thing to do. The vet returned to inform me how bad it was. You hear about athletes tearing one ligament in the knee and it is a big deal. Poor Monty had torn all of them. Monty must have jumped off of something very high to have an impact injury like that. He has a mysterious life! However, the treatment that the veterinarian recommended was to keep him inside for two weeks—an intervention which was rather torturous for him. He missed his mysterious lifestyle, and it was also rather unpleasant for his parents, who had to hear him screeching to go outside. Even years later, Monty's knee still does not appear to bend normally, but he has a good quality of life; the cat starts purring loudly just when we make eye contact with him across the room. That being said, the $330 MRI was not life-saving and probably unnecessary. It certainly did not seem to drive the recommended treatment. And for humans, Beever et al. (2004) concluded that there is tremendous evidence that we over-utilize technology, and its expense goes well beyond its value for our U.S. citizens. They report that medical technology spending has been growing at a 20 percent increase for five years and diagnostic imaging was a $100 billion-dollar business at the time of their publication.

The behavior of our citizens (e.g., smokers), the behavioral economics of our pharmaceuticals, and the use of technology in healthcare are driving up costs to the point of causing grave inefficiency in the U.S. healthcare system. Other lifestyle behaviors, isuespecially those causing Type II obesity, are also putting a dramatic burden on our modern healthcare system. So as not to add to the cultural problem of fat shaming individuals whose bodies are obese, let me clarify that obesity does *not* cause Type II diabetes. A poor lifestyle of being sedentary and eating unhealthful foods causes both obesity and Type II diabetes. Leung, Carlsson, Colditz, and Chang (2017) used the Medical Expenditure Panel Survey from 2008 to 2012 to examine trends in Type II diabetes and the burden this is costing the U.S. By 2011, it is estimated that 20.8 million or 9 percent of U.S. citizens had Type II diabetes. Given ongoing trends, the CDC (2010) projects that 33 percent of citizens in the U.S. will have diabetes by 2050. The estimated cost of diabetes in 2012 for the U.S. was $245 billion including $69 billion in reduced productivity and $176 billion in direct medical costs (American Diabetes Association, 2013). Leung et al. (2017) found in their samples that individuals with class III obesity (i.e., body mass index above 40) had a six-fold increase in developing diabetes. Marking the age of fifty as their anchor, they found that individuals with diabetes had three times the annual healthcare expenditures ($13,581) compared to those without diabetes ($3,954). Thus, we need to target the combined effects of sedentary lifestyle and our dietary habits (McGinnis & Foege, 1993). Sedentary lifestyle accounts for 23 percent of U.S. deaths from chronic diseases (Hahn, Teutsch, Rothenberg, & Marks, 1990). Detrimental dietary habits are associated with four out of ten of the leading disease causes of death in the U.S. including coronary heart disease, stroke, some cancers, and Type II diabetes (CDC, 1997; USDHHS, 2000). Consequently, if behavior is driving the disease processes, which are very costly in our healthcare system, it would make sense that we target citizens' lifestyle behavior to promote overall health, as well as a method for ending the fat stigma that harms many people. Behavior change could address these problems.

Walsh (2011) includes promotion of regular exercise and dietary recommendations as two of his *Therapeutic Lifestyle Changes* (TLCs). These are changes in Americans' typical lifestyle behaviors that have excellent scientific support to be able to improve both mental and physical health, yet are underutilized by U.S. citizens on their own—as well as underutilized by healthcare clinicians for the patients that they see. Consequently, there is a disconnect between what the science says makes people healthier and what healthcare providers are recommending to their patients to make them healthier or keep them well. We are relying on imaging, pharmaceuticals, and surgical procedures that are very expensive, when we have cheaper options that work very well. We rarely hear about this in the media or reports on our healthcare politics. Beyond exercise, the other TLCs that Walsh describes are nutrition and diet, time in nature, relationships that include emotional intimacy, religious and spiritual involvement, relaxation and stress management, and altruism or service to others. He does a wonderful job of contextualizing many modern-day mental health issues by noting that we humans have evolved to need all of these therapeutic lifestyle behaviors. In fact, they should be *ordinary lifestyle behaviors*!

Yet, many people live in artificial environments devoid of these behavioral habits or in environments bereft of such essentials. The discrepancy between the conditions in which the human mind and body evolved and how contemporary humans live, results in psychological distress and mental illness for many people. Walsh advocates that healthcare professionals educate themselves on the science behind these effective interventions that improve mental health—as well as physical wellbeing and quality of life for their patients—and counsel them with empirically supported therapeutic interventions. These effective lifestyle change therapies include motivational interviewing, cognitive behavioral therapies (CBT), dialectical behavioral therapies (DBT), interpersonal therapies (IPT), and acceptance and commitment therapies (ACT). I would add that mental health professionals need to weigh the efficiency, cost-effectiveness, and likelihood of the win-win side effects of these TLCs over our heavy reliance on psychotropic medications for diverse mental health issues. As Whitaker argues in his scholarly book, *Anatomy of an Epidemic* (2010), the rise in use of psychotropic medication in the past quarter century has *not* been met with a significant decrease in mental illness in our society. Instead he blames—with a sound compilation of science—that the increase in our burden of mental illness is *because* of our overuse of these medications. We have a treatment paradigm that not only does not work well, but causes more harm in the long run. We need a return to healthy lifestyles instead. Advocating for more fitness through exercise and healthful eating, as well as attention to the other TLCs proposed by Walsh (2011), is a much better path of intervention for individuals who are overweight or obese. This is especially better than fat shaming and pushing for weight loss interventions that normally fail to create long-term weight loss, fail to improve physical health, and can even worsen mental health. Body snarking and fat shaming cause significant harm. They are not the solution to Americans' sedentary lifestyles that are driving up rates of diabetes and subsequent healthcare costs. We need to focus on behavior change for our U.S. citizens and be more thoughtful with healthcare reform if we are going to have a positive impact on the health of our nation.

Body Snarking of Women in Popular Culture

Body snarking also has explanatory origins in evolutionary psychology. Called intrasexual competition, snarking is a form of interpersonal, indirect aggression towards women as a means for other women to achieve more social power and attract high status mates (Buss, 1988). Historically, boys and men have engaged in physical aggression with one another as intrasexual competition for mates. This explains the history of humans' historical admiration of sports and the men who show the most strength and athleticism. Girls and women, on the other hand, have historically protected their bodies for reproduction, and thus engaged in gossip and other forms of verbal aggression as means of rendering their females in intrasexual competition as less socially and physically attractive (Buss, 1988). While body snarking is inexcusable, there are modern-day research studies showing that young women can, indeed, enhance their dating status by using verbal aggression towards their peers (Pellegrini & Long, 2003; Vaillancourt, Brendgen, Boivin, & Trembley, 2003). Owens, Shute, and Slee (2000) found that female adolescents' envy about another young woman's appearance can be an important trigger for them engaging in body snarking towards her. Further, Leenaars, Dane, and Marini (2008) found an interesting gender interaction in teenagers in how level of attractiveness related with being a victim of indirect aggression. The young men who were considered to be highly attractive were less likely to report victimization of indirect aggression by other teens compared to those who were less attractive. On the other hand, the female adolescents who were considered to be highly attractive reported a 35 percent increase in the odds of being victims of indirect aggression compared to those considered less attractive. Young attractive women may be considered more threatening rivals for other young women who are competing for young men's romantic attention. Consequently, body snarking others is a way that some individuals manage personal insecurities and gain social status through harming other women.

Regrettably, the modern-day media has created the foundation for this public, oftentimes anonymous, form of bullying of women. This has become a genuine public health problem that maintains sexism and misogyny in our society. Female celebrities are, unfortunately, frequent targets of snarking, which makes this form of indirect aggression seem normative and acceptable. But it doesn't always go unchallenged. For example, in 2007 journalist Maureen Dowd and a number of female celebrities came to the defense of Jennifer Love Hewitt when an online photo of her wearing a bikini while she vacationed with her partner in Hawaii provoked fat shaming comments from the public. The actress herself responded confidentially, refusing to fall prey to such absurd criticism.

A size two is not fat! Nor will it ever be. And being a size zero doesn't make you beautiful. To all girls with butts, boobs, hips, and a waist, put on a bikini—put it on and stay strong [White, 2007].

We conducted a survey assessing clothing size in a sample of age and racially representative individuals in the U.S. population and found that average clothing size ranged between 14 and 16 for women (Maphis, Martz, Bergman, Curtin, & Webb, 2013). Thus, a size two for Jennifer Love Hewitt is *tiny* compared to normal women in our culture. Presumably just to produce and sell provocative press, that situation took the body snarking way too far.

More recently, Leopold (2016), who reports for CNN, noted how multiple celebrities, including comedian Amy Schumer, have faced body snarking on social media. Historically, only certain professionals, like fashion models, necessitated utmost concern for their attractiveness since it was a part of their job description to maintain a certain appearance. Modern media is obsessed with how women look, regardless of their occupation, even if their careers have absolutely nothing to do with physical appearance. This obsession, and the snarking it inspires, is maintaining unnecessary sexism and misogyny in our culture. In this generation of selfie postings on Instagram, Facebook, etc., this pressure to look better than others, or to always look one's best in public has become a preoccupation for many individuals. As my own research team reflected when we were running a study about selfies on Instagram, some of the pictures reek of pride and some were rather pitiful. My lab coined the term *body narcissism* to label this type of self-exploitation and attention seeking. One of my research team's favorite survey items that we created to code these Instagram pictures was, "How likely do you think this woman would want her grandmother to see this picture?" Grandmother would probably love the picture of granddaughter playing with a puppy. On the other hand, her grandmother might feel a little different about seeing the picture of her in her sexy bikini making the duck face provocatively in front of the bathroom mirror. Evolutionary psychologists would categorize the latter picture as a prime example of modern-day intrasexual competition, as these pictures draw sexual attraction from the men who view them.

Mazziotta (2016), who writes for *People*, covered Amy Schumer's response to a picture published when she and her boyfriend were vacationing in Hawaii (have you caught on that celebrities like to vacation in Hawaii?!). Amy is featured in a one-piece bathing suit returning to the beach from the ocean. This was meant to be a private moment for her and the picture was published without her permission. In response to the reporter's story and the picture, Amy posted,

> I meant to write "good morning trolls!" I hope you find some joy in your lives today in a human interaction and not just in writing unkind things to a stranger you've never met who triggers something in you that makes you feel powerless and alone. This is how I look. I feel happy. I think I look strong and healthy.

Further, when Schumer was featured, without her permission, in *Glamour* magazine's special issue on plus size celebrities, she responded,

> I think there's nothing wrong with being plus size. Beautiful healthy women. Plus size is considered size 16 in America. I go between a size 6 and an 8. *@glamourmag* put me in their plus size online issue without asking or letting me know and it doesn't feel right to me. Young girls seeing my body type thinking that is *plus* size? What are your thoughts? [Mazziotta, 2016].

Again, if the average size for American women runs from 14 to 16 (Maphis et al., 2013), then why do we allow the media to fat shame celebrities who wear sizes 4 to 8? I am glad that Amy Schumer is fighting back with some sense of dignity and humor. Also in response to media fat shaming, actor Melissa McCarthy has launched her own design label called Seven7 with women's clothes that range from sizes 4 to 28 in response to the fact that malls and clothing stores have often segregated the lower size stores from the plus size stores (White, 2015). In her typical comedic fashion, she said,

> It's an odd thing that you can't go shopping with your friends because your store is upstairs hidden by the tire section. We'll put you gals over there because we don't want to see you and you probably don't want to be seen.

Melissa McCarthy's intent for Seven7 is to enable women to express themselves in chic pieces of clothing that have been designed with style, wit, and confidence. Actor and comedian Rebel Wilson, who starred in the *Pitch Perfect* films, has also recently launched her own plus size clothing line (Denee, 2017). She says that every piece that she has designed is meant to "celebrate the figure, not hide it, and give the wearer the confidence to be her own Rebel." She is also quoted as saying,

> I know how hard it can be to find the cool, quality fashion I want to wear, even with the help of Hollywood stylists … I'm so proud to be creating this collection with The Mamiye Group, and to give gorgeous ladies everywhere amazing clothes that empower them to express their confidence and chic attitude.

We need more influential women like McCarthy, Wilson, and Schumer who represent role models that are actively resisting the body snarkers and creating support for larger women in our society.

Another recent example of body snarking—this time pulling in the reputation and agenda of feminists—is Emma Watson, the young actor most known for her portrayal of Hermione Granger in the *Harry Potter* films. She was recently the victim of public critique about her photos promoting her acting role in *Beauty and the Beast* (Andrews, 2017). Photographer Tim Walker and stylist Jessica Diehl produced some very artistic photos of Watson including one that slightly revealed her breasts. One of the body snarking tweets critiqued Watson's very public and historic support of feminism, yet was now showing her body and her beauty. The aggressive tweet was putting words into Watson's mouth that she did not say herself—"oh, and here are my tits!" In response to this public snarking, Watson proudly proclaimed that

> Feminism is about giving women choice. Feminism is not a stick with which to beat other women with. It's about freedom. It's about liberation … It's about equality.

First, I admired J.K. Rowling's character of Hermione Granger in the *Harry Potter* series. Hermione is a very smart, precocious child and teen who is also sensitive to others and knows how to problem solve with her intelligence and magic skills. What a wonderful role model for young girls! Watson herself appears to have many of the same qualities for the character whom she played. I am so pleased that she has reminded us that "feminism is about choice," especially considering the political backlash against women's choices threatened by our nation's leaders at this time.

Another example of body snarking in social media involves Grammy-winning singer Kelly Clarkson sending out a message on Twitter wishing her followers a happy Fourth of July. A troll responded to her tweet by saying, "You're fat." Clarkson told a reporter following the birth of her daughter, which included some natural weight gain from her pregnancy, that

> I don't obsess about my weight, which is probably one of the reasons why other people have such a problem with it … There are just some people who are born skinny and with a great metabolism—that is not me. I wish I had a better metabolism. But somebody else probably wishes they could walk into a room and make friends with everyone like I can. You always want what someone else has [Schwartz, 2015].

Speaking of which, I wish that I had her voice. I have to play the music very loud in my car for my voice to sound remotely decent when I sing along. Kelly Clarkson has reminded us that we could all find *something* to complain about. It is the straight hair, curly hair scenario over and over. We could always find ourselves very satisfied or very dissatisfied in our thoughts about ourselves. I am pleased to see these famous role models pushing back, publicly, in response to their experiences with body snarking. They could have been personally and publicly wounded by these comments instead.

In scientific documentation of body snarking in the media, Fouts and Burggraf (2000) analyzed 18 prime-time TV situational comedies (e.g., *Friends*) that aired in Calgary Canada in 1997 and coded characters' sex, body weights (i.e., below average, average, or above average), dialogue, and the audience responses such as laughter. They found that male characters made more negative comments about appearance to the heavier women and that 80 percent of those comments were followed by audience reactions of giggles or "oohs." The researchers expressed concern that such behavior, which would now be named body snarking or fat shaming, was being modeled by men towards these larger women and that the audience reactions were further reinforcing this association. Moreover, Fouts and Burggraf (1999) documented that in these situational comedies the thinner the female characters were, the more positive comments the male characters made about their appearance. Together, these results suggest that popular TV shows are modeling the thin ideal and reinforcing discriminatory attitudes towards larger women. Television is telling us that these aggressive and harmful comments are not only normative but funny. This makes the public backlash delivered by McCarthy, Schumer, Clarkson, and Watson in response to this nasty way of treating women even more timely and important for a feminist agenda.

Body Snarking and Sexism in Politics

While it is highly unpleasant to acknowledge how women such as actors and comedians are victimized by these cultural rituals, it is even more unfortunate to see how this type of sexism and misogyny can impact U.S. politics, our leadership, and thus policies, laws, and customs that impact all of us. Having attended the Women's March in Washington, D.C., in 2017, I felt the collective power of a feminist agenda to represent the needs of girls and women in our nation. Sexism is palpable, as is the energy behind the many feminists who are fighting for change. We need more politicians, especially women and individuals who represent oppressed groups, who will stand up to the White patriarchy and fight for equality of all people in our nation. Later in this chapter, I will argue that body snarking and the expectations of women's gender roles are social forces preventing women from garnering the votes that leverage the resources that they need for success in politics; yet body snarking is only one way that society threatens women's power. There are other contemporary threats to women's equality in our patriarchal nation. Again, some of this sexism has evolutionary explanations. Buss (1996) suggests that throughout human ancestry men were much more likely to be successful in mate selection and reproduction if they could acquire and demonstrate adequate resources to care for a potential family. Consequently, there are still many people in our culture that hold traditional values about men's career and financial success, while harboring disrespect for women who acquire these resources also. And our current federal administration has been deliberately trying to sabotage women's resources as a means of gaining more supremacy themselves.

As an example of proposed policy aimed at disenfranchising women, there are continued threats to defund and dismantle Planned Parenthood by our current federal administration. Our political leaders, such as Vice President Mike Pence, devise these threats based on the fact that Planned Parenthood offers abortions to women. However, of the services offered by Planned Parenthood, 42 percent include screening and treatment for sexually transmitted infections, 34 percent prescribe contraception, 9 percent are cancer screens such as pap tests for cervical cancer and mammograms for breast cancer, and only 3 percent are for abortions (Planned Parenthood, 2014). Moreover, abortions at Planned Parenthood have *never* been covered by taxpayer dollars. They are paid for by their patients or through outside donations. I am a routine donor to this organization as payback for the wonderful medical care they gave me in reproductive control and eventually during the pregnancy of my first son while I was making a mere $8,000 per year as a graduate student. I could not afford fancy healthcare then. Planned Parenthood cares for so many other women, and men, who are in similar situations. People need affordable healthcare and evidenced-based sex education and services. In fact, this organization provides services to 2.4 million people per year, with an estimated one in five women having used them for healthcare at least once in their lives (Planned Parenthood, 2017). If these 2.4 million women, and the men, who use Planned Parenthood for their healthcare and contraception lose these services, what an adverse impact this would have on the welfare of so many U.S. citizens—not to mention the harmful impact this could have on our economy.

Women and men who can only afford very low cost contraception are not the people who can afford very high cost pregnancies and children. Vasel (2017), who writes for *CNN Money,* reported on a document released by the U.S. Department of Agriculture that estimates the cost for raising a child by middle-income parents is now $233,610! And this is the amount before factoring in the cost of a college education, which the College Board (2017) estimated to be close to $100,000 for a four-year public university. When people do not have access to contraception, many more unplanned pregnancies occur, which result in unwanted children, infanticide, or women seeking unsafe abortions. Why would our politicians want to take away women's access to contraception? It seems like some politicians want to take away women's choices in hopes of taking away women's life options and—by doing so—take away women's power. If women lose their power, then men gain more—consequently, the gap in equality between women and men would grow. The threat to defund Planned Parenthood is a serious feminist issue. How we make decisions about our political candidates and the policies that they endorse has an exponential impact on many of us personally and our society as a whole. We need more leaders who embrace equal rights for all of our citizens because right now our country does not have enough feminist representation in our government.

By 2015, women composed 51 percent of the population of the U.S., but our representation by women in positions of power lags far behind our numbers (U.S. Census Bureau, 2015). Also, based on the salaries of full-time workers in 2013, women earn 78 cents compared to their male counterparts' $1.00. These factual metrics suggest women are nowhere near achieving equality with men in the U.S. In a 2006 Inter-Parliamentary Union survey (IPU, 2006) of women's representation in legislative and executive branches of the world's governments, the U.S. ranked 69th in the world, with only 16.8 percent of the House of Representatives and 16 percent of the Senate comprised of women. By 2017, women were holding a total of 19.6 percent of the total seats in the U.S. Congress, broken down to 19.3 percent of the House of Representatives and 21 percent of the Senate. Could Americans' tendency to view women as objects of sexualized beauty rather than objects of power and leadership affect women's lack of representation in government?

Hayes, Lawless, and Baitinger (2014) conducted an experimental design exposing a sample of 961 U.S. adults from Amazon's Mechanical Turk (MTurk) to news coverage of two hypothetical candidates for Congress. They varied gender and whether the candidates' appearance was covered negatively, positively, neutrally, or not mentioned at all. Results showed that offering negative commentary about physical appearance had an adverse effect on participants' opinion of the candidates' professionalism. However, they did not find gender differences when the candidates were portrayed negatively in their appearance or their perception of the candidate's professionalism. These results suggest that if the media make critique of political candidates' appearance salient, then it could have an impact on how citizens feel and vote. Fechette (2012) noted the harsh criticism Hillary Rodham Clinton faced during her presidential campaigns. First, she was criticized for wearing pantsuits, which tend to symbolize male power, as opposed to skirts and dresses that would be considered more lady-like. Rather than take this criticism as insult, she later used this condemnation in her favor by creating the *Pantsuit Nation* with the mission, "To build a foundation for a more equitable and engaged democracy" (https://www.pantsuitnation.org/mission.html). Later, she was criticized for wearing a skirt again. The media would not allow her to be at peace in her own clothing choices. Further, Hillary Rodham Clinton was criticized for her appearance and age. While men tend to be viewed as more distinguished, experienced, and authoritative with physical signs of aging, the reverse is true for women. Regarding Hillary Rodham Clinton, radio host Rush Limbaugh was quoted as saying, "So the question is this. Will this country want to actually watch a woman get older before their eyes on a daily basis?" (Dowd, 2007). Hayes et al. (2014) focused on hypothetical candidates for Congress in their research. However, could these prejudicial forces affect Americans' votes for critical, real-life leadership roles in our country—that of the presidency and vice presidency?

Geraldine "Gerry" Ferraro was the first woman to run for Vice President alongside Walter Mondale for the Democratic Party in 1984 (they lost to Ronald Reagan & George Bush). Elizabeth Dole originally ran for the Republican ticket for president in 2000, but pulled out of the campaign in 1999 before the primaries. Other than Dole, the presidential elections were devoid of women candidates until the 2008 election when Hillary Rodham Clinton ran for the Democratic nomination for president against Barack Obama (who won), and Sarah Palin, who was chosen for the Republican ticket as the vice-presidential running mate alongside John McCain. The campaign presented Americans with a real life "natural experiment" to see how citizens viewed women in politics, especially in that these women represented *both* parties. Kathleen Hall Jamieson (1995) presents us with a dilemma that befalls women in these elections, a predicament to which male candidates are conveniently immune. This could help explain why men have *always* won. Jamieson states,

> Women who are considered feminine will be judged incompetent, and women who are competent, unfeminine … [women] who succeed in politics and public life will be scrutinized under a different lens from that applied to successful men [p. 16].

Both Sarah Palin and Hillary Rodham Clinton took public stances that they were both "candidates that happen to be women" when they were faced with questions from reporters about whether or not sexism was a factor influencing their campaigns. I can see why each was professing this, but the fact that they were women was at the forefront of media attention that they attracted. Carlin and Winfrey (2009) conducted a communications analysis through the lens of sexist media portrayals of Hillary Rodham Clinton and Sarah Palin during the 2008 presidential election based on stereotypes of professional women, research on the impact of sexist language, research methodology on media framing, and lessons learned from the campaigns. Thus, they borrowed from scientific methodology from previous communications literature that has been proven to capture sexism and, if it exists, to bring it to the forefront and used it to see if sexism was operating in the 2008 election. From their research, Carlin and Winfrey documented pervasive sexism faced by *both* candidates. Of the categories that they analyzed, they asserted that the category of "sexiness" portrayed the worse gender bias as this was often the topic of content for both of them, while other qualities such as their knowledge or political experience were ignored or tossed aside. Consequently, as women both candidates were placed under a media microscope evaluating their sexiness, whereas male candidates rarely face this type of scrutiny. Whether sexism in the media existed during the 2016 presidential campaign or not, I failed to hear questions about how qualified Donald Trump was in the category of sexiness. I would remember, because I would have gagged!

After establishing that both Hillary Rodham Clinton and Sarah Palin were evaluated on their sexiness, Carlin and Winfrey (2009) found that the direction of the scrutiny over the perceived sexiness of the two candidates diverged. Palin was heralded for her attractiveness and beauty pageant background, and the press attempted to disregard any other positive qualities that she possessed because of her beauty. I recall having very mixed feelings when I heard Palin speak, as I struggled to discern her credibility and did not favor her policies, yet I found it painful to view how she was objectified and treated like a doll by the press. Maureen Dowd (2008) of *The New York Times* called her "Caribou Barbie." After what we learned about Barbie from chapter two, we now know that this was not a very nice thing for a woman of influence to call another woman. Not only was Sarah Palin objectified—she was sexualized. Reuters created an image that shot her backside showing only her legs and black high heels with a young male voter framed between her legs (Sheppard, 2008). Hmm, I wonder what subliminal messages they were going for in that image?! Although Palin was criticized for dressing to be pretty as opposed to dressing to be powerful, she was *not* dressing in revealing ways to appear sexual. She may have used her attractiveness, and certainly there was scandal over her $150,000 clothing budget supported by the Republican Party. However, Palin, and likely her stylist, chose very tasteful, attractive, nonsexual professional clothing—nothing like what Barbie would wear to a nightclub.

Hillary Rodham Clinton, on the other hand, dressed to appear credible and powerful, and was consequently critiqued for completely different reasons. They criticized her for wearing unfeminine pantsuits, often minimal makeup, and for having thick ankles (i.e., "cankles"). She was also under the microscope about her weight. Cartoonist Nick Anderson, who published with the *Houston Chronicle,* drew Hillary Rodham Clinton in a dark pantsuit with an exaggeratedly heavy bottom and the caption "What you gonna do with all that junk, all that junk inside your trunk?" which was taken from a Black Eyed Peas song that was popular at the time (Heimer, 2007). Carlin and Winfrey stated that Hillary Rodham Clinton was in a "clear double bind" for how she dressed (p. 332). When she wore a dress that was more feminine and showed more cleavage, Robin Givhan of *The Washington Post* wrote, "There was cleavage on display Wednesday afternoon on C-SPAN2. It belonged to Senator Hillary Rodham Clinton" (Givhan, 2007). I looked at this picture and thought she looked professional. Some of her cleavage was revealed, but not in a sexual way. It reminds me of Emma Watson having to defend her photo shoot as previously discussed. Women have bodies that are different than men's. Are we supposed to look like women, or are we supposed to suppress and hide our feminine features? It is exhausting to consider this double bind. Hillary Rodham Clinton's image certainly fell victim to this. Her intelligence, drive, and competitiveness were intimidating to people who thought executive leadership should not be a woman's role. Carlin and Winfrey (2009) report that there was even a Facebook group called "Stop running for president and make me a sandwich" about Hillary Rodham Clinton that had tens of thousands of members.

Consequently, the presidential election of 2008 was won by Barack Obama, with Joe Biden as his vice president. In an unprecedented natural experiment, our nation got to entertain the idea of having a woman as president or a woman as vice president. Obviously, Americans chose neither. Could the factors of media gender stereotyping of Hillary Rodham Clinton and Sarah Palin have had an impact on the way our nation voted? Jed Nedeau (2008) observes,

> Both women came from completely different political points of view. Both women presented themselves in completely opposite ways on the national political stage. But, both women experienced the wrath of a society seemingly afraid to see a woman in power ... While there has been no lack of critique, analysis and conversation about how sexism played a role in both Senator Hillary Rodham Clinton and Governor Sarah Palin's campaigns, one thing that has not been well-identified is the resolution of how society will proceed and one day elect a female commander-in-chief [para. 2, 4].

Fortini (2008) concluded that sexism was alive and well in this campaign, and not just "in the minds and hearts of right-wing crackpots and Internet nut-jobs, but it ... flourished among members of the news media." Although portrayed very playfully and humorously in the *Saturday Night Live* skits featuring Tina Fey and Amy Poehler playing Sarah Palin and Hillary Rodham Clinton respectively, could the media's body snarking and other gender stereotyping have cost them the election? Hearing these biased opinions in the daily news certainly seemed to normalize extant prejudices in the American public. Lawless (2009) found that at least 25 percent of those polled believed that most men are better suited emotionally for politics than most women. Further, Hillary Rodham Clinton exuded confidence, was incredibly articulate in her debates, and was an intelligent high achiever. Unfortunately, these are perceived as masculine personality traits that are considered by many to be appropriate for men but not for women (Bem, 1987; Constantini & Craik, 1972). Further, Dolan (2005) has shown that voters prefer more masculine traits in their elected leaders. So, in this case, Hillary Rodham Clinton had the requisite style of an elected leader, but many voters probably disliked her for behaving in a masculine manner. Based on perception by the public, Hillary Rodham Clinton was in a "damned if you do, damned if you don't" situation. Bligh et al. (2012) called this dilemma a paradoxical challenge. Eagly and Karau (2002) have argued that this perceived incongruity between traditional gender roles and stereotypical leadership traits increases prejudice towards women leaders by 1) generating less favorable attitudes about women's potential leadership because leadership ability is considered stereotypical of men and not women, and 2) by creating less favorable attitudes of women leaders because instrumental behaviors are perceived as less desirable for women than for men.

Since most voters never meet the candidates personally, and many people do not watch them speak extemporaneously in televised debates, they have to base their impressions on the information (often in brief "sound bites") *handed* to them by the media. The way this information is framed or presented to the public by the media is critical. Devitt (2002) conducted a content analysis of newspaper coverage of four 1998 gubernatorial races and showed that women candidates received more coverage about their personal characteristics such as their age, personality, and dress, whereas the men candidates received more coverage for their stances on public policy like healthcare, taxes, and education. Further, Kahn (1994) found that information on appearance, marital status (i.e., Hillary Rodham Clinton had to *pay* for indiscretions conducted years ago by her husband, Bill Clinton, in her later campaign years), and parental status dominated the media coverage of female candidates, whereas the newspapers covered more about experience, occupation, and accomplishments for the male candidates (Robinson & Saint-Jean, 1995). Even Hillary Rodham Clinton is named in popular press as a function of her marriage. Legally, her name is still Hillary Rodham to this day. It was during Bill Clinton's campaigning that his team began referring to her as Hillary Clinton or Mrs. Clinton to enhance his appeal for traditional voters. Thus, female politicians tend to be trivialized by the media no matter how serious their qualifications may be (Braden, 1996). Further, Carroll and Schreiber (1997) analyzed the content of media coverage on the female members of Congress and concluded that they were rarely treated as individuals, as male Congresspersons were usually depicted, but instead the media focused on their collective contributions (e.g., "Today the women in Congress voted together on…"). This double standard on how media treat male versus female leaders makes it very hard for women to become elected in today's culture. This is a feminist issue. How can girls and women receive the political representation that every citizen deserves when achieving a voice in modern politics is an uphill battle?

I heard Senator Kamala Harris speak at the Women's March in Washington, D.C., in January 2017. Harris obviously has strong feminist political views, yet when she spoke, she made a very important point (C-SPAN, 2017). In her roles as District Attorney of San Francisco, Attorney General of California, and U.S. Senator from California, Harris was either the first woman or the first Black woman in each of these distinguished leadership positions. She said that when people would greet her and say, "Kamala, let's talk about women's issues," she would respond as follows:

> And I'd look at them and I'd say, I'm so glad you want to talk about the economy. I'd say great let's talk about the economy because it's a woman's issue. You want to talk about women's issues, let's talk about national security ... let's talk about healthcare ... let's talk about education. Let's talk about criminal justice reform ... let's talk about climate change ... If you are a woman trying to raise a family, you know that a good paying job is a woman's issue. If you are a woman who is an immigrant who does not want her family torn apart, you know that immigration reform is a woman's issue. If you are a woman working off student loans, you know that the crushing burden of student debt is a woman's issue. If you are a Black mother trying to raise a Black son, you know that Black Lives Matter is a woman's issue. And if you are a woman period, you know that we deserve a country with equal pay and access to healthcare including a safe and legal abortion protected as a fundamental and constitutional right. So all of this is to say my sisters and brothers that we are tired as women for being relegated to simply being thought of as a particular constituency or demographic. We together are powerful and we are a force that cannot be dismissed or written off to the side lines.

Kamala Harris gave a very powerful speech, and I loved her point that feminists are *not* narrowly focusing their concerns on women's issues *only*. As 51 percent of the U.S. citizenry, *every* political policy affects us as women. Note the quote that I saw on a sign at the Women's March that is featured as the epigraph to this chapter: *"Equality is the radical notion that we are all human."* Yet historically, few men in politics have been concerned with the issues that tend to be more salient for women like reproductive control, paid family leave, access to quality child care, access to higher education, safety for our children, etc. We need more feminists—regardless of their gender—advocating for our rights in local, state, national, and international politics. I like Kamala Harris's point that feminists need to be concerned with everything in politics because everything affects everyone. Feminists need to make sure that we elect leaders who have the best interests of 100 percent of the U.S. population in mind—especially the interests of the 51 percent of U.S. women—as well as other groups that have been marginalized and neglected. Our current federal administration is not treating 100 percent of our citizens in the spirit of equal rights for all, and most of their proposed policies are, in fact, attempting to move us in the opposite direction. We could use more leaders like Kamala Harris. But can we get them elected?

In research determining how powerful media coverage of women candidates can sway opinions, Bligh, Schlehofer, Casad, and Gaffney (2012) surveyed 172 college women and 169 college men from state universities in southern California. They read a scripted vignette of a real woman senator from Maryland, whom most California college students knew nothing about. Her story was framed positively or negatively as an independent variable and they counterbalanced her political affiliation from Democrat to Republican. They based the content on farming issues and the need to conserve water, which are topics that are considered to be gender neutral, and they modeled their vignettes from an actual newspaper article. They found that participants' pre-existing attitudes towards female political leaders were strongly related to their perception of this female senator. They rated her more favorably when the article was framed positively than when it was framed negatively. Her depicted political party did not affect her ratings of warmth and competence. They found that ratings of a female candidate's competency were inversely related to their perceptions of her warmth. They likened this to how Senator Hillary Rodham Clinton was portrayed in her first run for president as competent, yet cold. On the flip side, Sarah Palin was depicted as warm and likable, yet incompetent in other abilities that are necessary for the presidency. Regardless of who it is, it appears that female candidates are perceived as lacking two of the requisite qualities to be worthy of serving us in office—competency and warmth.

In their second study, Bligh et al. (2012) used the same vignette but with a fictitious senator where the content was again framed either positively or negatively as the first independent variable and her political party was again counter balanced. For the second independent variable, the newspaper article either focused on her capability or her personality. They surveyed 223 women and 83 men from two southern California public universities. Results found that the female senator was viewed as more competent than warm when the media message focused on her personality, but was negatively framed. When the media message focused on her personality, viewers looked to see if she was warm. Findings varied as a function of the positively versus negatively framed content. When it was framed positively, the senator was deemed to be warm, which is consistent with expected gender stereotypes. However, when it was negatively framed, she was deemed to be cold, unlikable, and even incompetent, albeit the latter qualities were not even mentioned in the article. The authors concluded that media messages and how they are framed are powerful indicators in how voters form opinions of female political candidates.

Bligh et al. (2012) were also able to show how negative critiques of these women can serve as double-edged swords if they tap into either the traditional gender stereotype of expecting warmth or the traditional leadership stereotype of expecting competency. It appears that women leaders are not allowed the flexibility or luxury of holding both requisite characteristics. Bligh and her colleagues note that the media has the ability to sway votes, but their approach to candidates, based on these gendered stereotypes, can *also* have an impact on other important campaign variables such as financial donations, leadership ratings, how conversations are framed to others in "why I don't like her," and other political behaviors. This suggests women candidates walk a tightrope of "damned if you do and damned if you don't," because masculine and feminine stereotypes make the game more challenging from the start for women who run in politics, as compared to men. It reminds me of how Barack Obama was respected for his intellectual competency and ability to articulate himself in front of the media. Then he could smoothly shift into playful humor, or genuine empathy for others who were suffering. He could be a leader and be warm without provoking questions about whether or not he was correctly adhering to stereotypes of masculinity. It is no wonder that both Hillary Rodham Clinton and Sarah Palin tried—but not successfully— to run for positions as "candidates who just happened to be women." People are not blind to the gender of candidates; the saliency of their gender evokes complicated inherent biases in voters. It is easier for men to be immune to these biases because men are supposed to be masculine; leaders are supposed to be masculine. Women candidates, on the other hand, face some no-win consequences when they run for political office.

No doubt that the 2016 presidential election brought out magnified sexist stereotypes about our candidates. In Donald Trump we have a tall, rich (presumably), powerful businessman, claiming immunity to the Washington insiders' game of politics, married to a former fashion model who is 24 years younger. He speaks his mind with powerful nonverbal behaviors that indicate confidence, if not arrogance. Further, he was unafraid to boldly embrace multiple prejudices that brought out a surprising number of supporters (i.e., people who had likely been quietly harboring these same prejudices). Trump's opponent, Hillary Rodham Clinton, was obviously more competent and schooled in methods of politics/the workings of our federal government, articulate and knowledgeable, connected, and more interpersonally appealing to many of us. But again, she was still a *woman*. In what Goldmacher and Schreckinger (2016) called the biggest campaign upset in U.S. history, multiple experts attempted to analyze what happened.

In her article aptly titled, "Every Woman Is the Wrong Woman: The Female Presidency Paradox," Anderson (2017) asserts that Hillary Rodham Clinton was very qualified to be our president and the first woman president. Yet Anderson said Hillary Rodham Clinton may have been unelectable because of what she calls another *change campaign* possibility occurring in 2016 in our nation, after 2008 had already brought us a dramatic change campaign when we elected the first African American president in U.S. history. While results of 2008 delighted many people and felt socially progressive, there were also individuals who felt slapped by the national vote and harbored racist resentment as a result of the outcome. To the latter demographic, the voters went too far to the political left—the change was too much for them. And racist beliefs tend to coincide with sexist attitudes. Anderson (2017) blames sexist stereotypes about leadership roles for Hillary Rodham Clinton's loss and asserts that many people were afraid to consider a woman president when we had just been through the tenure of our first African American president. For conservative voters, President Obama was very successful at producing liberal and progressive agendas and policy. Even the goal of the Patient Protection and Affordable Care Act (i.e., Obamacare) was to provide insurance coverage to 100 percent of our citizens, as opposed to healthcare coverage for only the rich and gainfully employed citizens (i.e., overrepresented demographic of White men).

Obama's two terms were clear gains for liberal-minded Americans. The possibility of now having another liberal, this time also a woman, was just too risky for many individuals, particularly individuals harboring private prejudices of misogyny, racism, or neophobia in general. Over 90 percent of U.S. voters reported their willingness to vote for a qualified female presidential candidate (Malone, 2016); so then why did we not vote in the affirmative for Hillary Rodham Clinton, the person who Barack Obama called the most qualified candidate to ever run for office? Orstein and Mann (2016) have positioned part of the Donald Trump appeal to many voters as simply a nationwide conservative backlash against Obama as the first Black president. Obama was successful in leading many liberal and progressive accomplishments during his two terms. Some U.S. citizens feared that we were becoming too progressive and that we needed to return to baseline—the normative White male hegemonic presidency—in order to save traditional American values. If some believed Americans went too far with Obama, then Americans should certainly not err and vote in a woman, as this would be a progressive change election three presidential terms in a row (Anderson, 2017).

Unfortunately for Hillary Rodham Clinton, this sociopolitical climate and the ongoing backlash made her very thorough qualifications a major *threat* to many people. Given this, it is no wonder that the abrasive, yet elementary and easy to understand qualities such as "liar" and "corrupt" were used so frequently in the campaign. Even after being elected president, Donald Trump continually brings up Hillary Rodham Clinton in his speeches and welcomes his fan base by chanting, "Lock her up. Lock her up." Who knew that so many people could embrace such hate? Yet given these public displays, it makes more sense to me how simple it was for many individuals to justify preventing a woman from being elected to our presidency.

Unfortunately, what many Americans feared was that which excited some of the rest of us. Caughell (2016) speaks to the fact that during her campaign, Hillary Rodham Clinton was portrayed as the woman who could break the ultimate glass ceiling and become the first woman President of the

United States. The idea gave me goose bumps and reminded me of how
thrilled as I was when Nancy Pelosi was elected Speaker of the House of Representatives. As a teen, I went to a summer camp in Virginia called Girl's
State where we learned about and ran a mock government. Because my friend
nominated me (Thanks Leslie! ... said sarcastically, because I was terrified),
I was elected and served as the Speaker of the House during the week of Girl's
State. The collective group had some wonderful ideas for progressive laws to
better serve girls and women in Virginia. It also gave me more respect for
the challenges of politicians. Having served in that mock role, however terrifying it was for shy younger me, had amplified the great respect that I held
in my heart for this important leadership position in our federal government—a role that had *always* been held by men. Nancy Pelosi's rise to become
the first female Speaker of the House made me feel proud to be a woman.
Even though I was involved in a successful career at the time, it gave me a
whole new sense of hope. Women could get there! As Hillary Rodham Clinton
was gaining momentum in the campaign, many of us were anticipating that
she would break a very important glass ceiling and that Americans were about
to make history again. Keep in mind, it is easy to have a false consensus effect
and feel like everybody is liberal when working on a university campus. While
this does not prove true for *everybody*, the stereotype about professors' politics
tends to be accurate. I was so wrapped up in my selfish splendor for Hillary
Rodham Clinton that I had no idea how deep the fear and hatred of her ran
in circles of other people. Meanwhile, there were Americans who supported
Donald Trump and some who just did not want to see another Clinton in
office again. Breaking history, or the second potential change election, was a
new fear for Americans who thought the culture had already gone too far.
Having had a Black president and now a woman president could further agi-
tate the whole white male supremacy norm in our culture. When we hold
social privilege, it is often hard to see it until that privilege is threatened or
taken away. It is clear to see how Donald Trump accrued some of his fan
base.

    As one more additional, and disgusting, example of backlash against
Hillary Rodham Clinton's attempt to go into a sphere where many individuals
believe women do not belong, Chemaly (2016) notes that such women can
be downgraded by "pornifying" them, which is the internet's equivalent to
slut shaming. Chemaly points out how people have created pornographic
posts using the names or typical dress of women leaders. She notes that you
can type into Google the names of male leaders, such as Donald Trump, Ted
Cruz, etc., along with the word "porn" and the search discovers little. However, if you type in the names of female leaders like Hillary Rodham Clinton,
Nancy Pelosi, or Condoleezza Rice along with the word "porn," then one
finds a gold mine of images of individuals in various sexual acts with the

names of these women, or images of people dressed up to resemble them while performing sexual acts. Instead of treating these leaders with respect, these women have been sexualized, objectified, and "pornified." I found this to be horrifying!

As a political communication scholar, Anderson (2017) says that she is frequently asked what could Hillary Rodham Clinton have done any differently, or what do future women candidates need that Hillary Rodham Clinton did not have? Anderson responds,

> Nothing. There is literally nothing that women have not tried in their one-hundred-plus-year quest for the Oval Office. The problem lies with the culture rather than with the candidates [p. 135].

On the Friday evening after the 2016 election, I watched one of my favorite talk show hosts, Chelsea Handler. They had pre-taped a celebration on her stage *assuming* Hillary Rodham Clinton would have won by time the show aired. They ran the tape of the celebration anyways, but the production was surrounded by a very solemn mood. Chelsea and her guests on the live show were in shock and Chelsea was crying. For me, the reality sunk in after a week's worth of busy work. I think I had been too stunned to feel anything during the weekdays following the election on Tuesday night. I cried myself to sleep that Friday night. The pride that I had felt when Nancy Pelosi was voted as Speaker of the House was shattered that night by a new "punched in the gut" emotional reaction. It felt like all of our feminist progress had come to an abrupt halt on Election Day. Not too long after that, I had friends planning to make the trip to the Women's March in Washington, D.C. It felt like we feminists were, at least, planning something as an antidote for the anguish. Thank you, Lisa and Beth!

As a bit of an aside about Chelsea Handler's show, I recall thinking that as Chelsea's talk show season progressed, despite her natural acerbic humor, her focus had become more and more left-wing politically. She was an obvious fan of Hillary Rodham Clinton and an obvious mocker of Donald Trump. I recall commenting to my partner and friends about this. I thought she was being brave as a comedian to become so serious and so political. I did not mind it at all, but I was acutely aware that others might not appreciate it. Sure enough, I watched her Netflix ratings decline across the season. In some ironic way, this was a metric foreshadowing how voters were feeling and what was about to happen in our country's election.

We are still learning about situational influences of the 2016 presidential election in the U.S. as journalists, attorneys, and politicians continue to investigate the various complicated factors at work. Misogyny and American's concerns about how a woman could do harm in the White House was only one force. However, Hillary Rodham Clinton's loss could be one of the most powerful and adverse outcomes of sexism in recent history. Consequently, body snarking may be even more insidious for feminism as a whole, in addition to the harm that fat talking causes us personally and within our social circles. Fat talk has the potential to harm our self-esteem, our body image, and our physical and psychological health—while body snarking, on the other hand, has the potential to harm others and appears to have had an impact on our entire political system. We feminists need to end both. The question is, "How?"

7

"Other Women Like Fat Talk, But I Don't!"

"What do we Want?
Evidence based science
When do we Want It?
After peer review."—Women's March sign, 2017

Merriam-Webster (2017) defines a norm as "a widespread or usual practice, procedure, or custom." In her ethnographic interviews with Caucasian middle school girls, Nichter (2000) found fat talk to be both normative and common. This appears to be true for girls and has also been documented in adult women of all ages in the U.S. Nevertheless, my lab and others have found an interesting disconnect between the established normative nature of fat talk and our collective, but personal, desires *not* to own the norm. This chapter will examine the social psychological theories of the third person effect and pluralistic ignorance to help readers better understand why fat talk has been maintained as a societal norm. I will elaborate on the studies supporting this thought-provoking detachment between women's personal beliefs about fat talk and what they think other women accept.

First, the *third person effect* is a robustly documented social psychological phenomenon defined as individuals' tendency to view others as more vulnerable and influenced by undesirable media effects than they are. As an example, I could be watching a political advertisement that criticizes the person for whom I intend to vote. I think to myself that I will not be swayed by this negative advertisement, but worry that many people, who formerly intended to vote for my favored candidate, will now change their minds. This third person effect has already been documented as it relates to the influence of western culture's thin-ideal. Multiple studies have found that women overestimate the norm of the thin ideal for other women (Cohn & Adler, 1992; Fallon & Rozin, 1985; Jacoby & Cash, 1994:

115

Rozin & Fallon, 1988). In other words, "*They* prefer thin women, but *I* hold a more flexible, diverse standard." When female college students viewed idealized media images and then were asked how likely these pictures would affect body image, self-esteem, and vulnerability for an eating disorder for themselves and for others, they believed that other women would be more influenced than they would (David & Johnson, 1998; David, Morrison, Johnson, & Ross, 2002). This illustrates the idea that thin-ideal media is a problem for *other* women, but not for *oneself.* This makes the influence from the media even more insidious. We underestimate how much it could be harming us, even though it does.

Second, *pluralistic ignorance* is the social psychological phenomenon whereby "people erroneously infer that they feel differently from their peers, even though they behave similarly" (Prentice, 2007, p. 2). As an example, imagine that you are in a large crowded store and you notice an angry parent beginning to spank their crying child. You know that you are opposed to child abuse and that what they are doing is wrong. However, nobody else is reacting as people are all minding their own business. Even a store clerk turns and walks away from the scene. You absorb their social cues in an effort to *not* overreact. You conform and follow the behavior of the crowd. Later, however, you leave feeling disturbed, believing that you were the only bystander who was upset by witnessing this scene. Those other people must not care about childhood violence because they did not react. Pluralistic ignorance makes the *plural* (i.e., us) *ignorant* and unwise.

When it comes to the social psychology of fat talk, it appears that both pluralistic ignorance and the third person effect play a role. In other words, "Other girls and women—*They* fat talk with one another. *They* will conform and participate also, but *I* like women who are positive about their looks and *I* would not just conform and join in fat talk just because others are doing it." Social psychology is defined, in part, by the study of how powerful the environment is on human behavior—particularly the social aspects of the environment. And without us knowing it, the environment or situation is often more powerful in influencing our behavior than our personality or attitudes. Social psychology is a fun subject to teach, because students learn that what the science *shows* us is not always what they *think* the data will reveal. Even astrophysicist Neil deGrasse Tyson has noted on *Real Time with Bill Maher,* "The good thing about science is that it's true whether or not you believe in it" (Maher, 2011). What students often guess will happen in many of the classic social psychology experiments is not what was observed in human behavior in the actual social environments. Thus, individual women may dislike fat talk even though they think that other women approve of it. Further, many women think they would not participate in fat talk until they are placed in a social environment that encourages them to join in this type of conversational dialogue. Many of us do things around other people that we would not do when we are alone.

Park, Yun, McSweeney, and Gunther (2007) recruited 49 female and 39 male college students who were currently in dating relationships from a large Midwestern university. They found that both women and men overestimated the norm of ideal thinness preferred by others of the same sex and others of the opposite sex. Everyone thought everybody else preferred more slenderness in women than they themselves did. They concluded that this norm of ideal feminine thinness is now a documented social norm that is subject to pluralistic ignorance. Although there has been minimal research directly assessing whether fat talk is subject to the third person effect or pluralistic ignorance, Shannon and Mills (2015) were the first to propose these theories as an explanation for some of the research findings in their review article on fat talk. The following studies have found this curious separation between what women think of themselves and how they perceive what other women value in fat talk.

Britton et al. (2006) surveyed both male and female college students who read a vignette of four college women studying for a biology exam together. The content of their dialogue drifts from New Year's resolutions about making better grades to New Year's resolutions about wanting to lose weight. Three of the four women started the fat talk conversation. Participants were asked, using several different choices, how the fourth woman, named Jenny, would respond. The choices included a self-accepting response ("I'm pretty happy with my weight. I don't think I should diet or anything"), a no information response (plays with her pen and makes no comment), or a self-degrading/fat talk response ("Yeah, I'm pretty unhappy with my weight also; I should really go on a diet too."). Participants were asked which option would most likely lead *other women* to like Jenny, and students acknowledged the fat talk norm, as the majority of both men and women chose the self-degrading/fat talk option. Participants had very similar responses when asked *what would most women say?* in this situation; again, they thought most women would choose the fat talk option. Young men and young women are clearly aware of the fat talk norm, but they think the norm applies to others.

Conversely, when women were asked to put themselves into Jenny's shoes and pick the response that they would give, there were no statistically significant differences between the self-degrade/fat talk option, the no information response where she plays with her pen and makes no comment, and the self-accepting responses. Therefore, these women think other women would fat talk and that other women would like Jenny most when she fat talked, but their personal choices did not match these beliefs. At that time in my lab, my research team contained all women with the exception of one young man named Michael. As we ran the study, Michael suggested we add an item of what response would lead *most men* to like Jenny. In an ironic twist, 39.8 percent of the women and 28.5 percent of the men thought that men would like Jenny the most when she made self-accepting comments rather than using fat talk. Only 4.1 percent of the women and 6.5 percent of the men thought men would like her most when Jenny fat talked. We deemed this gender effect the "Michael effect." Consequently, college men and women seem to acknowledge that men either prefer positivity and/or do not like women's fat talk.

While we documented this disconnect in U.S. college students, Strandbu and Kvalem (2014) found very similar results when interviewing groups composed of female and male adolescents in Sweden. They conducted mixed-gender focus groups with twenty-three 17-year-old Norwegian girls and fourteen 17-year-old Norwegian boys. The researchers assert that the advantage of focus groups is that the teens speak to one another, more so than the group moderator, and use their own language. Their prompts included the following questions:

1. What are the dominating body ideals among young people?
2. What is the impact of these body ideals?
3. How are body ideals expressed?
4. What are the sources of body ideals?
5. Are there any subcultural differences in young people's body ideals?

Their responses were transcribed and subjected to a thematic analysis. Examples of themes that were coded by research assistants included "the ideal female body" and "fat talk." The body ideals for girls and boys, as described by the adolescents, were as expected and very similar to the ideals noted for U.S. norms. They did comment that they thought boys were less concerned than girls about living up to an ideal standard. In fact, one of the girls stated, "all girls strive for the things they have not got. No girl is happy with herself" (p. 630). Commenting on the normative nature of fat talk, one of the girls said that in "typical girl talk … you should always mention negative things. And then the girlfriends are like … oh-no-you look good … You boost each other's self-esteem" (p. 631). Both the boys and the girls acknowledged girls' pressure to participate in fat talk. The girls also commented on what it meant to engage in excessive fat talk. In response to a girl that they knew who did this, one girl commented that she thought this was more about being insecure than normal. A boy responded, "I don't know of any guys who think that's attractive or okay" (p. 632). The girls also reported some disapproval of fat talk, but more sympathetic understanding for why it occurs. Further, the boys reported disapproval of the girls' body snarking one another, and the boys said they do not do this to one another. When the boys engaged in body talk, it was about exercising and health. Strandbu and Kvalem (2014) concluded that the girls thought that fat talk was normative in that it was "easy to fall into," yet they expressed some disapproval about fat talk and body snarking.

Young women and young men are clearly knowledgeable of the normative nature of female fat talk in social settings. Yet, note that the vignette we used of four college women studying for a biology exam described three women who were *already* fat talking and then we had participants consider how Jenny would respond. This led my research team to wonder whether fat talk is normative because of conformity pressure. Nichter and Vuckovic (1994) surmised that one of the positive functions of fat talk is to afford a sense of self-acceptance in a group of girls. In his classic perception of line size study, social psychologist Solomon Ashe (1956) showed that people sometimes conform to a norm to be accepted by a group and/or avoid being rejected by a group. Ashe brought men into rooms where they looked at lines on a blackboard and had to pick a line size that matched the line length presented by an experimenter. Ashe had multiple men who were trained confederates publicly select the *incorrect* answer *together*. I still remember seeing a textbook picture of one of the poor guys squinting as he looked at the lines while the other men sat there looking confident and undisturbed. Did he follow his instincts and give the correct answer? No—most of the participants conformed to the wrong answer because that is what the other young men had done. Norms are very powerful. Lines on blackboards are not very important; thus, imagine the peer pressure when it is about something germane to one's appearance to others and to social relationships. Research on gender differences within conformity suggests that women tend to conform to one another more than men, but for positive social functions including acceptance by the group and to preserve social harmony (Eagly & Chrvala, 1986; Insko, 1983; 1985). Further, women may conform in groups of other women as a means of establishing identity or self-definition—the *we* believe or *we* think as a means of knowing who *I* am (Santee & Jackson, 1982).

As the first to examine whether women fat talk as a function of conformity, Tucker et al. (2007) had college students interacting in pairs with another woman who was really a confederate. When the confederate self-derogated/fat talked about her body, participants gave the lowest ratings of their own personal body image. Moderate ratings occurred when the confederate self-accepted, and they gave the most positive personal body rating scores when the confederate had self-aggrandized about her own body. Thus, the participants conformed in their personal body image responses to the tone of what they heard from the other woman. DeStephano (2007) analyzed both the transcripts and nonverbal behavior of these participants on videotape, looking for discomfort, and found that this conformity occurred in a genuine and composed manner. Interestingly, Tucker et al. (2007) had measured the participants' own body image prior to the dyadic interviews and found that their personal body esteem also predicted their public ratings of their bodies in front of the confederate, as did the previous dialogue and body image ratings of the other woman. It appears that women's body talk can be both true to themselves and nudged in the direction of what they are hearing from others. As such, fat talk can perhaps be tactful bonding with others.

In the second test to examine whether fat talk is just conformity, Tompkins, Martz, Rocheleau, and Bazzini (2009) used the same vignette with Jenny and three other college women who were studying for a biology exam that transgressed into fat talk for the negative body talk condition. However, we altered the dialogue in an alternative condition, as the first independent variable, so that the three women were saying positive versus negative things about their bodies to one another. As a separate independent variable, Jenny joins in at the end and either fat talks or says positive things about her body to the other three women. Therefore, Jenny either conformed or did not conform to the group. We had participants rate Jenny's likability as themselves (*personal*) and as they thought *other women* would perceive her likability. In *personal* ratings of Jenny's likability, participants favored her more when she spoke positively, rather than fat talked, regardless of whether the other three women were fat talking or speaking positively about their bodies. In contrast, participants thought *other women* would find Jenny to be most likable when she conformed to the valence of the group's body talk, especially when they were engaging in positive dialogue. Hence, these women thought they were less prone to engage in behaviors that sustain the fat talk norm. From this data, we concluded that there is an alternative norm for women to be more self-accepting of their bodies in our culture, as well as the known norm to embrace fat talk. Further, perhaps some women are simply conflicted. For example, Rubin, Nemero, and Russo (2004) ran focus groups with female participants that held feminist values. Most of these women believed that women should reject popular media's emphases on perfect bodies and female sexual objectification, yet many also expressed personal body image concerns. Further, many reported having had struggled in situations that were naturally more objectifying, like clothes shopping.

Given the previously mentioned results, Tompkins et al. (2009) proposed there could be two possibly competing norms in U.S. culture for women—a fat talk norm and a feminist norm that women should be self-accepting of their appearance and body image, much like many African American women have already embraced (Fiery et al., 2016; Webb et al., 2013). As additional evidence that U.S. culture could hold more than one norm about body talk, Payne et al. (2011) compared U.S. adults and young adults from the United

Kingdom on various forms of body talk (i.e., negative, self-accepting, & positive). Men and women from the U.S. reported hearing more self-accepting and positive body talk than participants from the United Kingdom. We interpreted this cross-cultural difference to mean that individuals from the U.S. tend to pride themselves more on self-acceptance and/or that individuals in the United Kingdom adhere to more humble norms.

Salk and Engeln-Maddox (2011) also documented a significant third person effect on fat talk for 168 college women surveyed at a large Midwestern university. Although 93 percent of these women acknowledged their own participation in fat talk, they believed that other women did this more frequently than themselves. Becker et al. (2013) similarly documented a third person effect while examining both fat talk and "old talk" (i.e., how women express and respond to aging concerns) in their online sample of 759 U.S. women. They believed that family, friends, and media modeled more fat talk and more old talk than they did.

Finally, in their "Chatting with Friends" study about friendship dyads' reactions to media depictions of women's appearance, Cruwys et al. (2016) classified their participants as either adhering to a "pro-fat talk" norm or an "anti-fat talk" norm. Participants rated their friend after ostensibly hearing (i.e., privately viewing their text chat) the other friend engage in fat talk, positive body talk, or neutral body talk. Pairs of friends who adhered to the pro-fat talk norm liked their friend more after she engaged in fat talk compared to neutral talk. Interestingly, participants who reported that they owned the pro-fat talk norm indicated that they liked their friend more when she engaged in positive body talk rather than the neutral body talk, even though this was the opposite of the fat talk norm. This suggests two norms in our culture even for individuals who seem to embrace a norm about physical appearance critique.

If there are two competing norms, one to fat talk and another to say self-accepting things about appearance to others, what is maintaining the fat talk norm? Previous literature suggests that for women with body dissatisfaction, sharing this dissatisfaction with others temporarily makes them feel better. Once fat talk has been initiated, some of the responses from others could be simple conformity. Women know the norm and believe that other women should follow the fat talk norm. They themselves, however, do not always favor it. In fact, they tend to prefer the self-accepting norm. The latter is more aligned with feminism.

Since previous research has documented the separation between what we think other women prefer versus what we personally prefer, this begs the question: is fat talk more personally disliked, or does hearing self-accepting talk generate personal positivity? Do we have separate norms, or are these two behaviors on a bipolar continuum? Further, we do not know how these two norms are related. The next study attempted to investigate this question. Rocheleau, Martz, Walker, Curtin, and Bazzini (unpublished manuscript) used the same body talk vignette of four college women studying for a biology exam when the dialogue transgresses into body talk. The target is, again, named Jenny. In the fat talk condition, Jenny responds, "But seriously, I'm with y'all. I have been feeling bad about my body. I should really go on a diet, too." In the self-accept condition, she responds, "But seriously, I'm not with y'all on this one. I have been feeling good about my body. I don't need to go on a diet or anything." To create a unique anchor, this study created a non-body talk condition where the target was simply considered to be an ideal college student. They were instructed to think of Jenny as "someone that you would find likable and with whom you would want to be friends." As the dependent variable, we created a 40-item personality trait questionnaire where respondents rated 1–"*Does not describe Jenny at all*" to 5–"*Describes Jenny completely.*" Factor analyses of these items revealed the following clusters: confidence (e.g., has high self-esteem), interpersonal awareness (e.g., humility), social undesirability (e.g., cowardly), and responsibility (e.g., mature). The final design was a 2 (Gender independent variable: women vs. men) × 3 (Target woman independent variable: fat talk, self-accept, vs. control) with four dependent variables (confidence, interpersonal awareness, social undesirability, & responsibility).

Participants were 280 college students (46.1 percent women; 53.9 percent men) who were primarily Caucasian (87.9 percent) from a comprehensive public university in the Southeast. Results suggested that when Jenny self-accepted her own body, she was viewed to be closer to the ideal college student than when she was fat talking. Again, this suggests there may be a norm in our culture to voice more positive impressions of our appearance to others rather than a tiresome pull to complain, critique, and publish about our appearance flaws.

In her seminal work on the topic, Nichter (2000) also noted the interpersonal nature of fat talk, especially for middle school girls with their friends and with their mothers. Indeed, Cooley, Toray, Wang, and Valdez (2008) documented how mothers' body image dissatisfaction was correlated with the same dissatisfaction felt by their daughters. How people in families feel about their own bodies could be modeled in a way that is somewhat contagious to others. Two other studies support this relationship between mothers and daughters as it relates to their fat talk behavior. Arroyo and Andersen (2016) examine how the reported fat talk of mothers and daughters was significantly related. Both mothers' and daughters' fat talk was personally related to their ratings of their body image, and mothers' reported fat talk was positively related to the reported bulimic behaviors of their daughters. MacDonald, Dimitripoulos, Royal, Polanco, and Dionne (2015) have developed a Family

Fat Talk Questionnaire that contains a section to complete as oneself and a section to complete as a family member would. Example items for the subscale on Self include, "When I'm with my family members, I complain that I am fat." An example for the perceived family members dialogue would be, "When I'm with my family, I hear them complain that they are fat." They surveyed 83 female participants and found the Self and Family subscales to be moderately associated (r = .34). Participants were allowed to choose a family member for the questionnaire, and 80 picked their mothers, 52 their fathers, 37 sisters, 37 brothers, 5 partners, and 27 selected "other family members." The authors did not specifically report the correlation between these young women's self-scores and their mothers separate from the other family members.

Hence, previous studies have documented a link between young women's report of fat talk and that of their friends and mothers. Rogers, Martz, Webb, and Galloway (2017) conducted an additional study examining the reported fat talk of young, primarily Caucasian college students from a public comprehensive university in the Southeast. They had 120 women complete a Fat Talk Questionnaire as themselves, and they were asked to complete it two more times—once as if they were their mothers, and once as if they were their best friends. Unique to this study (compared to the ones mentioned above), they also sent the Fat Talk Questionnaire and collected data on the actual mother's reported fat talk and the actual friend's reported fat talk. Using simple correlations, these participants reported fat talk was minimally related with both the friend's actual reported fat talk (r = .31) and the mother's actual fat talk (r = .22). Stronger correlations were found for participants' fat talk and their friend's perceived fat talk (r = .55) and their mother's perceived fat talk (r = .52). We then conducted hierarchical regression analyses that included these five measures together to see which one best predicted the college women's own fat talk. The final model accounted for 34 percent of the variance with only her perceived mother's fat talk and perceived friend's fat talk predicting her own fat talk. Thus, perception trumped reality. The modeling of fat talk from significant interpersonal relationships may be one method of fat talk's contagion, but it appears that the perception better explains one's inheritance regarding frequency of fat talk. We interpreted this within a false consensus effect (Ross, Greene, & House, 1977) whereby people tend to—sometimes falsely, but sometimes truthfully—assume that individuals in intimate social networks hold attitudes and beliefs the same way that they do. When it comes to the contagion of body image, Wasylkiw and Williamson (2012) suggested that perception might trump reality, in part due to our tendency to project our own sense of self onto the habits of others. For fat talk, this is yet another potential disconnect documented in the literature that could explain how the norm is maintained. If women are able to justify in their own minds that their personal ownership of fat talk matches their mothers' and their friends', then there is no threat or dissonance. Without dissonance, then there is no need to question one's behavior and, therefore, no need to spur change in these conversational habits. This information suggests that interventions could target this false consensus or pluralistic ignorance to change individuals' sense of the commonness of fat talk. Chapter nine will discuss *The Body Project*, which is an effective cognitive dissonance-based program that improves women's body image and self-esteem and prevents eating disorders by having women challenge their own beliefs.

A final disconnect evident in the literature is the difference in how men seem to perceive women's fat talk. If fat talk were truly an accepted norm, then men who know the norm would find it appealing in women. This is not what the few studies examining this have found. Research exploring how men perceive and respond to women's fat talk is in its infancy. Warren, Martz, Curtin, Bazzini, and Gagnon (2013) conducted qualitative work on college men's and women's responses to fat talk in various situations. They found that women would respond supportively to other women's fat talk and men would do the same for other men. However, both genders tended to report a response of silence if body talk came from a person of the other sex. Although the study did not allow for an explanation of this, we interpreted this silence to indicate discomfort, a sense that they did not know what to say, or that responses to the opposite sex's body talk could be construed as flirtation in heterosexual individuals. Similarly, recall that Britton et al. (2006) found that the target woman's response was most attractive to men when she said self-accepting things about her body image, compared to when she engaged in fat talk. Mikell and Martz (2016) surveyed 103 college men who were predominantly Caucasian (89 percent) from a Southeastern public university and had them respond to a dating scenario as if they were attracted to a target women named Brittany and were about to ask her out. As one independent variable, the male participants overheard Brittany in class speaking to her friends and she either engaged in fat talk or self-accepting talk. In a one-item Likert metric, these men found Brittany's mental health to be less healthy when she fat talked and healthier when she said self-accepting commentary to her friends.

In conclusion, despite evidence that individuals are aware of the normative nature of fat talk for girls and women in our culture (especially as a Caucasian norm), we can see how the third person effect and pluralistic ignorance operate. There appears to be a personal distancing from individuals from embracing this fat talk norm, as opposed to what women think other women will accept. Both men and women know that heterosexual men do not appear to favor fat talk behavior in romantic situations. We also have evidence for an alternative norm that fits better with feminist ideology, as well as for girls and women to be more accepting and positive about their appearance. Therefore, this literature provides some clarity on how girls and women can begin to personally break away from this pathological behavior, as well as how we can advocate and create community and public health interventions to reduce fat talk behavior on a larger normative scale.

8

Feminism and the Personal
Effects of Fat Talk

"A woman's place is in the revolution."—Women's March sign,
2017

When I was in college, I took the equivalent of a minor in Women's
Studies courses. This addition to my psychology education has influenced
me personally, in my clinical work with clients, how I teach my courses, and
the manner in which I conduct my line of research. Carol Hanisch's 1970
paper titled "The Personal is Political" that was published in *Notes from the
Second Year: Women's Liberation* (Hanisch, 2009) continues to resonate with
me. As a political argument and catch phrase for the second wave of feminism,
the maxim defines connections between individuals' private lives and the
broader social and political culture in which they live. In her paper, Hanisch
speaks about what were called "therapy" groups that people were attending
in the 1960s and 70s. She clarifies that many of these individuals identified
more with feeling political compared to needing psychotherapy in the traditional definition. Psychotherapy is normally needed for someone who is sick.
In that sense, Hanisch says she was offended by the term:

> Women are messed over, not messed up! We need to change the objective conditions,
> not adjust to them. Therapy is adjusting to your bad personal alternative.

As a psychotherapist and as a woman who relates with the personal and cultural
pressures that have created and maintain fat talk and body snarking, the *personal
is political* speaks to my feminist sensibility about our feminine enemies. Like
many primitive, behavioral drives that we have inherited from human evolution,
we must use modern, enlightened values to build awareness and override these
human inclinations. I feel cultural pressure to fat talk. I have heard it all my life,
so it seems natural. I want to fit in with my friends. I want to be perceived as
effective but humble. I want to have a witty response when I overhear a friend

or acquaintance disparage her appearance in front of me. At times, I even think fat talk can be funny. In her stand-up show *Freezing Hot* (2015), comedian Iliza Shlesinger performs a bit on why women are cold all the time:

> We're not allowed to eat as much as we want in one sitting. Trying to get another girl to admit that she is hungry between two girls it's like a standoff. You can't admit you're hungry. That's admitting weakness. That's admitting defeat.

In her description of two girlfriends who are out on the town together, she states,

> "Are you hungry? Me neither. So."
> "Are you hungry? No, I ate last week!"

I laughed hard when I first heard this. Then, I felt guilty for laughing at fat talk. Then, I laughed some more. The primitive part of me wants to laugh, while the feminist part of me wants to end this. It captures my own cognitive dissonance on this subject. Iliza Shlesinger, as a comedian, has sharp insights into the inner worlds of girls and women. She makes the sad facts humorous. If you like acerbic humor and can laugh at gender role insights, I recommend that you check out her work.

As the personal is political, some women reading this book may have realized that they participate in mild fat talk and this new awareness will inspire them to cease the behavior rather easily. Others may wish to stop the behavior, but struggle, like I have, in what to say or do instead when responding to friends who have initiated the conversation. As I will address later, some women may find reading about fat talk to be triggering in a way that reveals they are seriously struggling with an eating disorder and need help. Learning about fat talk and knowing it has a name will make many readers more aware of it when they hear it in their own lives. How this affects readers personally will vary, and what readers wish to do about their own participation will likely vary as well. At this point, researchers have not studied the best means of handling fat talk, especially a method that is guaranteed not to harm relationships.

In our first study on fat talk (Britton et al., 2006), we had created an option for our target woman named Jenny who plays with her pen and makes no comment in response to the other three women's fat talk. I remember thinking, "It sure would be nice to have the opportunity to play with one's pen and say nothing at times in life." Avoidance is not my modus operandi, but the fantasy of escaping an uncomfortable situation sure is pleasant. Women know that they are supposed to respond in a reassuring way when they are prompted by another's fat talk. Nichter (2000) called it a bonding ritual for the middle school girls that she interviewed. It seems that there is a pull to reassure and a push to not avoid it. Nichter and Vuckovic (1994, p. 116) reported that a girl saying that "she didn't diet would be an admission that she didn't need to work on herself—that she was satisfied." Even the middle school girls were feeling the pull to fat talk in order to not look "stuck up." By adulthood, "stuck up" morphs into being called a "bitch." Similarly, in college students, Warren et al. (2013) used a qualitative analysis of body talk and found that both men and women knew that the right thing to do is to respond with reassurance to a friend of the same gender's body talk. The nature of the dialogue was different in that the young men responded by offering support for workouts and tips on how to build muscle; the women, on the other hand, were focusing more on nutrition or exercise for weight loss or weight management. That pull to reassure somebody in this circumstance is a powerful one. I can identify.

There is a gap in research on what women are supposed to say in response to fat talk when they do not wish to participate. I have heard suggestions, but that takes me back to my scientific skepticism of do we really know that this works? Of the suggestions, a woman could comfort her friend on an emotional level and inquire more about what is really going on. The friend who says, "I feel fat today!" probably needs a response like, "Hey, what is going on? You seem like you are having a rough morning!" Finding middle ground where we do not appear to be stuck up for ignoring fat talk and figuring out how to sensitively comfort friends or family when we hear this dialogue is a challenge. All of us have insecurities and vulnerabilities. How do we share them and get reassurance for ourselves without the habitual reliance of critiquing our physical appearance? Ambwani, Baumgarner, Guo, Sims, and Abromowitz (2017) surveyed 283 undergraduate women on their body dissatisfaction and their baseline tendency to fat talk. One week later, they were shown a vignette of two women either engaging in fat talk or a vignette that *challenged* fat talk by showing one woman fat talking and the second woman responded with a feminist statement. As examples of the challenge talk, the second woman responded, "I think feeling healthy and happy with who I am as a person is so much more important than focusing on how I look," or "It's not fair to compare ourselves to those models." After viewing their vignette, participants completed a measure of mood, their likability of the target women, their engagement in fat talk, and their tendency to attempt to make positive impressions on others. As predicted, they found that participants reported more fat talk after viewing the vignette that featured it over the vignette challenging fat talk. Also, participants assigned to the challenge condition had a more positive impression of the target woman and had less negative affect compared to those assigned to the fat talk condition. Finally, participants were asked, "If you were a part of this conversation, what would you say next?" Two research assistants, who were both blind to the experimental manipulation, then coded these responses for fat talk, positive body talk, empathic statements, neutral or ambiguous responses, and feminist talk. The latter was identified for responses that rejected the thin-ideal or body objectification, critiqued unrealistic cultural standards for appearance, emphasized the importance of physical health, or reflected a sense of connection and respect for one's body. For the fat talk condition, 38.2 percent of the responses were considered positive body talk, 37.4 percent were feminist responses, and 26.8 percent were fat talk. On the other hand, for the vignette that challenged fat talk, 60.2 percent were deemed to be feminist responses, 31.4 percent were positive body talk, and only 17.8 percent were fat talk. Therefore, exposure to fat talk begets more fat talk. However, hearing a woman challenge fat talk freed more of the participants to respond in a way that was feminist in nature or more reflective of positive body talk. Again, this suggests that fat talk is, in part, conformity or a norm that is subjected to pluralistic ignorance. Ambwani and colleagues have offered us a nice alternative for responding to fat talk. There is much work to be done in this area of figuring out the best ways to deflect fat talk while maintaining compassion and positivity in relationships.

Fat Talk and Eating Disorders

Previous chapters showed literature that connects fat talk and eating disordered symptoms (Ousely et al., 2008; Tzoneva et al., 2015), and some women reading this book may be struggling with body image issues or a diagnosable eating disorder. I have worked with many teenagers, women, and even some men struggling with eating disorders, and it is a nightmare of a lifestyle. I remember speaking with a father of a daughter whom I was treating for an eating disorder. He asked, "Is this about vanity? Because she is beautiful." He was asking with genuine curiosity and concern, but the implicit message was "let us tell her she is beautiful and this eating disorder will magically go away." I wish it were that easy. Chapters one and two explained both the evolutionary and sociocultural reasons why we tend to care about our appearance. But there is a difference between normal concern and obsession. Interestingly, not caring at all is a sign of severe mental illness. When conducting a mental status exam on clients, I was trained to comment whether or not they appear to be their stated age, because looking older than one's age means severe neglect in self-care. Further, I was trained to comment on how well-groomed individuals appeared. Poor grooming, again, means poor self-care, which is often a symptom when a person has not been grounded in his or her own reality. Thus, there is what is considered to be a normal level of thoughtfulness about physical appearance—too much obsessive caring *or* neglect in regards to appearance are both signs of psychological disturbance.

Eating-disordered worries usually reach a level of obsession, driven by some other form of misery such as anxiety, depression, or severe damage if they have been physically and/or sexually abused. The behaviors often begin as a way to comfort one's self and attempt to feel better. A woman who feels fat might feel a bit better once she loses a little weight, yet the behaviors often escalate and become life consuming. When I first meet clients struggling with eating disorders, I certainly want to bond with them and establish a relationship, but in my head I am usually asking, what is this *really* about? I also ask, how are they stuck? What is the pattern? Is it like an old vinyl record that was stuck on repeat? They can't get the nudge that would bump them back into a continuous groove. Instead, they go in circles. I look for opportunities to help them break the loop. Knowing that persistent negative emotions and a style of behavioral or emotional avoidance tend to be at the root of many psychological disorders, I also ask myself, what are they avoiding? If I can get them to see how the avoidance is maintaining the problem, then we can develop a plan to either expose them to what they are avoiding or figure out an alternative way of dealing with it. The treatment of eating disorders occurs in multiple stages. Although radical change can happen for these individuals, successful recovery usually involves a thousand baby steps out of the struggle. Ideally, each step moves them closer to health with a minimal experience of anxiety in between. Assessing the client to determine where she is currently operating is critical to match interventions to current needs and readiness to move forward.

The *Diagnostic and Statistical Manual of Mental Disorders, Fifth Edition* (DSM-5; APA, 2013) describes the three eating disorders as anorexia nervosa, bulimia nervosa, and binge eating disorders. Technically, the newest edition has expanded this section to include feeding disorders such as the new Avoidant and Restrictive Food Intake Disorder for which my colleagues have created a measure of adult picky eating (Ellis, Galloway, Webb & Martz, 2016). In this book, I will focus on only the three classic eating disorders.

Anorexia involves severe food restriction that leads to significantly low weight for individuals considering age, sex, physical health, and their developmental trajectory. These individuals have an intense fear of gaining weight or becoming fat despite their low body weight. They also have serious body image disturbance in that their self-esteem is disproportionately determined by their size and they tend not to be appropriately concerned about the danger of their low body weight. Subtypes of anorexia include the classic food restriction type as well as a subtype that can involve some binge eating and/or some purging. I have seen a lot of college students with anorexia rely on compulsive exercise with the specific intent to burn calories consumed. Exercise seems more socially acceptable than skipping meals or counting calories. I recall telling some students that I like to take personal and professional problems out on a run or out on a bike ride. I usually return with some ideas for a solution. A particular student of whom I was quite fond was trying to make a very difficult life decision. She told me that she took the problem on a 14-mile run but the solution did not come to her. I laughingly said that my solution must come by mile three because that is when I stop. So if the solution has not surfaced by mile three, it is not there for the taking.

Anorexia can often fall into a pattern much like obsessive compulsive disorder because these individuals obsess about their bodies, engage in all kinds of bodily checking behaviors like frequent weighing or checking their bodies in the mirror. I recently watched a movie called *To the Bone* (Noxon, 2017). In this movie, Ellen—who later wishes to be called Eli as symbolism for defining herself—is a woman in a residential eating disorders treatment center. According to some of the buzz on social media, this movie is already causing controversy among professionals who treat eating disorders. I will not delve into the controversy here, but I do want to make a point about checking behaviors. Eli would engage in checking behavior by placing her hand around her upper arm (i.e., biceps, triceps & humerus bone). If she could wrap her fingers around her arm in this way and have her thumb touch her index finger, she felt safe in her anorexic mind. If she could not touch these fingers together, she felt fat and unsafe then would want to restrict her food even more. Eli spent a good bit of time with her hand around her upper arm.

Individuals with anorexia usually have very distorted thoughts about food and their weight and often develop multiple superstitions. The compulsive behavior can involve obsessive counting of calories, counting steps in compulsive exercise, or counting skipped meals. It is a disorder of obtaining massive control over one's physical body and biological needs that often ends up controlling the whole person. Human biology has a way of reacting, preserving its homeostasis, and preserving lives. Again, this is an evolutionary adaptation to humans' many encounters with food shortages and starvation across our ancestry. To help my clients and students relate to how severe deprivation backfires and can make any of us engage in what would be considered "crazy behavior," I give the example of severe dehydration. If we had been hiking through a desert climate, ran out of water, and could not find some to replenish, we would get desperate (e.g., Reese Witherspoon gives a great depiction of this in *Wild* [Hornby & Strayed, 2014]). We would obsess about water during our waking hours. We would dream about water in our sleep. We may also feel hungry, but higher order biological needs like sex drive, would wash far away from our thoughts. If we saw a muddy hole full of water with bugs floating in it, we would get down on all fours and relish drinking the muddy water. We would get primitive and we would—by modern civilized standards—look rather disturbed. This is what happens when individuals with eating disorders become malnourished and/or dehydrated. It forces their behavior into abnormality. I had a client ask her parents to deposit only $4 into her checking account twice a day so she could buy food with the money. Since it was limited to only $4, she could not afford binge food quantities. Unfortunately, $4 was not enough food to sustain her, but she liked that it forced some restriction. Biologically, her starvation was increasing. She eventually started dumpster diving for food to eat—an act that left her feeling even more disgusted with herself. To understand that bizarre behavior, we have to backtrack and appreciate what the behavior is reacting against. Such behavior is adaptive considering the abnormality of the situation and how she had stressed her own body. Individuals with eating disorders get so stuck and so sick.

Consequently, inpatient hospitalization is often needed to compel the individual's behavior towards normalcy while her body and mind heal. I had a client cry and beg me to not send her to the hospital, even though our contract stipulated hospitalization would be required if she continued to lose weight. She was terrified they would make her gain weight when she had put so much tormented energy into her weight loss. Her family and physician agreed it was time for her to go, but she was particularly mad at me for overriding her desire to refuse hospitalization. It is not a good feeling to be a psychologist and have to do these things. I feel like I have made tough decisions working with clients who are suicidal, but my toughest decisions have been over hospitalizing my clients with eating disorders. This same client, who was so reluctant to try inpatient care, later thanked me for the hospitalization once she had healed from the inpatient experience. She told me that I took control when she thought she was in control, but was actually consumed and controlled by her eating disorder.

Bulimia nervosa is the diagnosis for individuals who regularly engage in binge eating, which involves the rapid, out-of-control consumption of a large quantity of food in a discrete amount of time (APA, 2013). To relieve the fear, anxiety, or guilt from calories consumed during the binge, these individuals then engage in unhealthy compensatory behaviors such as self-induced vomiting, fasting, compulsive exercise, and abuse of laxatives, diuretics, or diet pills. They also struggle with body image issues in that their self-worth is overly influenced by their body shape and weight. When binge eating begins, it is often to serve some psychological function of comfort, like taking a drug to dissociate, or to escape the here and now. It is the misuse of food as reward. Binges tend to grow in amount, so eventually the binge amount reaches a level that creates disgust, fear, anxiety, and a desire to undo or compensate for what just happened. This is when that person begins looking for an escape plan and he or she starts purging, abusing laxatives or diet pills, exercising in excess, or makes a commitment to fast. Rather than *undo* the damage from the binge, such behaviors actually *intensify* the eating disorder. These behaviors are very dangerous and can be life threatening in and of themselves. Self-induced vomiting or laxative abuse can seriously alter the blood's electrolytes (e.g., sodium, potassium & calcium) that regulate human hydration and pH levels that balance fluids and allow for nerve conduction. Consequences can include confusion, weak muscles or muscle cramps, kidney failure, and heart failure. If the human body does not have the minerals to muster up nerve conduction to the heart, the heart stops beating. Whenever I work with clients who have eating disorders, I always ensure that they are under the conscientious care of a physician who knows there is an eating disorder involved. The physician cares for their medical well-being, while the psychologist treats the behavioral aspects of the condition. Behaviorally, we conceptualize the purging behavior as negative reinforcement— "negative" in that it is *subtracting* the anxiety and creating a sense of relief. It is the escape or attempted undoing of the intense anxiety created from the binge, and it is "reinforcement" because then the binge episodes either increase in frequency, amount of food consumed, or both. Exposure therapy is based on the premise that this negative reinforcement cycle tends to maintain the eating disorder. To reverse and intervene in this negative reinforcement cycle, the therapist leads the client in what is called "exposure and response prevention" sessions, whereby the client has to face the feared thing (e.g., eating pizza) without being allowed the habitual escape behavior (e.g., purging to try to undo the calories consumed.) These interventions can be very effective in breaking habitual cycles.

Binge eating disorder is the most recent disorder to be classified in the *DSM-5*. It was considered a provisional diagnosis for almost ten years in the *DSM-4* while researchers gathered more data to determine its validity. Binge eating disorder is characterized by repetitive binge eating—defined by rapid consumption of a large amount of food during a discrete period of time. It is normally done secretively, and the person ends the binge episode because of pain or by falling asleep (APA, 2013). These individuals often eat when they are not hungry, usually because they are bored, lonely, tired, or upset, and tend to experience shame, guilt, or disgust about themselves following the binge episode. Unlike bulimia, these individuals do not engage in compensatory behaviors following the binge. Further, frequent binge eating can lead to rapid weight gain, and the large quantities of food traveling through the gastrointestinal tract puts a great deal of physical stress on the body. Treatment of binge eating disorder fairs much better when the focus is on the behavioral parameters initiating and controlling the compulsive eating, as opposed to focusing on restriction and weight loss.

By attempting to control weight or move closer to the cultural thin ideal with self-induced torture, eating disorders are a cultural representation of our devaluation of women. They also reflect women's tendency to take issues out on themselves, when it is our society that needs to change. Recall Hanisch's quote that "Women are messed over, not messed up!" Not surprisingly, eating disorders have a long history of garnering feminist attention. It makes some sense that individuals who are suffering might believe that improved appearance could make them happier. We receive those messages in the media every day. We are also told that the body is malleable. If you do not like your body, you just need the right diet and the right exercises to change it. A feminist perspective pierces through these myths and clarifies how our culture promotes these disorders. Ironically, for some people—especially girls and women who are suffering psychologically—eating disorders are a socially acceptable outlet or coping mechanism compared to other unhealthy coping behaviors like drug use or cutting behavior. As I mentioned earlier, when I first assess a client referred to me for an eating disorder, I may make the diagnosis, but I also back up and think about what I am really treating. Is this depression? Is this obsessive-compulsive disorder (OCD)? I had a very young client who was starving herself but wanted to reach puberty and grow curves. You would think one would want to eat a lot if that was their body image goal, not starve themselves. But she was restricting her food intake and, at times, would feel overwhelmed when she did eat, so she would then make herself vomit. But her body image goals were the opposite of her eating disorder behavior. She was really struggling more with social anxiety and anxiety management. Unfortunately, she had learned that food restriction and vomiting after eating could help quell her anxiety. Once she learned how to more effectively tolerate and manage her anxiety, her eating disorder faded away.

I worked with a young man who was on a path to becoming a minister. He had become fixated on the Bible quote in Corinthians, "Do you not know that you yourselves are God's temple, and that God's spirit dwells in you?" Any time he would consume food that was considered unhealthy (he mainly focused on food with fat in it), he was committing sacrilege against God. Then he would question if he was a good Christian. He questioned if he was pure enough to become a minister and lead others. He was tormented and losing weight rapidly. It took some cognitive work to restructure his thoughts and convince him that if the body is a temple, we should probably nourish it well in respect for God. We had to do some exposure therapy that involved eating pizza together. He had a lot of anxiety about consuming the pizza, but he got through it. Neither of us went to hell that day, so I think that God did not mind. This young man's eating disorder was really a form of obsessive-compulsive disorder. He also needed some serious discernment—without the complication of the food superstitions—about whether the ministry was right for him. This client is a good example of the fact that eating disorders can be culturally driven, or an outlet for other psychological disorders like depression or OCD.

Given that we live in a culture that promotes eating disorders, it is not surprising that eating disorders have a long history of attracting feminist attention. At the most basic level, we deserve to eat and nourish our bodies. Suffering so intensely that a person refuses to engage in such simple self-care as normal eating is a statement about their self-worth. We live in a culture that provides blatant privilege for men, including obvious privilege for White men. Eating disorders demand feminist attention. Even though my treatment approach is transdiagnostic—i.e., borrowing from multiple clinical orientations like cognitive behavioral therapy, acceptance and commitment therapy, and interpersonal therapies—I am always aware of the feminist context. Susie Orbach's *Fat Is a Feminist Issue* (1982) focused on understanding compulsive eating (i.e., now called binge eating) and why girls and women can have complicated relationships between their needs and their food. Patricia Fallon, Melanie Katzman, and Susan Wooley's *Feminist Perspectives on Eating Disorders* (1994) calls eating disorders "a gendered disorder" and encourages integrating feminism into treatment and the prevention of eating disorders and the cultural issues that promote them. Linda Smolak, Michael Levine, and Taryn Myers's "Feminist Theories of Eating Disorders" (2015) posits how feminist beliefs serve as a protective factor for the development of eating disorders, and considers how feminist ideology can inform prevention programs. In "Feminist Multicultural Perspectives on Body Image and Eating Disorders in Women" (2012), Kashubeck-West and Tagger focus on causes and treatments for eating disorders within a feminist perspective, with careful integration of multicultural perspectives as well.

In a nationally representative sample of U.S. adults, Hudson, Hiripi, Pope, and Kessler (2007) found that between 50 to 63 percent of individuals suffering from an eating disorder had sought treatment for their disorder, meaning that at least one third had never sought treatment. For those individuals considering entering or returning to psychotherapy, I encourage you to do so. I especially encourage any reader who is suffering from anorexia, bulimia, binge eating disorder, or a blend of any of these eating disorders to seek professional help from a psychotherapist, a physician to check your medical health, and a registered dietician to help guide nutrition. Eating disorders are very dangerous. They create significant impairment (Stice, Marti, Shaw, & Jaconis, 2009), and they are the most lethal of all of the psychological disorders in the *DSM-5* (Crow et al., 2009). As an example, using the National Death Index and eating disorder criteria from the *DSM-IV*, Crow et al. (2009) found that crude mortality rates were 3.9 percent for bulimia, 4.0 percent for anorexia, and 5.2 percent for "eating disorder, not otherwise specified" (i.e., *DSM-5*'s unspecified feeding or eating disorder). These disorders are not about vanity, and the individuals who suffer from them or family and friends who know of someone struggling should not take them lightly. Getting professional help can be a matter of life and death. The organization called *Someday Melissa* was developed by Judy Avrin (2017), a mother who lost her daughter Melissa to an eating disorder. Melissa's pediatric gastroenterologist told Judy about her daughter's eating disorder, but Judy and her husband were in some type of denial. In her journal before her death at age nineteen, Melissa wrote,

> Someday, I'll eat breakfast. Someday, I will keep a job for more than three weeks. Someday, I will have a boyfriend for more than 10 days. Someday, I'll love someone. Someday, I'll travel wherever I want. Someday, I will make my family proud. Someday, I'll make a movie that will change lives.

She had simple goals, including things that most of us accomplish on ordinary days, and she had ambitious goals as a filmmaker. Sadly, Melissa died before she could accomplish any of these life goals. In addition to forming the group *Someday Melissa*, Judy Avrin spearheaded a documentary by the same name that is hopefully changing some lives. Through her activism, Judy has fulfilled some of her deceased daughter's hopes and dreams.

If eating disorders are acknowledged and correctly diagnosed, there are effective treatments for those individuals willing to seek help. My former student Courtney and I have written an article specifically for physicians and other healthcare providers on how to screen for body image issues and eating disorders in medical practices where these patients may present with cryptic symptoms such as fatigue or heartburn (Martz & Rogers, 2016). The secrecy of eating disorders often keeps individuals from disclosing them to their healthcare providers. Instead, they may present with vague symptoms like lethargy, dizziness or fainting, gastrointestinal upset, cold intolerance, etc. We recommend that the physicians indeed listen to the reported symptoms, but also ask directly about laxative use, self-induced vomiting, food habits, and if the patient is trying to lose weight. We emphasize the need for suicide screening in these situations also as this is a common means of death for individuals deep into the eating disorders struggle. Unfortunately for many of them, suicide becomes the only hope of ending the misery. When patients arrive at healthcare settings, it is a prime opportunity for intervention. Yet, the physicians need to know how to ask questions to identify what is really going on.

After making an eating disorder diagnosis, healthcare providers are given information on stepped care and how to find a treatment program fitting their patient's level of suffering and severity. Stepped care is a way of delivering an intervention to patients starting with simple type of effective treatment at a lower cost (e.g., outpatient psychotherapy once per week), then assessing outcome to see if the patient needs to be stepped up to more intensive and costly treatment in order to be effective (e.g., round the clock inpatient hospital care). Once healthcare providers make the eating disorder diagnosis, they then are provided information about stepped care and how to find a treatment program matching their patient's level of suffering and severity.

There are psychotherapies for eating disorders with scientific evidence for effective treatment. For individuals who might be interested in seeking treatment, I will give a brief description of these therapies and how they work. Cognitive behavioral psychotherapy (i.e., "CBT") helps individuals understand how an eating disorder functions for them in their lives. Therapists examine what prompts various eating disordered behaviors and their consequences.

A while ago, I treated a client struggling with anorexia who initially reported that she could *not* eat because she was feeling nauseous most of the time. Yet her food restriction was the defining feature of her anorexia. I was able to draw on my own experience with morning sickness during pregnancy. By the time I became nauseous, it was usually because of the effects of the hormones on an empty stomach. I learned to keep food in my stomach at all times to stave off the nausea (i.e., even involving some night-time, sleep-walking snacks). Therefore, the worst thing that my client could do was interpret her nausea as "My body is telling me that I must not eat." Once we recorded her behavior/feelings over time and saw the pattern, then we were able to determine that she was nauseous *because* she was not eating. In this reframe of the problem, her not eating was fueling both her nausea and her anorexia. Eating more frequently was the solution to both.

Examining the antecedents, behavior, and consequences (i.e., ABCs) of problematic behavior can be eye-opening. Another common pattern is that a person starts the eating disordered behaviors initially because of weight gain. For example, the slightly overweight teen who loses some weight might receive compliments from significant others in her life. Such reinforcement can feel addictive, thus prompting further weight loss. CBT also considers a person's stress and ineffective/destructive coping behaviors in order to replace the unhealthy coping with improved ones. For example, engaging in food restriction helps some individuals feel in control of their lives by controlling what goes into their mouths. Moreover, CBT examines how these individuals have maladaptive thoughts, such as "eating any fat will make me fat" to more functional thoughts like "eating dietary fat is necessary for life and I want to live a healthy life."

Individuals with eating disorders are frequently stuck in patterns of avoidance. They could be avoiding very painful memories of sexual or physical abuse, avoiding conflicted relationships, avoiding negative emotions, etc. Usually there are deeper issues underlying the disturbed eating. The behavioral aspect of CBT uses principles to understand the ABCs of behavior and how problematic behavior functions or is needed for that person. As an exposure and response prevention technique, I have worked with clients with bulimia and had them intentionally binge eat in front of me. Doing this behavior in front of another person builds awareness of the behavior that is normally done in secrecy and in a mindless or dissociative state of mind. After the client engages in the binge eating, then the habitual response of self-induced vomiting is prevented—hence the treatment's name, "exposure and response prevention." Preventing purging elicits a great amount of anxiety because now they are terrified about the calories that they have just consumed in the binge episode. They do not get their typical escape. If done over and over, they habituate to the anxiety and thus can reduce their binges or eat more normal portions without feeling that learned impulse to purge. Without the purging behavior serving as a negative reinforcer, the frequency and/or amount of food in the binge episodes are no longer reinforced and thus decrease. Essentially, it was only okay to mass consume 5,000 kilocalories in one sitting if—and only if—one intended to get rid of them. If one cannot get rid of the calories, there is no reason to consume to excess. Although there are many other interventions conducted when using CBT for bulimia, this exposure (i.e., to the binge) and response prevention (i.e., no purging allowed) technique is one example of an effective intervention.

The scientific evidence for these interventions is quite strong. In a meta-analysis, which is a study of compiled studies on a topic, CBT was found to be superior to medications alone and effective in treating bulimia nervosa (Whittal, Agras, & Gould, 1999). CBT also showed strong treatment effectiveness for bulimia in an additional meta-analysis (Hofmann, Asnaani, Vonk, Sawyer, & Fang, 2012). A meta-analytic review that compared CBT and medications to treat binge eating disorder found strong effects for CBT, medium effect sizes for antidepressant medications, and no additional effect for psychotherapy and medication in combined treatment (Vocks, Tuschen-Caffier, Pietrowsky, Rustenbach, Kersting, & Herpertz, 2010). An updated review for the treatment of anorexia nervosa found that a combination of renourishment plus cognitive behavioral and interpersonal psychotherapy was recommended (Watson & Bulik, 2013). I am a professional member of the Association for Behavioral and Cognitive Therapies, which is a community of psychologists who study scientific research and apply it to help individuals through Cognitive Behavioral Therapy or Acceptance and Commitment Therapies (ABCT, 2017). The organization's website has a list of psychotherapists trained in these modern, evidence-based therapies that could be helpful to those of you in need.

Body Image Treatments for Eating Disorders

Since fat talk is the interpersonal extension of poor body image, and fat talk ostensibly normalizes obsession about appearance or makes disordered eating behaviors seem commonplace, this section will overview research and clinical techniques for treating body image dissatisfaction. Troubled body image is one of the most robust gender differences that researchers see in psychology (Feingold & Mazzella, 1998), and poor body image is often a starting point for individuals who begin eating disordered behavior. Consequently, knowing how to help girls and women with body image struggles is a feminist issue. It is often an important therapeutic component of eating disorders treatment. As an example of using CBT to treat body image anxiety, I often do mirror exposure therapy with clients. As in any exposure therapy intervention, one must obtain very motivated consent from clients to begin treatment. If we were to start exposure therapy and the client quits because she gets too upset or scared, then we have fueled the fire and likely made the problem worse. Clients must understand what they are agreeing to do and make a commitment to follow it through. Therapists must explain what they are asking and how the therapy technique works, as well as persuade the patient regarding the proven effectiveness of the treatment. It is also good to share with them that I have used this treatment with former clients who have found it to be very helpful. Once that consent has been obtained, I begin by pulling out a full-length mirror, in front of which the client must stand and look at herself in normal clothing for approximately 40 minutes. Ideally, we tip her anxiety level to the highest level possible. When prompted, the client regularly reports a "Subjective Units of Distress," or SUDS rating from "1 = no anxiety" to "10 = tremendous anxiety." Ideally, we get up to 10 and have her endure or *expose herself to that which she fears*. Clients with body image issues are accustomed to doing the opposite. They get worried about their appearance so they go and check their body. They check on the scale, check in the mirror, or check their arm size like the young woman in *To the Bone*. One would hope that the checking behavior would reassure them, allowing them to move on and have a good day. However, the checking behavior usually backfires. They check and get anxious. Then they escape the anxiety (i.e., look in the mirror, get upset then leave the room). This is the "negative" in negative reinforcement. What has been reinforced in this instance is the original body image anxiety. Therefore, this is their normal pattern that maintains their body image issues or makes them worse. Mirror exposure does the opposite. Initially, my clients get to wear normal clothing. They stand there and the anxiety is inevitable. I have them voice thoughts and feelings, which gives me a much better understanding as to how their cognition is maintaining poor body image and the eating disorder. The thoughts are often vicious and abusive. I had one teenage client say, "You fat bitch, you lazy ass bitch who needs to go to the gym." I asked if she would say these things to her friend and she responded, "Of course not." When I asked why she did not speak to her friend that way, she said, "Well, because the words are abusive." She made the connection. Her own thoughts were abusive to herself. This was the start to finding neutral words that accurately reflected her appearance in the mirror. After we had done several exposure sessions and she was able to alter the words in her mind, she could stand in the mirror without anxiety and say things like, "I have a curvy body. I am healthy with my curves. I'm not flat like some other girls." While doing the exposure sessions in front of the mirror, we often have to find creative ways to heighten the anxiety and push their SUDS rating towards 10. The more we do that, the quicker they get better. I have had clients wear their bikini bathing suit in my office, and I have them do nude sessions in the privacy of their homes. A recent client with social anxiety found that my standing behind her noticing what she was focusing on and seeing that I was looking at her moved her anxiety to the top. The process can be very painful for them, but the return on therapeutic investment is well worth it. Eventually these individuals can look in the mirror at themselves without any anxiety, they say more kind words in their minds when they view themselves, and the compulsive need to check the mirror, or the scale, or their measurements, ceases. Once the body image improves, often their drive to restrict food or their tendency to binge and purge improves as well.

Cook-Cottone (2015) presents a model of body image treatment that can be used in and of itself to improve self-esteem or can be an important component in the treatment of eating disorders. The model borrows from interpersonal therapies and dialectical behavioral therapies, but unlike traditional models focused on treating pathologies, her program pulls from positive psychology, particularly the body appreciation literature.

The ultimate goal is to achieve body acceptance and body love, which is the comfort and respect for one's body just as it is (Frisen & Holmqvist, 2010; Tylka, 2012). Cook-Cottone and Vujnovic (2015) conceptualize eating disorders as comprised of disordered food and body-related cognitions, poor self-regulation, and dysfunctional eating behaviors. Cook-Cottone (2015) suggests that central to these disorders are problems in how individuals experience their body, how they care for it, and how they accept it. Instead of attempts to *fix* the body by changing it so a person can be happy with it—which is the body image struggle that often fuels the eating disorder—she describes the positive psychology goal that individuals aim for *flourishing*, which involves awareness of both one's body and actions (Tylka, 2012). Cook-Cottone (2015) proposes that body flourishing entails two critical ways of living one's life: 1) having a healthy, embodied awareness of the internal and external aspects of self, and 2) practicing mindful self-care. The former strives for purposeful attention to the inner aspects of the self, including the physical body, the emotional experiences, and the cognitive domains. So many individuals, especially those struggling with eating disorders, are attempting to either ignore the inner self or to fight their natural sensations (e.g., trying not to feel hungry). It is very common in clinical work to begin psychotherapy with clients who have been fighting their negative emotions and wanting them to just go away. In other words, "I don't want to feel anxiety. I don't want to be depressed." Pharmaceutical advertisements try to convince us that it is our earthly right to not feel these persistent negative emotions. Clients come to me after having fought these emotions for a while and hope that I will be the magical person to wipe them away. It is a big shift to learn that physiology, emotions, and thoughts are natural, and they *will* happen. It reminds me of the brief therapy maxim that many of us, especially those who use Acceptance and Commitment Therapy, know very well: "The problem is not the problem. The problem is the person's persistent, well-intentioned but off-target attempts to solve that problem." Trying to make the thoughts or feelings simply go away does not work. I recently treated a wonderful client who is very smart, and she responded to me with something like, "What, am I supposed to respect my emotions?" to which I suggested, "Yes, they are natural, and what if they are offering you an important message?"

Having an embodied awareness of the internal aspects of oneself related to our hunger, our eating, and knowing when we are satisfied after eating is called *intuitive eating* (Tribole & Resch, 2012). Most Americans do not engage in intuitive eating, which is a way of paying respectful attention to one's hunger and eating accordingly. I am always amazed—but no longer surprised—when I ask for a show of hands in my class at the number of students' hands raised in the "clean your plate club." Oftentimes the "clean your plate" rule is an ancestral guideline that has trickled down from relatives who survived the Great Depression. When there is not enough food, humans don't want to waste any of it. Unfortunately, as a contemporary practice, this rule causes its victims to overeat. Ideally, intuitive eating coincides with the purposeful pursuit of healthy foods most of the time while allowing flexibility for cravings and environmental constraints on food availability. In my health psychology class, before I cover eating disorders and nutrition, I ask students to develop a definition of healthy eating. They usually arrive at a characterization that involves what we call 1) intuitive eating, and 2) making healthy choices that 3) involve diverse food choices to cover nutritional needs fully. Once we arrive at a definition of normal healthy eating, it becomes easier to understand 1) why many Americans are overconsuming calories, protein, and fat, which is adversely affecting their health, and 2) what goes awry in individuals who develop eating disorders. Babies arrive in this world instinctively engaging in intuitive eating. Breastfed babies get fed the right amount, as long as Mom feeds them upon hearing their hunger cries. Bottle fed babies, on the other hand, tend to get overfed. I had the opportunity and luxury of breastfeeding one of my sons. Due to environmental constraints, I was not able to breastfeed the other. I still harbor both guilt and resentment about that situation. (Sorry, my little Buddy!) However, having breastfed my other son because the environmental circumstances were more supportive, I can attest that we know when the milk is released and the baby responds with appreciation, but it is not easy to tell how much volume the baby is consuming. It is a very sweet bonding experience (i.e., my son hummed while he nursed). Moms only know how much milk is released if they pump a meal. Conversely, when babies are bottle fed, not only do the feeders know exactly how much volume is consumed, but many of them end up pressuring the child to finish. Imagine you just made eight ounces, but the baby detaches from the bottle at about six ounces. Many feeders would respond with something like, "Come on now, you need to finish this meal … after all, this formula is *very* expensive. We shouldn't waste it. Finish it up, little one." As a pressuring technique, this is often the baby's first step in being led away from intuitive eating. Imagine a lifetime of these forces—people eat according to parents' encouragement, what is available to them, time of day, emotional experiences, knowing when they will be able to eat again, and how much is served to them at a restaurant or in a fast food order. It is easy to eat for many reasons other than natural hunger. It is better to tune in and listen carefully to one's hunger and satiety.

One of the ways we can facilitate gravitation towards more intuitive eating is called *appetite awareness training*, which is when clients record their eating behavior and rate their hunger on a 1 to 10 scale, where 1 = no hunger and 10 = ravenous hunger. A rating of 5 means ideal hunger and time to eat intuitively. After eating, they then rate their satiety from 1= not satisfied, still very hungry to 10 = uncomfortably full (i.e., the person with bulimia would want to purge). They are coached to stop at a rating of 5, which means nicely full and satisfied. Using these ratings, intuitive eating would look like close to a 5 on hunger for initiation of eating and close to a 5 on satisfied after eating most of the time. Clients are often surprised how often they eat when they are not really hungry, which is indicative of boredom, loneliness, or stress eating. They often end up overfull on satiety because they were not really hungry in the first place and they have not satisfied emotionally what their minds were trying to tell them they really need (e.g., interpersonal company or rest). Clients who are fasting and trying to lose weight usually push their hunger way past 5 and head towards the higher, ravenous end of the scale. Guess what happens to them once they eat? They tend to overdo the meal because their hunger communicates, "Hey, who knows when she will feed me again ... it's erratic and unpredictable ... better chow down now!" They, too, progress well beyond a 5 in satiety towards a sensation of 10 when they are bloated and in pain. Intuitive eaters hit the 5s frequently on hunger and on satiety. They listen to their bodies and moderate the hunger and satiety well. Those who do not engage in intuitive eating tend to eat when not really hungry or when they are extremely hungry. Isn't it interesting that both forms of non-intuitive hunger errors tend to result in overeating? This helps us understand why so many Americans are in the habit of overeating. Appetite awareness training is only one of the interventions that therapists conduct to help individuals rediscover the intuitive eating style that they likely owned as newborns. See Tribole and Resch (2012) if you would like more information on this therapeutic process.

Intuitive eating is only one example of what Cook-Cottone (2015) would recommend for individuals to improve their relationship with their internal lives. There are certainly many other interventions that therapists offer to people who need healthier relationships with their emotions and their thought processes. Cognitive behavioral, dialectical behavioral, and acceptance and commitment therapies all address this awareness in the therapeutic process. While each approach uses slightly different strategies to address the feelings or thoughts, all of them work. Cook-Cottone (2015) describes the external or outer aspects of the self as containing the 1) microsystem (i.e., friends & family), 2) exosystem or community, and 3) the macrosystem or culture. She calls attunement the "reciprocal process of mutual influence and co-regulation" (p. 159) between the internal processes and the external forces. A healthy relationship occurs between the two when an individual respects and nurtures internal needs while also negotiating effectively within the context of family, community, and culture. Although many Americans struggle to find the embodied self and undergo this process smoothly, individuals with eating disorders usually harbor a very dysfunctional relationship between the internal and external. In fact, the common pattern is they are trying to please family and cultural values at a grave expense to respecting personal feelings, thoughts, and physiology. By definition, eating disorders involve brutal disrespect for an individual's hunger and satiety needs.

The second essential aspect of Cook-Cottone's (2015) program to promote body flourishing entails practicing mindful self-care. Clearly linked to the awareness processes of both internal and external forces described above, this process advocates for a loving-kindness or compassionate approach to one's self. She lists multiple interventions that include mindful awareness, self-soothing, spirituality, physicality including healthy eating, getting enough rest, exercise, and hydration, and knowing when the body or mind needs to seek heath care. As an example of an effective intervention that accomplishes this, Cook-Cottone, Beck, and Kane (2008) showed that a yoga-based program specifically targeting improvement of the mind and body connection, body image, emotion regulation, and critical examination of media influences was able to decrease eating disorder symptoms in individuals who suffer from them. Many individuals with body image issues, especially those struggling with eating disorders, are in the habit of fighting themselves or trying to please external forces, and they have given up on, or never learned how to engage in healthy self-care. As I tell my students and my adult clients, certainly our parents were responsible for giving us care as babies and children, but as individuals negotiate the teen years and approach adulthood, the responsibility becomes theirs. If only the "self-care fairies" would visit us regularly! In other words, "Now dear, it's time for you to run; here are your shoes. Look, I drew you a warm bath so you can relax. You have worked so hard today! Here is your coffee and a healthy breakfast … you know, the most important meal of the day, dear." My favorite is the hypothetical chardonnay fairy: "Here Sweetie, an ice-cold glass of wine so you can sit back and relax while I cook dinner and take care of the entire household." I may jest, but this is a very common problem for people—especially for women who were raised to take care of others before taking care of themselves. Many clients pay me good money to give them *permission* to prioritize self-care. Like many in my profession, I enjoy the airplane analogy: The safety video rolls. They inform us if in the unlikely event that the airplane loses cabin pressure, oxygen masks will drop automatically. I'm usually thinking, "In the unlikely event that the airplane loses cabin pressure, we are *all* going to *die*, violently. We are about to die!" Actually, I am not afraid of flying; it is just that I cannot control my morbid thoughts. So the video rolls, the oxygen masks are down, and they instruct us capable adults to place our mask on *our* face first so we can breathe in the life-saving air and be capable of helping others, like the adorable small child sitting next to us. If we pass out and die, we will not be able to help others. The message is to take care of ourselves first, *then* we will have the ability to take care of others later. I have seen this over and over in my clients and I have felt the pull in my own personal life to take care of others first in lieu of self-care. Thus, I tell clients and encourage my students to take care of themselves first or they will burn out. The burn out commonly expresses itself in depression, anxiety, drug use, eating disorders, etc. Meanwhile, those very unpleasant emotions and behavioral problems are really a strong message to one's self. The message being that these individuals needs to rethink their relationship with their body, their feelings, and their mind, and they need to find better ways of nurturing themselves, thus, enabling them to function and take care of the people in their lives.

I have known a lot of women, myself included, who find it easier to feel empathy and compassion for other individuals before we can feel these things for ourselves. Women can be pretty hard on themselves at times. Self-compassion is defined as a multidimensional construct that acknowledges that failure, suffering, and inadequacy are merely a part of the human condition and that all people are worthy of compassion (Neff, 2003). Self-compassion has three dimensions:

1. Self-kindness, which is being kind and understanding oneself rather than being critical and self-judging;

2. Mindfulness, which involves holding aversive thoughts and feelings in balanced awareness rather than over-identifying or following their commands; and

3. Common humanity that involves seeing one's own experiences as a natural extension of humankind, as opposed to feeling the personal experience as isolating and separate as if one is suffering alone.

Kelly, Miller, and Stephen (2016) studied 92 college women who agreed to complete daily surveys for seven nights of their daily social interactions, self-compassion, body image, intuitive eating, and emotions. Their fat talk measure was called "frequency of interactions with body-focused others," and was factor analyzed into three subscales: diet focused, body focused, and exercise focused. They found that on days when women were reporting less self-compassion than was typical for them, their attention to their bodies and their fat talk were associated with less intuitive eating, less body appreciation, more body image concerns, and more negative emotions. Yet, these same relationships were either absent or inversed on days where these women were reporting more self-compassion than was usual for them. This suggests that self-compassion is fluctuating—not trait-like—and can have important buffering effects for young women's body image and eating behavior when they are exposed to excessive fat talk.

In a review of 28 studies, Braun, Park, and Gorin (2016) found that self-compassion was associated with less eating disordered behaviors and seemed to be a protective factor for poor body image and eating pathology. This bodes well for both prevention efforts and treatment interventions for poor body image and eating disorders, because compassion-focused therapy has been shown to be as effective as behavioral therapy and more effective than a control condition for the treatment of binge eating disorder (Kelly & Carter, 2015). Goss and Allan (2014) describe compassion-focused therapy as a trans-diagnostic approach to psychological disorders including eating disorders—more specifically by targeting shame, self-criticism, and self-directed hostility. Dickerson and Kemeny (2004) note that shame is a complicated perception characterized by emotions such as anger, anxiety, contempt, and disgust, behavioral reactions such as behavioral inhibition, submissiveness, and escape, as well as physiological responses such as elevated cortisol levels. Gilbert, Clarke, Kempel, Miles, and Irons (2004) define two types of self-criticism: 1) focusing on mistakes and a sense of inadequacy, and 2) focusing more on feelings of self-disgust and hate and wanting to hurt oneself. They found that this state of self-criticism could result in attempts at behavioral coping that involve self-directed hostility or attempts at improvement. Goss and Allan (2014) suggest that compassion-focused therapy is a logical addition to traditional cognitive behavioral therapy that involves: Socratic dialogue, mindful monitoring of thoughts, emotions, and behaviors, behavioral experiments, diary keeping, exposure to difficult situations, learning emotion-focused regulation strategies, problem solving, and out-of-session homework to practice the skills that generalize to real life.

Additionally, compassion-focused therapy reduced eating concerns and weight concerns more than the behavioral therapy or control conditions. Kelly and Tasca (2016) tracked 78 eating disordered patients across a 12-week treatment program. Whenever patients experienced more of a sense of shame, their eating pathology worsened. However, when their sense of self-compassion increased, it lowered their experience of shame. The authors conclude that training in self-compassion can help break the reciprocal relationship between feeling shame and engaging in eating disordered behaviors. Kelly, Carter, and Borairi (2014) studied 97 patients within a 12-week eating disorder treatment program and found that those with greater decreases in their sense of shame during the first four weeks of the program had greater decreases in eating disorder symptoms by the end of the program. Again, those patients who showed more of an increase in their self-compassion levels were the ones to decrease their sense of shame the most across the treatment program.

In addition to treating the classic eating disorders, compassion-focused therapy has been used to reduce stigma, normalize unhealthy eating patterns, and increase quality of life in women struggling with overweight or obesity. Palmeira, Pinto-Gouveia, and Cunha (2017) studied 73 women with overweight/obesity without binge eating, who were randomly assigned to the Kg-Free intervention group or a control group. The intervention was named Kg-free because it focused on promoting mindfulness, acceptance, and self-compassion, as opposed to focusing on losing kilograms or pounds of weight. Kg-Free was comprised of 12 total sessions and the results were promising. Participants' pre- to post-intervention data suggested more improvement than the control group for health-related quality of life, physical exercise, reduction of weight self-stigma, body size, self-criticism, and weight-related avoidance. They found that an increase in self-compassion showed a trend towards predicting this improvement, but an increase in mindfulness was not significant.

Finally, Halliwell, and Diedrichs (2013) have found that body image interventions that create higher body acceptance have the positive side effect of helping girls increase their resilience to the thin ideal in popular media. Halliwell (2013) studied the effect of exposure to media featuring ultra-thin female images for 112 primarily Caucasian college women from the United Kingdom. They were categorized as high and low in body appreciation, using a median split on that variable, as well as those higher or lower in internalization of the thin ideal, using a median split on that variable also. Participants were led to believe that they were taking part in a study on how images in advertising affected their attitudes. In the experimental condition, they were exposed to five print images of ultra-thin models featuring a product for sale. In the control condition, print images showed only the product and did not feature the female model. The dependent variable was a body image scale composed of appearance discrepancies. Those with more discrepancies between the ways they perceived themselves compared to how they wished they looked had poorer body image. Halliwell (2013) found that women higher in body appreciation did not report negative body image effects after exposure to this type of media. The women who were high on internalization of the thin ideal and low on body appreciation experienced the most negative body image effects after exposure to the ultra-thin female images versus women in the control group. Yet for those women who were high on both internalization of the thin ideal and body appreciation, the positivity of their body appreciation buffered the harmful body image effects of media exposure, and there were no differences for them compared to the control group, which was not exposed to the ultra-thin female media images. Halliwell concluded that interventions should focus on improving women's body self-acceptance as a method to help make them more resilient against the potentially damaging effects of the thin ideal in media.

In summary, this section has reviewed multiple interventions shown to improve body image with the ultimate goal of helping those who are suffering from eating disorders recover. There is hope. Recall that Hudson et al. (2007) found that at least one third of individuals who were suffering from eating disorders had never sought treatment, and that individuals with eating disorders face a serious risk of death (Crow et al., 2009); consequently, it is my hope that anybody who is reading this who recognizes how fat talking or body shaming fuels poor body image and disordered eating finds help for themselves. Just because we live in a culture that supports these toxic feminine enemies does not mean that we have to accept the damage that they cause. Note that Association for Behavioral and Cognitive Therapies (ABCT) and National Eating Disorders Association (NEDA), have websites with resources for finding qualified professionals who can help.

Body Image and Its Relationship with Exercise

I established in earlier chapters how evolutionary biology/psychology and culture influence women's tendency to objectify their physical appearance. Franzoi (1995) proposed an object-process dichotomy in his observation of gender differences in body esteem. Girls and women are socialized in our culture to focus on their bodies for appearance or their "body as object." Conversely, boys and men tend to be raised to focus on what their bodies can do or their function, which is called "body as process." Much like attitudes concerning fat talk, Franzoi also found that college students hold more favorable attitudes towards the "body as process" than towards "body as object." Women can borrow from this approach as a means of improving body image. Wasylkiw and Butler (2014) studied 143 primarily Caucasian undergraduate women and assessed their exercise behavior, body esteem, and body appreciation, and expanded upon their measure of fat talk to include both weight loss talk and exercise talk. As expected, these women more strongly endorsed the "body as object" orientation than the "body as process" attitude. Further, they found that women who reported more frequent exercise were more likely to hold the "body as process" attitude. I get it. It is a healthy way of thinking about exercise or athletic training.

Years ago, an undergraduate majoring in exercise science talked me into training for my first sprint triathlon because she knew I was a lifelong runner. I thought it would be a wonderful way to program a "mid-life crisis," so I did it. Thankfully, it introduced me to the bike, and I have enjoyed road biking and mountain biking ever since. Swimming, on the other hand is not an exercise in propulsion for me, but rather a continuous task of *not* drowning. I prefer the running and biking. Like many others who love exercise, I find that it keeps me sane and allows me to focus and concentrate. It is a wonderful stress reliever, and I have learned that I can problem solve much more effectively when I am moving. I also have a competitive spirit, so these road events allow me to push myself and release that personality trait. When I was training for my first sprint triathlon, I saw a friend that I had not seen in a while. When she found out about my training, she asked me immediately, "Why are you trying to lose weight?" Her question threw me by surprise. It had nothing to do with trying to lose weight. It had everything to do with wanting to successfully be able to swim that much, bike that much, and run that much, and especially to be able to combine them (i.e., bike to run is worst on lead legs!), while pushing myself as competitively as possible. I was approaching this from the "body as process" and was surprised she was viewing it from the "body as object" standpoint.

Homan and Tylka (2014) studied 321 college women recruited from both a small liberal arts college and a large public university to study how exercise affected aspects of positive body image. They emphasized that their construct of body appreciation is not merely the absence of body image dissatisfaction. They found that women who engaged in moderate and intense exercise frequently reported higher levels of body appreciation, higher internal body orientation (i.e., the opposite of self-objectification), and higher functional body satisfaction (i.e., what the body can do). They also measured if these women engaged in exercise for appearance-based motivations, which is very similar to the body as object construct mentioned above. For the women who exercise for weight or shape control, the researchers found weaker relationships between all of the positive body image measures and exercise. Consequently, they recommend that interventions that encourage increased exercise in women focus on the stress relief and enjoyment aspects of exercise.

Many individuals who have eating disorders tend to exercise very compulsively, obsess about burning calories, and focus on how exercise could change their bodies. Knowing this, Calogero and Pedrotty (2004) designed an exercise program for individuals with eating disorders that deliberately tried to shift their focus and motivation for exercise to be healthier and more respectful of their body image. They used a mindfulness-based program to help participants see how exercise could rejuvenate rather than deplete their body's energy, establish a healthy mind-body connection, and help remedy mental and physical stress. Their intervention increased healthy weight gain in individuals suffering from anorexia nervosa and reduced a need for obligatory compulsive exercise attitudes for all participants.

Wasylkiw and Butler (2014) found that weight loss talk—which I would call fat talk—was associated with less body appreciation, whereas exercise talk was positively associated with body appreciation. Further, they showed that the relationship between conversation topics and body image was mediated by body attitudes and body orientation. Women who engage in exercise talk tend to view their bodies more positively and adopt a "body as process" orientation that then contributes to body appreciation. Conversely, the women who spend more time focused on weight loss, or engaging in fat talk, tend to view their bodies more negatively and have less body appreciation.

Girls on the Run is a developmentally-focused youth sport program for girls from 3rd to 5th grade. The program is intended to improve their self-esteem and body image through group-focused running. The program also features therapeutic discussion sessions that proceed through a standardized curriculum. The program runs for 12 weeks in the fall and the spring. Groups meet twice per week, and the curriculum includes 24 lessons with each session beginning by discussing the lesson of the day, followed by a warm up, time running, then a group processing discussion and closing. By the end of the program, the girls run a 5-kilometer road race together. There are three stages of the curriculum. The first is called "All about me: Getting to know who I am and what I stand for," which focuses on the girls' self-awareness. They examine their values, their likes and dislikes, and think about whom they wish to be in the future. The second stage is called "Building my team: Understanding the importance of cooperation," which targets team building, being supportive of others, how to listen and cooperate, and developing a sense of community. The third stage, "Community begins with me: Learning about community and designing our own community project," incorporates lessons about contributing to one's community, as well as becoming aware of negative messages that girls receive from the media and/or peers. There are several pre- to post-intervention studies that have examined the impact of Girls on the Run. Sifers and Shea (2013) conducted pre- and post-intervention surveys of a "Girls on the Run/Girls on the Track" program with girls ages 8–11. They found that body image and self-perceptions of appearance significantly improved. Their discrepancy between real and ideal body size decreased. Thus, results showed that multiple measures of body image improved. The program did not change outcomes of behavioral or emotional functioning. Program satisfaction was high among the girls' parents. DeBate and Thompson (2005) also found significant improvements in the girls' self-esteem, eating attitudes/behaviors, and body size satisfaction for girls who completed Girls on the Run. DeBate, Zhang, and Thompson (2007) found significant improvements in the girls' positive attitudes about physical activity and their commitment to engage in physical activity. DeBate, Gabriel, Zwald, Huberty, and Zhang (2010) studied more Girls on the Run councils in various geographical regions and found significant improvements in the girls' self-esteem and body size satisfaction, as well as in their attitudes about vigorous physical activity. Gabriel, DeBate, High, and Racine (2011) improved upon the previous three studies that were non-experimental by using pre- and post-intervention surveys on three different groups. The control group was never exposed to Girls on the Run; a second group had been previously exposed to the program; and the third group had just completed the Girls on the Run program. At pre-intervention, the girls who had been previously exposed—versus those who had never been exposed to Girls on Run—had higher commitment to physical activity and engaged in more physical activity. From pre- to post-intervention, the self-esteem of girls newly exposed and previously exposed improved, whereas the self-esteem of the control girls declined. Commitment to physical activity increased significantly in the previously exposed group, and even more so in the newly exposed group. Further, body size satisfaction improved significantly in the newly exposed group. Consequently, Girls on the Run appears to be effective in helping adolescent girls navigate a potentially tumultuous time of life while setting them up for continued mental and physical health.

Exercise interventions also seem effective for adult women's body image. Three meta-analyses have shown that exercise-training programs improve women's body image. Hausenblas and Fallon (2006) conducted a meta-analysis on studies examining how exercise relates to body image and grouped 121 studies into interventions (i.e., exercise versus control groups), single group (i.e., pre- and post exercise interventions), and correlational studies. They found that exercisers had more positive body image than non-exercisers. Individuals who began exercising had better body image scores post-intervention than pre-intervention. In the experimental studies, those who began exercising, relative to control participants, had better body image. Also, for the experimental studies, they found a greater effect size for the women ($d = .43$) compared to the effect size for the men ($d = .39$). The largest effect size ($d = .45$) was found for participants who engaged in both aerobic and anaerobic exercise with smaller effects for those who participated in only one kind of exercise (aerobic only, $d = .25$; anaerobic only, $d = .27$). Campbell and Hausenblas (2009) examined 57 publications resulting in 98 comparisons of studies that met their inclusion criteria. They found that exercise interventions had a small ($d = .29$) but consistent effect on improving individuals' body image. There was a larger effect for women ($d = .32$) than for men ($d = .19$). Finally, Reel and colleagues (2007) conducted another meta-analysis on 35 studies, including 60 effect size comparisons, and found that exercise, again, was associated with better body image. However, they found a much stronger effect ($d = .64$) for individuals engaged in weight training than those who only did aerobic exercise ($d = .40$).

The three meta-analyses described above produced some conflicting results on what type of exercise is more beneficial for women with poor body image, however. Ginis, Strong, Arent, Bray, and Bassett-Gunter (2014) recruited young women from a university campus who felt dissatisfied with their bodies and/or needed help following through with their New Year's resolutions. The 48 women who participated were randomly assigned to an aerobic training group or a strength training group. Both groups participated in exercise sessions three days per week for eight weeks. They measured body image in three ways: Social Physique Anxiety Scale, Appearance Evaluation, and Body Areas Satisfaction. Both exercise programs yielded significant improvements on each of these body image scales. Yet, the aerobics exercise program produced a better effect—in fact, twice the statistical effect size on the social physique anxiety. Improvements in all three body image scales were associated with perceived changes in body fat and aerobic endurance. Actual changes in fitness were unrelated to the body image constructs.

In conclusion, this chapter began with the feminist adage that the "personal is political," which means that how women feel about our body image and how this may seep out into our interpersonal conversations of fat talk are feminist concerns. How can we begin to strive for equality when fat talking reinforces the enemies within ourselves? For women who have identified that they participate in this harmful dialogue and wish to change their fat talk, this chapter has reviewed multiple therapeutic approaches. Cognitive behavioral therapies, compassion-focused therapies, intuitive eating, and exercise interventions have been shown to help people feel better about themselves and their bodies by moving them from self-loathing to compassion and self-appreciation for their bodies and what their bodies can do for them. For readers who identify with some of these problems, I hope that you will explore these scientifically supported interventions further to see what could be helpful for you. The feminist movement needs our sisters to be strong, healthy, and happy, not only for themselves, but in order to fuel needed social change. We women can take personal responsibility for our well-being with the ultimate goals of taking better care of others and having the energy to initiate greater feminist change in our communities, our nation, our world, and for our planet.

9

Feminism Targeting the Feminine Enemies in Our Culture

"We march because we care. Women's rights are human rights. Women power everywhere."—Women's March sign, 2017

The evidence is clear that fat talk and body snarking are feminist problems for many of us personally and on a cultural level. Per earlier chapters, both fat talk and body snarking are understandable given evolutionary psychology and modern misogynist cultural forces. However, our feminine enemies are not excusable! To date, there have been more attempts to reduce fat talk than attention paid to reducing body snarking, and the development of effective community interventions to reduce fat talk is in its infancy. What can feminists do on a large scale that can have a positive impact on our culture? Most importantly, what can we do that has been shown through science to be effective and ensures that we have not harmed anyone? Just like pharmaceutical medications can be very effective in treating a symptom, yet harbor serious side effects that cause more harm than the original symptom, scientists must be careful to study our behavioral interventions to make sure that the benefits outweigh the risks as they attempt to help people. This chapter will review some of the ongoing feminist activism targeting women's fat talk. The intent of this activism is respectable. However, I will also include critical review concerning the effectiveness of these interventions.

My students know that I am not a fan of what seem like "good ideas" when we should be approaching problems scientifically. Sometimes good ideas backfire—particularly when activists attempt to design community interventions that they think will serve multiple levels of prevention at the same time for target audiences. *Primary prevention* helps individuals who are healthy stay healthy. For fat talk, this could mean targeting girls or individuals who have reached their teenage years, which is when most fat talk seems to begin. An example of this is the NYC Girls Project, which I will discuss at the end of this chapter. This media campaign was aimed to increase the self-esteem of pre-teenage girls in New York City. *Secondary prevention* helps individuals with signs or symptoms of problems to prevent these from moving into diagnosable psychological disorders or medical disease. For fat talk, this would mean targeting individuals who engage in this form of dialogue habitually, such as some sorority members, where the behavior could be starting to take a toll on their body image, self-esteem, or eating behaviors. Crandall's (1998) study, which will be mentioned later in this chapter, illustrates how social groups like university sororities can establish norms associated with eating disorders. Although he did not measure fat talk during this study, he found that eating disordered behaviors were contagious within these groups of young women—and my bet is that the contagion was spread by fat talk. *Tertiary prevention*, usually referred to as *treatment*, helps individuals with diseases or disorders from worsening with the ultimate goal of preventing more disability and death. For fat talk, these community interventions would seek to target individuals with poor body image, poor self-esteem, those who are being fat shamed, and those with eating disorders to secure the professional help that they need. Before I discuss what has been done to target fat talk in our communities, I will overview some wisdom about how effective community psychology interventions are developed, implemented, and evaluated.

Community psychologists know that scientists are not very good at developing one single, universal intervention that effectively targets primary, secondary, and tertiary prevention all at the same time. As noted in the examples above, the individuals at these three levels are in very different circumstances and potential levels of harm associated with fat talking or body snarking. Figuring out what type of intervention to design and implement in hopes of helping people is only one part of good science in community psychology. We also need to figure out how to specifically target individuals who can benefit from interventions without wasting resources by accidentally targeting individuals who do not need those interventions. Further, we need scientific methodology to determine if the intervention works, for whom it works, and if it has any iatrogenic side effects. As a clinical psychologist who is versed in the American Psychological Association's ethical guidelines, it is our professional responsibility to ensure that the interventions that psychologists provide to individual clients and to people targeted in communities are borrowed from evidence-based practice. We want to deliver interventions that have been shown to work. Further, from a fiscally responsible standpoint, we should also be studying what works most effectively for the least expensive price in terms of professional time and resources, has the fewest iatrogenic side effects, and determine whether the intervention has any "win-win" helpful effects. An example of this is the fact that many physicians are unfamiliar with how to prescribe exercise, dietary management, and other self-regulation protocols to prevent or treat Type II diabetes (McMaughan et al., 2016). Instead they tend to rely on medications for treatment, most likely because pharmaceutical representatives are regularly recommending use of their medications to doctors. The pharmaceutical industry does not profit from people exercising or eating healthfully. Counseling patients with pre-diabetes in radical lifestyle changes would be cheaper and more effective in restoring their health than the typical way that our healthcare providers intervene.

When it comes to fat talk, it would be easy for me to say we should just stop it. However, that approach would be naive. How will we find the people most harmed by fat talk and help them stop? Will the intervention approach work? Will the intervention have possible iatrogenic effects like disrupting intimate relationships when others are seeking reassurance with their fat talk behavior? Can we target fat talk without also addressing body image or eating and exercise behaviors? Is an individualistic psychological approach the best way to address fat talk, or should we take a social psychological approach or design public health communications campaigns? How will we target body snarking and fat shaming? It seems like going after perpetrators would look very different than trying to help their victims. Once we start thinking ethically and scientifically about this problem, it begins to seem more complicated.

As an example of how a good idea can backfire, Mann and colleagues (1997) studied a commonly performed intervention meant to prevent eating disorders or build awareness about eating disorders on college campuses. My own campus favored this intervention once upon a time. I tried to voice my concern about what the science regarding this approach says to a group of practitioners, but my concern was not taken seriously. People liked the "good idea." The program features individuals either alone or on a panel of speakers who have recovered from an eating disorder. They tell their stories while the audience listens carefully and likely goes through an array of emotions in response to the poignant stories. Both the speakers and the individuals who invite them and plan the programs are very well intentioned. Yet, the net results could be exactly what the sponsors are trying to prevent. Most notably, these are stories of disordered eating *recovery*. What these stories also convey (albeit, unintentionally) is that one can experiment with eating disordered behavior, but then willfully recover and get healthier when ready to do so. What is *not* conveyed is how many individuals suffer from an eating disorder and continue to be disabled and miserable—or worse—those who have since died. As an example of the notable lethality of eating disorders, the *Something*

Fishy website displays candles where family members have memorialized loved ones lost to eating disorders (http://www.something-fishy.org/memorial/memorial.php). The introduction reads,

> In Loving Memory...
> Each candle is a lighted face,
> A soul, a time, a life, a place,
> Remember each, their smiles and grace,
> Each one who suffered ... each different case.
> All in common one they share,
> Their names left here to make aware,
> No longer feeling hidden pain,
> Their death in peace ... and not in vain.

As of 2018, the website featured 611 candles in recognition of memorial posts of parents who lost their daughters, individuals who lost their spouses or partners, men who lost their battles, and women who lost their babies in repeated miscarriages as they suffered from eating disorders. It is very sad. The recent movie *To the Bone* (Noxon, 2017) features a young pregnant woman in a residential eating disorders treatment program who accidentally miscarries her baby while she is purging in the bathroom. It is an incredibly painful scene as the woman is crying hysterically over her loss—one she has just caused with her self-induced vomiting. She wanted this baby, and her fellow friends, also in treatment for eating disorders, had just thrown her a baby shower. It is a heartbreaking scene. Yet, the scene illustrates that eating disorders can be about a total loss of control and can destroy lives. I show the *Something Fishy* website in my class during my eating disorders lecture, and the experience is always powerful and moving. This website features the very sad outcome of a student named Nicki who attended Appalachian State University. I do not think that we crossed paths, but I think about her whenever I show this website to my students. It always feels more poignant when these stories hit closer to home. Nicki's parents posted the following:

> Nicki was a beautiful, intelligent young girl who suffered from anorexia/bulimia since she was 13 years old. At age 22 she was hospitalized for the first of many attempts at recovery. She was hospitalized periodically for the next 6 years at every major eating disorder facility we knew of. She desperately searched for a reason for this terrible disease that plagued and ruined her life. She thought that she couldn't overcome the disease and said that it controlled 95 percent of her brain. In April last year she had a near death experience. As I held her close all night in bed, she took me on a journey to Heaven where she had no more pain, no one knew she was sick and she looked like everybody else. The next 9 months with my only child were a gift from God and together we experienced true unconditional love. She died 2 weeks after her 29th birthday of a massive heart attack.

I am so sorry for what this family had to endure. I remember the quote about the eating disordered thoughts controlling 95 percent of her brain, because that is a very effective reminder of how miserable eating disorders can make people. These stories are very real to the family and friends that have lost loved ones. Unfortunately, the stories of *recovery* that are used to build awareness of eating disorders on college campuses or other venues do not adequately tell the stories of *death*. This is an example of a place where what seems like an intuitive "good idea" deserves critical scientific study as a part of its use in community interventions. Perhaps it is not a good idea to feature these individuals who have recovered from eating disorders as speakers in community interventions aimed at primary, secondary, and tertiary prevention. What does the scholarship say about this?

Mann et al. (1997) performed a scientific study examining the effect of hearing classmates present their stories of eating disorder recovery on college women. They recruited 509 first-year female students from an Ivy League university on the west coast and surveyed them at three separate intervals about their demographics, eating behavior, body image, and self-esteem. The preliminary survey was referred to as Time 1. Three months later, half were invited to participate in an eating disorders prevention program, while the other half were not invited and instead served as a control group. The intervention sessions lasted 90 minutes with audiences of ten to twenty women at a time. One of the panelists suffered from anorexia nervosa and was still in recovery. The other had recovered from bulimia nervosa. The researchers then distributed Time 2 surveys four weeks following these intervention meetings and a Time 3 survey twelve weeks post-intervention. At follow-up, audiences exposed to the intervention—versus those in the control group—had slightly *more* symptoms of eating disorders. The "good idea" had backfired! Rather than reduce stigma associated with eating disorders, the authors suggested that the intervention might have unexpectedly normalized them. The intervention also conveyed that recovery is probable, which is very dangerous given the impairment and lethality of eating disorders (Crowe et al., 2009; Stice, Marti, Shaw, & Jaconis, 2009). In the real world, recovery is possible, but not probable, and in some cases absolutely unfeasible. Consequently, it does not appear that featuring the recovery panels is very effective if we are using them to target all three levels of prevention in a one-shot intervention program. Thank goodness Mann et al. (1997) chose to study this intervention using the scientific method. People thought the "good idea" would be *helpful*. The science showed it to be *harmful*.

In contrast, other researchers have studied eating disorder preventative interventions that really work. However, in order to know if these interventions or seemingly "good ideas" work, do not work, or backfire, they must be studied using the scientific method—ideally using the random assignment of participants, an intervention group as well as a control group, appropriate measures of outcomes, and appropriate inferential statistical analyses. Because body image dissatisfaction and fat talk are associated (i.e., see Mills & Fuller-Tyszkiewicz, 2017 for a review), another solution to reducing fat talk would include interventions that improve body image and prevent eating disorders. Becker and colleagues (2017) reviewed results of multiple studies on *The Body Project*, which is a cognitive-dissonance-based intervention that invites young women to critique our culture's thin-ideal beauty standard using written, verbal, or behavioral exercises. Hence, some of what they say or write is the opposite of fat talk, and the content often takes on a feminist tone when participants note the needed rebellion against cultural and perhaps even evolutionary forces. It is effective. Compared to control groups, women who participated in this intervention had less body dissatisfaction, less internalization of the thin ideal, less dieting, and fewer eating disordered behaviors. To be clear here, fat talk appears to breed poor body image, poor self-esteem, and eating disorders. Positive body talk, which often falls into the spirit of feminist philosophy, breeds body image satisfaction, self-esteem, and ideally social activism.

Drs. Carolyn Becker and Eric Stice have made *The Body Project* readily available for organizations to access and implement. *The Body Project Collaborative* website reads,

> What is the Body Project? The Body Project is a dissonance-based body-acceptance program designed to help high school girls and college-age women resist cultural pressures to conform to the appearance ideal standard of female beauty and reduce their pursuit of unrealistic bodies. The Body Project is supported by more research than any other body image program and has been found to reduce onset of eating disorders [http://www.bodyprojectcollaborative.com/].

One of the website's testimonials by a woman named Savannah states,

> Participating in Body Project training was honestly life changing … Just in the last 24 hours, my thought process has dramatically changed. I've always been aware of the harmful effects of the media's skewed portrayal of beauty ideals, but this program really helped me explore and challenge all of the messages the media is sending. The practice that we all got at handling "fat talk," negative comments etc. was incredibly helpful and educational.

Another participant by the name of Maci writes,

> The Body Project training has been amazing and eye opening … I will be more aware of fat talk going on around me and I will refrain from using these negative statements towards myself and those around me. The training has taught me to make a positive impact for myself and those around me.

In addition to guiding research showing that *The Body Project* is effective for women who participate in it, Becker et al. (2017) describe how the organization has engaged in quality community psychology methodology with multiple organizations such as sororities, the Eating Recovery Center Foundation, universities such as Arizona State, activism foundations such as the National Eating Disorders Association, and international organizations. Hence, they are using preventative interventions that really work while embracing marketing strategies for larger scale dissemination, such as scaling-up strategies, task-shifting to lay providers rather than professional experts, and developing partnerships with organizations with shared missions to improve body image and prevent eating disorders. This is an absolutely ideal example of scientists using their knowledge for positive activism. Students in my research lab and I were fortunate to attend *The Body Project* training, sponsored by our counseling center, this past semester. I applaud all that these professionals have done, and I am thrilled that my university has embraced this effective intervention!

Unfortunately, not all of these community interventions have been studied scientifically. An example of one such intervention is Caitlin Boyle's (2010) creation of a movement and website called *Operation Beautiful*. The back cover of her book reads,

> Tired of watching women pick themselves apart in front of the mirror, blogger Caitlin Boyle scribbled a note: "YOU ARE BEAUTIFUL," and slapped it on the mirror of a public bathroom. With one small act, she kick-started a movement. In a matter of days, women were undertaking their own feats of resistance, posting uplifting notes on gym lockers, diet shakes at supermarkets, weight-loss guides in book stores, and anywhere else a nagging voice of self-criticism might lurk.

To counter the negative messages that girls and women receive regularly from the media and the people around them, which they then later repeat habitually to themselves in their own thoughts, Boyle and her followers place Post-it notes with affirming messages in women's bathroom mirrors and other salient places for them to view. Her book and website are full of testimonials of women—many of whom were distressed and suffering with body image issues and eating disorders—who found the messages to be a pleasant surprise and quite uplifting. For example, one of these notes reads, "You are beautiful"; or one quoting Maya Angelou reads, "You alone are enough. You have nothing to prove to anybody"; another reads, "Don't be afraid to fail. Be afraid not to try." Boyle reports that she hears from individuals suffering from stress, depression, and eating disorders who become motivated to seek help after happening upon one of these notes. To date, thousands of these notes have been posted all over the world in different languages. The book and the online blog seem very positive, with great intentions, and include many positive anecdotal responses to this movement. I am pleased to hear about constructive reactions to *Operation Beautiful*. Keep in mind, however, that this type of intervention has not been studied scientifically.

Lynch (2011) conducted a critical analysis of *Operation Beautiful*'s book and website blog using communications research methodology that had been previously used to examine other popular media counter-discourses. A counter-discourse campaign is an attempt to counter or undo the harm created by common/normative media and marketing campaigns that take advantage of women's body image insecurities. Although *Operation Beautiful* intends to remove the dominating, narrow standard of beauty for women in the U.S. (i.e., hegemonic beauty discourse), Lynch's first observation is that Boyle refers to negative body thoughts or dialogue as fat talk. In fact, Boyle had contacted me personally while writing her book to interview me on my thoughts and research about fat talk. I am fine using the definition of fat talk to pertain to the broadly defined expression of critique about general physical appearance. Complaints about being fat are just one example of this type of dialogue. However, since *Operation Beautiful* is meant to encourage acceptance of diverse body types and denounce the hegemonic beauty ideal, Lynch criticizes the use of the term fat talk as it is attached more narrowly to fat stigma. Boyle is highly critical of fat talk and calls it "toxic," "damaging," and says it is "extremely triggering of unhealthy behaviors" on her website (http://www.operationbeautiful.com/meet-caitlin/). Boyle suggests that women should replace the fat talk with positive words. As an example, a woman could call her body "strong" instead of "stocky." This proposed solution is what psychologists call cognitive restructuring, which is a technique within cognitive therapy. Lynch (2011) also critiques Boyle's suggestions that women's misery such as depression, anxiety, or an eating disorder could be cured if these women thought of themselves as beautiful with the further assumption that reading a positive Post-it note will end in that effect.

I have taught clients with body image issues this same type of cognitive restructuring. I recall one teenage client's very harsh words about her own body. By the conclusion of her treatment, she would refer to her body as "curvy" rather than "fat and disgusting." While thought replacement or cognitive restructuring fit well into a cognitive therapy approach to change, it is often just one intervention embedded within other much more complex interventions in psychotherapy for these illnesses. Further, Acceptance and Commitment Therapy (i.e., commonly called "ACT") would take a different approach for the very same problem of fat talk thoughts. Acceptance and Commitment Therapy acknowledges that we humans cannot *not* think. Try not to think about something, and most of us—especially those of us good at obsessing—will think about it much more. In his classic experiment, Wegner (1994) asked participants to spend a few seconds thinking about anything they wanted to, but asked that they not think about a white bear. Give yourself a few seconds with your eyes closed and give it a try. For most people, the attempt to not picture or think about the white bear fails. Most of Wegner's participants were indeed thinking about a polar bear. He then asked them to not think about a white bear, but to try to think about a red fire truck. Go ahead and give yourself a few seconds with your eyes closed and try to not see the white bear, while trying hard to see the red fire truck. I do this exercise in my classes. My students always laugh when we do this demonstration, because when they close their eyes they see the polar bear in the road with the fire truck, or the polar bear driving the fire truck. The best is when they see the polar bear clinging and riding playfully on the back of the fire engine! Thoughts are additive. We cannot subtract them. We cannot *not* think. Some individuals engage in the practice of meditation and can do a good job of learning to quiet the thoughts in their mind, but it is not as if they can just turn them off like we do with the sound for a TV or the radio.

Consequently, rather than changing fat talk thoughts to make them more neutral or more positive, ACT therapists would help their clients learn to distance themselves from their thoughts, or defuse them. Many of us follow or obey our habitual thoughts regularly and this drives our feelings and our behavior. As an example, we say to ourselves, "I am hungry" and then we find ourselves problem solving to find food. The thoughts drive behavior and emotions. As a defusion technique, we train ourselves to become aware of thoughts without necessarily following them. This is akin to enjoying upbeat music in our ear buds, when the music is driving how we feel and what we think if we are singing along in our mind. You can pull the ear buds out and you may still be able to tell what song is playing and the place within the song. However, ear buds at a distance of several feet from our ears fail to captivate or control how we feel or what we think. It is also not very easy to sing along in our heads with the music at a distance. This is a cognitive defusion technique. As an example, for personal fat talk, a woman could think, "That ice cream has a lot of calories and will surely make my thighs fatter" and practice distancing from the thought, yet accepting that such thoughts do tend to habitually show up in her mind. She would then say to herself something like, "Yes, my mind often gives me thoughts about calories when I am about to eat something special. I would like to instead savor every bite of this ice cream and really taste how good it is." Cognitive behavioral therapy and ACT interventions overlap, but cognitive behavioral therapy aims to replace the thoughts with healthier, more rational ones. ACT does not try to change the thoughts, but instead attempts to distance oneself from the power of the thoughts. Thus, it is a way of accepting that thoughts are just thoughts. They need not dictate how one feels or behaves. We all have quirky, negative, and even dark thoughts. People who find these thoughts to be terrifying and try to make the thoughts go away are the people who suffer most from stress, anxiety, depression or other psychological disorders. People who realize that such thoughts are a quirky or random part of the mind's way of life are able to move forward and think about other things. It is the attempt to control thoughts that backfires and breeds worse issues for people. Allowing such thoughts to come and flitter through one's mind keeps the peace. My example is the "we are all going to die" thought when the flight attendant rolls the airplane's safety video. I can be scared by my own morbid thoughts, or I can simply chuckle and see the humor in them.

Both cognitive behavioral therapy and ACT ask individuals to build awareness of the power of their habitual thoughts. I like what Caitlin Boyle has in her motives for *Operation Beautiful*. Her activism is clearly feminist and humanistic in nature, yet I can also relate to Lynch's critique that feeling beautiful is not the answer to many women's woes and ending fat talk thoughts or dialogue is not as simplistic as it is presented. My friend Lisa and I pondered if feeling more beautiful would make us and the women we care about feel happier. As clinical psychologists, we came up with words that are more action oriented, such as "effectiveness, loving, caring, agency, capability, interpersonal sensitivity, etc." Yet, as we learned in chapter one, the evolutionary psychology literature tells us how important a sense of beauty is and why attractiveness is an important component of self-identity for many women across human history. So is it possible to end fat talk, or is it an expression of how we are wired? Before I review studies examining attempts to reduce fat talk, I will summarize research examining how disordered eating behavior is potentially contagious as women communicate with others about their values and then develop group norms.

Crandall (1988) was the first to document how women's eating behavior was shaped across an academic year for women in two sororities. The first sorority held a moderate binge eating norm, and the most popular women were those who binged moderately while the less popular women engaged in this abnormal eating much less or much more than moderately. In the second sorority, there was a pro-binge eating norm in that the most popular sisters were those who binged the most. Imagine a sorority sister ordering a large pizza delivery and showing her friends bags of chips and cookies and soda proclaiming, "Tonight Ladies, we get to splurge," as a welcoming prompt to binge eat together. Crandall hypothesized that binge eating behavior could be contagious for sorority sisters living in the same house. Indeed, he found that the women were more similar in their personal binge eating behavior at the end of the academic year than at the start. This similarity of binge eating increased as a sense of group cohesion developed among the women. Although it was not studied directly in Crandall's sororities, the norm formation that transpired was likely communicated woman to woman via fat talk dialogue. The term "fat talk" had not yet been coined in the 1980s; thus, Crandall certainly did not attempt to measure it.

As another example that our personal body attitudes could have some social contagion, Wood-Barcalow, Tylka, and Augustus-Horvath (2010) conducted a qualitative study from individual interviews of fifteen college students (seven Black, seven White, and one Asian) with positive body image to gather content on how they arrived at or maintain the positivity. They found multiple themes including: body appreciation, unconditional acceptance from relationships, body acceptance and love, religion/spirituality, taking care of oneself with healthy behaviors, filtering potentially negative information in a body-protective manner, inner positivity influencing their personality and demeanor, and holding a broad rather than narrow or hegemonic conceptualization of beauty. Further, these women with positive body image reported that they tried to surround themselves with other women who also expressed personal self-acceptance, rather than seeking friendship from women who habitually engaged in fat talk. Being around women who hold positive body image and make it public in their conversations makes this healthy attitude seem more normative. Thus, it would make sense that it was easier to feel that way about oneself when surrounded by people who feel the same way. Some of these women implied that they avoid others who fat talk as a preservation mechanism for their positive body image. Hence, these participants had some sense that attitudes about body image can be contagious among girls and women.

In the spirit of feminist activism, some women's groups are attempting to fight fat talk norms. Bonnie Rochman (2010), who writes for *Time*, first covered the story on how college campuses are fighting back to end the norm of the thin ideal and to help students find healthier and more realistic attitudes about their physical appearance. Trinity College psychology professor Dr. Carolyn Becker, who developed their Reflections Body Image Program in 2008, introduced this campaign. Since 2008, TriDelta (i.e., Delta Delta Delta) Sorority has initiated and maintained a social action week on its university campuses. Named *Fat Talk Free Week*, this social marketing campaign is meant to help build women's awareness and willingness to cease this harmful dialogue, as well as to promote healthy body positivity and self-care for students on their campus for one week of the academic year. This campaign relies on students' social media accounts on sites like Facebook and YouTube as well as signage in heavy trafficked areas of campus that read "Friends Don't Let Friends Fat Talk." Consequently, the intervention encourages these students to attempt to cease the fat talk in their own behavior. They have also made this an interpersonal intervention. If friends are normally supposed to reassure a friend who fat talks, as well as reciprocate, the signage about friends not letting friends fat talk gives them another response option if they hear it during this week.

Molinaro (2014), who wrote for *The Miami Student,* reported on how Miami University's chapter of TriDelta Sorority partnered with Operation

Beautiful for their Fat Talk Free Week. Sorority sisters posted affirming Post-it notes across campus on mirrors in women's bathrooms. Garnett and colleagues (2014) recruited two New England college campuses that were planning a Fat Talk Free Week for this pilot evaluation of the social media campaign. Students on these campuses were recruited to complete a 20-minute online survey two weeks prior to Fat Talk Free Week and again two weeks immediately following the conclusion of Fat Talk Free Week. Forty-eight percent of the women originally recruited for the pre-test completed both the pre-test (Time 1) and post-test (Time 2) assements. The surveys included a one-item *Self fat talk* response for their behavior in the past two weeks, a five-item *Fat talk exposure within peer network* scale originating from the Appearance Conversation with Friends subscale, a five-item *Peer physical comparison* scale that was borrowed from Thompson's Physical Appearance Comparison scale, as well as a scale named *Body-image-related risk factors* with items copied from several published scales. In their post-test survey, Garnett et al. included several items asking participants about the campaign's saliency and relevancy to them personally. Regarding the latter, participants were asked:

If Fat Talk Free Week was engaging?
Had a positive impact on their life?
Was an important social action week to have on their campus?
Was relevant to their life?, and
If it should be held at their university again for the following year?

Results found that post-test measures compared to pre-test scores showed decreases in self fat talk, decreases in fat talk exposure in their peer networks, less body dissatisfaction, and less physical comparisons with peers for the participants who completed both sets of surveys. Quantified in a different manner, 50 percent of participants reported "almost always" or "often" participating in fat talk at pre-test with 34 percent reporting this by post-test. Hence, their data showed that the goal of Fat Talk Free Week—to decrease personal fat talk as well as the behavior in social settings for women—seemed to have been achieved. Further, they found that a perceived sense of campaign saliency and relevancy was a stronger predictor of these changes compared to simple campaign event attendance. Therefore, participants' report of identifying with the goals of the campaign resonated in reports of their personal and network behaviors. This research is encouraging for feminist intentions to reduce fat talk in female communities.

As discussed in chapter seven, the research reviewed several studies that have documented what seems like two norms in our culture for women: one supporting fat talk, but then another norm encouraging self-acceptance dialogue. Pluralistic ignorance is operating, whereby many women appreciate hearing the higher self-esteem commentary and dislike the fat talk themselves, meanwhile *ignorantly* thinking other women hold the fat norm closer to their preferences. Although it was not tested directly in Garnett et al. (2014), Fat Talk Free Week could have helped to inform these college women that there are other women like themselves who would like to see a cultural norm shift. Called minority influence in the social psychological literature (Moscovici, 1980; 1985), this type of campaign has the potential to free young women's personal preference for speaking about and hearing other women's body positivity. Garnett and colleagues posit that this campaign could have changed the norm by making it acceptable to sanction fat talk behaviors. Yet, it could also have unleashed the alternative self-accepting norm. If women privately adhere to a norm of self-acceptance, but think other women comply with the fat talk norm, then it is quite enlightening to learn that some other women also embrace norms of esteem and positive body image. My bet is that these social psychological phenomena were driving the changes found in the frequency of fat talk after these young women were exposed to Fat Talk Free Week.

As a potential limitation to their study, Garnett et al. (2014) also acknowledged that demand characteristics, fitting best into a social desirability bias, could have been operating. In other words, some students may have reported less fat talk after Fat Talk Free Week intervention since they knew this is what was *supposed* to happen and would please the researchers. Further, it would have been wonderful if the researchers could have taken conversational, behavioral samples of dialogue of women in public places to see if they could document behavioral changes beyond the self-report nature of the research. Recall that the sorority posted signs that read "Friends don't let friends fat talk" in high trafficked areas across the campus. It would be interesting to see if these behavioral prompts really affected their conversational behaviors after Fat Talk Free Week compared to what they sounded like prior to the social action intervention. Regardless of these possible study limitations, college campuses are ideal communities to produce these communication interventions and to study their effects, given that participants are all part of a finite community, usually with salient social norms. Further, these social marketing campaigns are low cost and can be disseminated rather easily through social media. They can have direct effects for individuals participating personally in these events and/or indirect effects by the conversations inspired by those who identify with the campaign and speak with others about it.

We need more research to determine how often women adhere to fat talk versus self-accepting norms. Can individuals embrace both norms and access them behaviorally considering the type of situation that they are in? Is the fat talk norm really the majority norm? Further, is the self-accepting norm really the minority norm, in terms of how minority influence is defined in social psychology (Moscovici, 1980; 1985)? Worchel, Grossman, and Coutant (1994) noted two different ways that minority norms or groups are defined: one by sheer numbers, and a second way based on relative social power. Moscovici (1976) proposed that the ideal tactic by which a numerical minority can overpower the majority is if a minority person "boldly reveals in public what has been the case in private" (p. 69) and "openly adopts a behavior that most individuals would themselves like to carry out" (p. 70). Could Fat Talk Free Week be especially powerful if sorority women—who we might otherwise assume adhere to the fat talk norm set by their friends and sorority sisters—help buck the norm? Further, could celebrities like Amy Schumer, Emma Watson, and Melissa McCarthy—as discussed in the Body Snarking chapter—have this type of effect on women who privately hold the self-esteem/self-accept norm?

Kerr (2002) distinguishes between passive and active social advocates of the minority position. Active advocates are aware of the popularity of their opinions for their in-group, are interdependent with their in-group, and do expect to have conversations with others in the in-group about this topic. The celebrities named above fit here. We now expect them to espouse esteem in public and to fight back when internet trolls or reporters critique them about their appearance or their feminist beliefs. They are our anti-fat talk and anti-body snarking role models! Passive advocates, on the other hand, support an unpopular opinion (i.e., self-acceptance in a known fat talk culture), but they are *not* aware of the true popularity of their opinions within their in-group and they do *not* converse with their in-group members in a way that would reveal their personal beliefs or the opinion of others. My bet is that a lot of the women who have privately told us about their admiration of other women who are self-accepting in their body talk would fall into this passive minority subgroup. We need to tap into this resource. Perhaps researchers need to borrow from social marketing strategies or "word of mouth" marketing literature as scientists develop interventions and assess their possible effectiveness. Although Garnett et al. (2014) did not directly study why college women who were exposed to Fat Talk Free Week reported a decrease in their fat talking behavior, it is likely that these social psychological forces were operating. The campaign informed college students that it was acceptable to sanction fat talk. The use of Operation Beautiful signage, as adopted by some of the Fat Talk Free Week sororities, also informed individuals that it is appropriate to support other women's positive body image. This perhaps frees the minority influence for individuals who feel that way privately to now air the attitude publicly.

If we are motivated to break through pluralistic ignorance norms for fat talk, we can borrow from literature that has done so for college students' alcohol consumption. Miller and McFarland (1991) documented how college students, despite having the same public drinking behavior as their peers, held more conservative, anti-binge drinking attitudes. They thought they disapproved of binge drinking more so than their peers, despite drinking the same amount. In other words, "They think binge drinking is funny and fine. I think, however, that it is a bit immature and perhaps dangerous." Prentice and Miller (1993) found the same disconnect for college students across all four years of college. They believed themselves to be less comfortable about heavy drinking than they thought their friends and peers were. Prentice and Miller suggest that this cognitive error helps to maintain a pro-alcohol, pro-binge drinking norm on many college campuses. This is very similar to the disconnection that research has found for women's fat talk. Women believe other women share the fat talk norm, but they themselves prefer the woman who self-accepts (Becker et al., 2013; Britton et al., 2006; Cruwys et al., 2016; Salk and Engeln-Maddox, 2011; Tompkins et al., 2009). Schroeder and Prentice (1998) believe that pluralistic ignorance offers us an advantage for attitude change as the pro-alcohol norm is an injunctive norm that defines what people approve of or disapprove of in others. They recruited 454 first year college students from an Ivy League university in New England and randomly assigned them to an individual-oriented discussion on alcohol (control condition; $n = 77$) or a peer-oriented discussion that dispelled the pro-alcohol norm (intervention condition; $n = 66$), thus attempting to break through the ignorance or misinformation in pluralistic ignorance. It worked. Students were surveyed four to six months after participating in the groups. Female students were consuming 2.29 drinks per week if they participated in the peer intervention versus 4.02 drinks per week in the control condition. Male students were consuming 3.81 drinks from the peer intervention group versus 5.81 drinks per week from the control group. There were no group differences in alcohol abstinence, just level of consumption. Schroeder and Prentice were also able to document that this difference in level of drinking was a function of a change in their perceived drinking norms. Thus, norm perception was a powerful indicator of behavior.

McAdams (1997) defines a norm as the "informal social regularities that individuals feel obligated to follow because of an internalized sense of duty, because of fear of external nonlegal sanctions, or both" (p. 338). A norm of fat talk fits nicely into this definition. I have already established that the fat talk norm follows principles of pluralistic ignorance in that other women believe they should be fat talking and reassuring other women who fat talk, but that individuals, personally, tend to favor other women showing more body image esteem. Recall that TriDelta's Fat Talk Free Week is an intervention whereby women in a united group proclaim the intent to cease this behavior for at least one week. Further, they place "Friends Don't Let Friends

Fat Talk" signs in high trafficked areas on campus. This is a public and deliberate attempt to resist the assumed norm that women should fat talk. McAdams, who is a law professor, states that some laws work, not because of citizens' fear of violating the law and incurring penalties, but because they sometimes create a public expression or attitude of what is approved of or disapproved. As one example, he speaks about how normative it is for dog owners to use poop bags to clean up their dog's waste in public areas and public parks. As an owner of a large German Shepherd, I realize that my dog can produce some colossal poops. We always clean up after him. This new norm to clean up one's pet's waste was totally absent just a few years ago, however. The kiosks—including the trashcan, the free bags, and the signage— are very powerful prompts for shaping this sanitary behavior, even if there is neither a law requiring it nor any legal consequence for not doing it. People simply know that cleaning up after their dog is the right thing to do. Nobody wants to step in somebody else's dog's poop. Stepping in my Leo's poop would certainly serve to ruin anyone's day.

McAdams suggests that when these rules or laws express public opinion, such as antismoking laws including signage about "no smoking" outside a public building, this helps other individuals update their attitudes about the behavior (i.e., nobody should have to breathe a smoker's secondhand smoke). Such laws and signage make it more convenient for individuals to intervene. It might be easier for a bystander to point to a "no smoking" sign and comment politely, "You might want to put that out or move elsewhere," than it would be for a bystander to intervene if there were no law and no sign. The law and the sign convey that the public believes this is the right thing to do. Even though there could be zero legal consequences for the smoking behavior, the ease with which others can now intervene and show disapproval makes for less effortful social sanctions. Because people like to be approved of by others, such sanctioning can have a pleasant side effect whereby the smoker chooses to smoke elsewhere in the future—or better yet, decides to quit the behavior. Further, the passing of the smoking restriction law enables strengthening of the antismoking attitudes of its citizens.

Of course, I am not suggesting that we attempt to outlaw fat talk, as this would be absurd. However, we do need to hear more expressions of anti-fat talking examples or positive body talk examples if we intend to break fat talk norms. If women are privately attracted to more examples of female self-esteem, yet think all women like fat talk, then we need to make these many private attitudes public—and we need more public role models. Additionally, we need to support the writers, speakers, scholars, and activists who are deliberately fighting cultural norms of the thin ideal and fat talk. This is not an exhaustive list of these advocates, but it does inspire hope to know these professional women are making a difference in our world. Susie Orbach's *Fat is a Feminist Issue* (1982) examined many women's struggles with compulsive eating, now often diagnosed as binge eating disorder, through a feminist cultural lens. I show Diane Israel's documentary *Beauty Mark* (2008) in my classes, as she has approached our societal obsession with beauty from a feminist lens as well. She is able to explain the intersectionality between cultural beauty imperatives, interacting with perfectionistic and compulsive tendencies of elite athletes, and family systems explanations for how she developed her own eating disorder as a world-class triathlete. As mentioned earlier, Abigail Saguy's *What's Wrong with Fat?* (2013) takes a framing approach to deconstruct our culture's disdain of body fat. Naomi Wolf's *Beauty Myth* (2002) focuses on forces such as commercial marketing that hijack women's attention to their physical appearance at the cost of focusing on feminism and women's equality in our society. Wolf describes the "myth" as this false idea that if people achieve ultimate beauty, then everything could be perfect in their lives. She documents how the beauty myth finds itself in multiple arenas of our lives including hunger, violence, sex, vocation, and religion. Finally, actor and activist Geena Davis has created the Institute on Gender in the Media (https://seejane.org/) that subscribes to the maxim, "If she can see it, she can be it." This is a feminist, research-based organization that supports education, research, and activism to improve the lives of children, especially girls ages eleven and under, through collaborations with the entertainment industry. Finally, Bell (2014), who writes for *Huffington Post*, interviewed model Tyra Banks who has joined Special K's campaign "Fight the Fat Talk." Banks says, "Self-acceptance doesn't come from saying 'I have no flaws,' rather confronting what you're not happy about head on, and refusing to let it define you." Tyra Banks calls the way women speak negatively about their bodies "crazy negative" and states that they would not use the words that they say to themselves in their heads to their worst enemies. It is refreshing to see some of these writers, activists, and celebrities fighting against feminine enemies.

Dove's Real Beauty

Historically, advertising directed towards women's concerns about their appearance has used models and images to remind them that they are not living up to cultural standards of beauty. Thus, women buy lots of products to assist them in their pursuit of beauty. Kilbourne (1999) suggests this advertising strategy works very well. It has been an enduring marketing strategy by various companies to get girls and women to buy their merchandise. If the advertisement makes you question if you look good enough or that you could look better, then you might want to give that product a try. As an example, I have wavy hair. Although I sometimes wear it curly, I really like when my hair is straightened instead. You can get my attention immediately with a new anti-frizz cream, gel, or spray, or a fancy wand or brush that promises straight, smooth, wistful hair. It has been a lifetime pursuit. You would think I would have given up by now, but it is easy to succumb to the forces of corporate marketing. I am sure that I am probably influenced in ways that I am totally unaware. If you want to find yourself enlightened and angrier that you thought you could be, watch any of Jean Kilbourne's *Killing Us Softly* (1979) or *Still Killing Us Softly* (1987), or read her newest book *Deadly Persuasion: Why Women and Girls Must Fight the Addictive Power of Advertising* (1999). There are a lot of enlightened scholars who actively challenge these powerful advertising influences on American girls and women. Kilbourne (2018) is a feminist, speaker, and writer and has been a persistent and effective activist against the harmful effects that contemporary advertising has on girls and women in the U.S.

The marketing industry has a long history of peddling women's discord with their appearance, sometimes at the expense of their health. As a chronological example, Phillip Morris marketed cigarettes to women by borrowing language from the feminist movement (Weinstein, 1969). Virginia Slims launched the slogan "You've come a long way, baby" in 1968 to prompt associations with the women's liberation movement that was quite active at the time. The idea was that women had come such a long way in feminist activism towards equality that they could now enjoy cigarettes just as much as men have always been allowed to appreciate them. The advertisements featured colorful, fashionable, sassy looking thin women. Another slogan of the campaign said,

It's different now. Now there's a slim cigarette for women only. New Virginia Slims.

The "Slims" name of these cigarettes was not at all accidental. It reminds women that they wish to be slim and that a common reason why women smoke—especially why female smokers feel they cannot quit—is that cigarettes boost energy (i.e., temporarily and in a manner that backfires across time as one's cardiovascular health slowly fails) and quell appetite. It is easier for many women to smoke than to eat. The ads were also using feminism to tell women they had the choice to smoke—as a backlash to the culture in previous years where women would get in trouble with their parents, boyfriends, or husbands for smoking. The ads were selling choice and freedom. Commercials featured a catchy jingle:

You've come a long way, baby. To get to where you've got to today. You've got your own cigarette, baby. You've come a long, long way.

Although the "baby" add-on was obviously appealing to women's femininity, in hindsight it sounds quite patronizing. These were teenagers and grown women, not babies. Another magazine advertisement launched in 1978 featured at the top of the print a woman outside holding her laundry basket and placing clothing on the laundry line. The caption read,

> Back then, every man gave his wife at least one day out of the house [i.e., to dry laundry]. You've come a long way, baby. Virginia Slims—Slimmer than the fat cigarettes men smoke.

Below the woman, featured in black and white hanging up her laundry, was a much bigger picture of a tall, lean woman in a colorful silk gown smiling and looking sassy. Thus, the Virginia Slims campaign by Phillip Morris tried to tell women they could be slim and they could be feminists by buying their product. Although the logic seems absurd as I write it, the brilliant campaign was successful, sadly, and Phillip Morris was blamed for a spike in the prevalence of female smokers.

As another example of the advertising industry's knowledge of feminist dissent as a strategic marketing campaign, in 2004 Unilever launched a multi-million-dollar campaign called "Dove's Real Beauty." They were very aware that feminists were tired of seeing ultra-thin, heavily made-up women—who were then airbrushed or photoshopped in advertising images—designed to make them feel like they do not live up to those beauty ideals. By making women feel bad, many of them would then buy the product in hopes it would help them look more like the model in the image. As a backlash to the hegemonic thin ideal, Dove featured women of varied colors, shapes, and sizes in an attempt to align with feminist ideology. Billboard, television, and magazine advertisements featured women who were wrinkled, freckled, pregnant, fat, and those with stretch marks. Advertisements would ask provocative questions such as "Wrinkled or wonderful?" and "Flawed or flawless?" The campaign has been a financial success for Unilever and ironically, their flagship product, a firming cream, sold beyond their expectations. The campaign drew the attention of celebrities like Oprah and received massive media attention. Dove's *Evolution* video depicts an everyday woman placed in hair and make-up, then photoshopped with the final image placed on a city billboard. She looks like an attractive yet ordinary person at the start of the video, but then she appears to be a high-power fashion model on the billboard. I have shown this in class, and the evolving image does seem to have an impact. The take-home message is that what people are frequently viewing in advertising is not real. The video won two international advertising awards in 2007 (Waymark, 2007). It reminds me of watching the fashion model Cindy Crawford in a television interview that aired many years ago. The talk show host said something like, "Geez I wish I woke up looking like Cindy Crawford every day." Crawford had a wonderful response. She laughed and said something along the lines of, "Haha, I wish I woke up looking like Cindy Crawford every day too!" Meaning, even a model doesn't just "roll out of bed" each day with the look of a magazine cover model. I have a wonderful hair stylist named Sarina. She is able to give me that magical straight and wispy look that I can never seem to replicate at home. She has learned that I am joking, but I usually take her a picture of some model or actress (i.e., Reese Witherspoon's hair is a favorite … note that she has naturally straight hair!) and I *request* that I look *exactly* like the picture upon exit. Of course, I don't leave looking like Reese Witherspoon, but I usually leave looking like a much better Denise. Thanks, Sarina! It is nice to be pampered in that way every few months as a special grooming occasion, but I cannot imagine what it would be like to feel the need to take that much time and effort to achieve that same look every day. Advertisements are definitely *not* displaying pictures of natural women with the "just rolled out of bed" look.

Millard (2009) conducted focus groups with Canadian women about the Dove campaign. Responses in a group with older women were universally positive. One participant said,

> I think they did a tremendous job with this campaign. I personally do. Cuz it makes people realize it doesn't matter what you look like, or what color you are, or how big or how small you are, or how old you are, you're still beautiful [p. 157].

When asked if they thought the campaign could change minds, this same participant said it would. When asked how, another participant responded,

> It makes it OK to be different. To be different. To not be the typical size, height, color, age, whatever, you don't need to be that [p. 157].

Millard suggested that the campaign provided women with a means to join a fight against impossible beauty standards. The women acknowledged that the campaign was meant to sell products, but this did not bother them. One woman stated, "Even though it's a gimmick, I think it's a good gimmick" (p. 161). The women who had children were especially pleased for their children to be exposed to realistic images. Thus, these women in Millard's focus groups liked the message and saw through the intent to sell. They were positive about it and not very critical. Keep in mind that Millard's focus groups were just asking women their general impressions of the advertisements.

Taylor, Johnston, and Whitehead (2016) also conducted focus groups with women and asked them "Is the Dove campaign for Real Beauty *feminist*?" Overall, their respondents suggested this campaign was better than doing nothing. Many reported that at first it was refreshing to see images of real women in varied races, sizes, and shapes without makeup and without airbrushing or photoshopped alterations. As an example, one participant remarked,

Phew, it was a breath of fresh air. Something new, more realistic, that represented like, how people really are [p. 130].

However, as the discussions progressed, many of the women's initial positive impressions gave way to concerns about the larger meaning of the campaign. Another said,

At first I thought it was great, you know, celebrating women, but then I felt there was something really forced about it, something artificial [p. 130].

Another woman complimented the campaign and thought it would help other women's self-esteem and body image. But after some thought, this same participant became skeptical and commented, "There is nothing radical about saying bigger women can be clean too" (p. 131). That comment cracked me up! When asked if the campaign was *feminist*, the women offered that it felt like a type of faux feminism and that it felt inauthentic. Instead, they suggested that feminism should "shake things up, shock people out of complacency, and transgress accepted norms" (p. 132). They added that Dove's message that women should prioritize being beautiful was totally status quo and that it was not at all original. Taylor et al. (2016) reported that five of their six groups suggested there was nothing feminist or norm-busting about using women dancing around in their underwear to sell products. They also suggested that just resisting typical norms about feminine beauty would not be sufficient to initiate needed political or economic changes for women. They noted that women focused on themselves—on their beauty and their self-esteem—were not going to change the world around them.

Another campaign that was designed to deliberately help enhance young girls' self-esteem was called the *NYC Girls Project*. Hartocollis (2013) writes about a campaign launched in New York City, supported by Major Bloomberg, targeting girls ages seven through twelve mainly through advertisements on buses and in the subway that feature real happy girls with the slogan,

I'm a girl. I'm funny. Playful. Daring. Strong. Curious. Smart. Brave. Healthy. Friendly and Caring. I'm beautiful the way I am.

The program also offered physical fitness programs through their parks and recreation centers, self-esteem classes offered during afterschool hours, and a Twitter campaign called #ImAGirl. The twenty-one girls featured in the ads were not professional models, but real girls who happened to be daughters of NYC workers and their friends. One of the mothers of a featured girl commented that most of them worry that the preteen years can often be an age of a loss of innocence and self-esteem for many girls. Twana Cameron commented, "I think every Mom has those worries. We all can't be models, we can't all be super thin." I looked to see if anyone had done any follow up research to determine the impact of this month-long campaign. Most postings were in October of 2013 around the launch of the campaign; the website has since been archived. I wonder if it made a difference for girls in New York City. It sounded like a "good idea," and I hope researchers will take up projects like these in the future to determine if they really help.

In conclusion, there have been many feminists from a variety of backgrounds and careers who share my passion to reduce fat talk and body snarking and all that these feminine enemies do to harm women. My hope is that this book has increased readers' awareness of the toxic nature of the feminine enemies in our lives. How can women rise to their own personal empowerment when they are locked into a habitual pattern of fat talk which brings them down? And, how can we achieve gender equality in a society that tolerates public body snarking of female celebrities and other women on social media? This book features extensive scientific research explaining the evolutionary and cultural forces explaining our feminine enemies, as well as some social psychological theories and community psychology interventions on how to break free from these misogynist and noxious norms. Culturally, the beauty imperative is pushed at women from relentless angles—how thinness is considered to be the ideal and how fat is severely stigmatized, how advertising maintains traditional gender roles for women or recent attempts to use strategic advertising to spur cultural change. I love the intent for all of the activists in this mission. From a strategic community psychology or public health tradition, however, we have a long way to go. Only one study has shown Fat Talk Free Week helped sorority women reduce their fat talk (Garnett et al., 2014). Further, Becker and colleagues (2017) reviewed multiple studies on The Body Project showing how scientifically successful this intervention has been in improving body image and preventing eating disorders. Future research will want to link their work with fat talk dialogue to better study the relationships between these variables and find what is the best way to improve the lives of girls and women. In the meantime, let's try to reduce the fat talk that could be pulling us down personally and end the body snarking that is damaging womankind. Now that readers understand our feminine enemies, let us work together to make a difference!

Bibliography

Alviola, P. A., Nayga, R. M., Thomsen, M. R., Danforth, D., & Smartt, J. (2014). The effect of fast-food restaurants on childhood obesity: A school level analysis. *Economics and Human Biology, 12,* 110–119. doi:10.1016/j.ehb.2013.05.001.

Ambwani, S., Baumgarner, M., Guo, C., Sims, L., & Aborowitz, E. (2017). Challenging fat talk: An experimental investigation of reactions to body disparaging conversations. *Body Image, 23,* 85–92. doi/10/1016/j.bodyim.2018.08.007.

American Diabetes Association. (2013). Economic costs of diabetes in the U.S. in 2012. *Diabetes Care, 36(4),* 1033–1046. doi:10.2337/12–2625.

American Psychiatric Association. (2013). *Diagnostic and statistical manual of mental disorders (DSM-5)* (5th ed.). Arlington, VA: American Psychiatric Publishing.

Anderson, K. V. (2017). Every woman is the wrong woman: The female presidency paradox. *Women's studies in communication, 40(2),* 132–135. doi:10.1080/07491409.2017.1302257.

Andres, R. (1989). Does the "best" body weight change with age? In A. J. Stunkard & A. Baum (Eds.), *Perspectives in behavioral medicine: Eating, sleeping, and sex* (pp. 99–107). Hillsdale, NJ: Erlbaum.

Andrews, T. M. (March 6, 2017). "Feminism is not a stick with which to beat other women": Emma Watson tells off critics of revealing photo. *The Washington Post, Morning Mix.* Retrieved from https://www.washingtonpost.com/news/morning-mix/wp/2017/03/06/feminism-is-not-a-stick-with-which-to-beat-other-women-emma-watson-tells-off-critics-of-revealing-photo/?utm_term=.6bd9e78263f8.

Andreyeva, T., Puhl, R. M., & Brownell, K. D. (2008). Changes in perceived weight discrimination among Americans: 1995–1996 through 2004–2006. *Obesity, 16(5),* 1129–1134.

Anschutz, D. J., & Engels, R. C. (2010). The effects of playing with thin dolls on body image and food intake in young girls. *Sex Roles, 63,* 621–630. doi:10.1007/s11199–010–9871-6.

Areni, C. S., & Sparks, J. R. (2005). Language and power persuasion. *Psychology & Marketing, 22* (6), 507–525. doi:10.1002/mar.20071.

Arroyo, A., & Andersen, K. K. (2016). Appearance-related communication and body image outcomes: Fat talk and old talk among mothers and daughters. *Journal of Family Communication, 16,* 95–110. doi:10.1080/15267431. 1144604.

Arroyo, A., & Brunner, S. R. (2016). Negative body talk as an outcome of friends' fitness posts on social networking sites: Body surveillance and social comparison as potential moderators. *Journal of Applied Communication Research, 44(3),* 216–235. doi:10.1080/0090 9882.2016.1192293.

Arroyo, A., & Harwood, J. (2012). Exploring the causes and consequences of engaging in fat talk. *Journal of Applied Communication Research. 40(2),* 167–187. doi:10.1080/000909 882.2012.654500.

Arroyo, A., Segrin, C., & Harwood, J. (2014). Appearance-related communication mediates the link between self-objectification and health and well-being outcomes. *Human Communication Research, 40,* 463–482. doi:10.1111/hcre.12036.

Asch, S. E. (1956). Studies in independence and conformity: A minority of one against a unanimous majority. *Psychological Monographs: General and Applied, 70(9)*, 1–70. doi:10.1037/h0093718.

Asher, J. (2017). *Thirteen Reasons Why*. Penguin Group. Retrieved from http://www.thirteen reasonswhy.com/.

Aslam, S. (June 21, 2017). Instagram by the numbers: Stats, demographics & fun facts. Retrieved from https://www.omnicoreagency.com/instagram-statistics/.

Association for Behavioral and Cognitive Therapies (ABCT, 2018). How do I choose a therapist? Retrieved from www.abct.org/Help/?m=mFindHelp&fa=HowtoChooseTherapist.

Avrin, J. (2017). The story of an eating disorder, loss and hope. *Someday Melissa*. Retrieved from http://www.somedaymelissa.org/.

Bacon, L., & Aphramor, L. (2014). *Body respect: What conventional health books get wrong, leave out, and just plain fail to understand about weight*. Dallas, TX: BenBella Books.

Bane, V. L. (1999). *Dr. Laura: The unauthorizedbBiography*. New York: St. Martin's Press.

Barak, A. (2007). Phantom emotions: Psychological determinants of emotional experiences on the Internet. In A. N. Joinson, K. Y. A. McKenna, T. Postmes, & U. D. Reips (Eds.), *The Oxford handbook of Internet psychology* (pp. 303–329). New York: Oxford University Press.

Bardone-Cone, A. M., Balk, M., Lin, S. L., Fitzsimmons-Craft, E. E., & Goodman, E. L. (2016). Female friendships and relations with disordered eating. *Journal of Social and Clinical Psychology, 35(9)*, 781–805. doi:10.1521/jscp.2016.35.9.781.

Barry, V. W., Baruth, M., Beets, M. W., Durstine, J. L., Liu, J., & Blair, S. N. (2014). Fitness vs. fatness on all-cause mortality: A meta-analysis. *Progress in Cardiovascular Diseases, 56(4)*, 382–390. doi: 10.1016/j.pcad.2013.09.002.

Barwick, A., Bazzini, D. G., Martz, D. M., Rocheleau, C., & Curtin, L. (2012). Testing the norm to fat talk for women of varying size: What's weight got to do with it? *Body Image, 9(1)*, 176–179. doi:10.1016/j.bodyim.2011.08.003.

Bazzini, D. G., Curtin, L., Joslin, S., Regan, S., & Martz, D. M. (2010). Do animated Disney characters portray and promote the beauty-goodness stereotype? *Journal of Applied Social Psychology, 40(10)*, 2687–2709. doi:10.1111/j.1559-1816.2010.00676.

Becker, A. E. (2004). Television, disordered eating, and young women in Fiji: Negotiating body image and identity during rapid social change. *Culture, Medicine, and Psychiatry, 28(4)*, 533–559. doi: 10.1007/s11013-004-1067-5.

Becker, C. B., Diedrichs, P., Jankowski, G., & Werchan, C. (2013). I'm not just fat, I'm old: Has the study of body image overlooked "old talk"? *Journal of Eating Disorders, 1*, 6–18. doi:10.1186/2050-2974-1-6.

Becker, C.B. and Stice, E. (2017). From officary to effectiveness to broad implementation: Evolution of the body project. *Journal of Consulting and Clinical Psychology, 85*, 767–782. doi: 10.1037/ccp0000204.

Beever, C., Burns, H., & Karbe, M. (2004). US healthcare's technology cost crisis, strategy and business. Retrieved from www.strategy business.com/press/enewsarticle/enews 033104?pg=all&tid=230.

Bell, P. (March 14, 2014). Tyra Banks joins the "Fight Fat Talk" campaign: A new conversation about body image. *Huffington Post, Conversation changers*. Retrieved from http://www.huffingtonpost.co.uk/2014/01/16/tyra-banks-fight-fat-talk_n_4597942.html.

Bem, S. L. (1987). Probing the promise of androgyny. In M. R. Walsh (Ed.), *The psychology of women* (pp. 206–225). New Haven, CT: Yale University Press.

Bligh, M. C., Schlehofer, M. M., Casad, B. J., & Gaffney, A. M. (2012). Competent enough, but would you *vote* for her? Gender stereotypes and media influence on perceptions of women politicians. *Journal of Applied Social Psychology, 42(3)*, 560–597. doi:10.1111/j.1559-1816.2011.00781.x.

Blue, D. J. (2012). Who are the men who fat talk? Unpublished honors thesis. Appalachian State University. LD175.E5 No.826.

Body Image: An International Journal of Research. (2018). Retrieved from https://www.journals.elsevier.com/body-image.

Bove, C. F., & Sobal, J. (2011). Body weight relationships in early marriage. Weight relevance, weight comparisons, and weight talk. *Appetite, 57(3)*, 729–742. doi:10.1016/j.appet.2011.08.007.

Boyle, C. (2010). *Operation beautiful: Transforming the way you see yourself one Post-it note at a time.* New York: Gotham Books.

Braden, M. (1996). *Women politicians and the media.* Lexington, KY: University of Kentucky Press.

Brand, P. A., Rothblum, E. D., & Solomon, L. J. (1992). A comparison of lesbians, gay men, and heterosexuals on weight and restrained eating. *International Journal of Eating Disorders, 11(3),* 253–259. Retrieved from http://eds.a.ebscohost.com.proxy006.nclive.org.

Braun, T. D., Park, C. L., & Gorin, A. (2016). Self-compassion, body image, and disordered eating: A review of the literature. *Body Image, 17,* 117–131. doi:10.1016/j.bodyim. 2016.03.003.

Britton, L., Martz, D., Bazzini, D., Curtin, L., & LeaShomb, A. (2006). Fat talk and self-presentation of body image: Is there a social norm for women to self-degrade? *Body Image: An International Journal of Research, 3,* 247–254.

Brown, Z., & Tiggemann, M. (2016). Attractive celebrity and peer images on Instagram: Effects on women's mood and body image. *Body Image, 19,* 37–43. doi: 10.1016/j.body im.2016.08.007.

Bureau of Labor Statistics. (2014) Consumer price index. BLS online database. Retrieved from http://www.bls.gov/cpi/data.htm.

Buss, D. M. (1988). The evolution of human intrasexual competition: Tactics of mate attraction. *Journal of Personality and Social Psychology, 54,* 616–628.

Buss, D. M. (1989). Sex differences in human mate preferences: Evolutionary hypotheses tested in 37 cultures. *Behavioral and Brain Sciences, 12(1),* 1–49. doi:10.1017/S0140525 X00023992.

Buss, D. M. (1996). Sexual conflict: Evolutionary insights into feminism and the "battle of the sexes." In D. M. Buss & N. Malamuth (Eds), *Sex, Power, Conflict: Evolutionary and Feminist Perspectives* (pp. 296–318). New York: Oxford University Press.

Buss, D. M. (2008). Attractive women want it all: Good genes, economic investment, parenting proclivities, and emotional commitment. *Evolutionary Psychology, 6(1),* 134–146. Retrieved from http://epjournal.net.

Buss, D. M., & Barnes, M. (1986). Preferences in human mate selection. *Journal of Personality and Social Psychology, 50(3),* 559–570. doi:10.1037/0022-3514.50.3.559.

Cafri, G., Strauss, J., & Thompson, J. K. (2002). Male body image: Satisfaction and its relationship to well-being using the somatomorphic matrix. *International Journal of Men's Health, 1(2),* 215–231.

Cafri G., Yamamiya Y., Brannick M., & Thompson, J. K. (2005). The influence of sociocultural factors on body image: A meta-analysis. *Clinical Psychological Science Practice,12(4),* 421–433. doi:10.1093/clipsy/bpi053.

Calogero, R. M., & Pedrotty, K. N. (2004). The practice and process of healthy exercise: An investigation of the treatment of exercise abuse in women with eating disorders. *Eating Disorders: The Journal of Treatment and Prevention, 12(4),* 273–291. doi:10.1080/10640 260490521252.

Campbell, A., & Hausenblas, H. A. (2009). Effects of exercise interventions on body image: A meta-analysis. *Journal of Health Psychology, 14(6),* 1–14. doi:10.1177/1359105309338977.

Carlin, D. B., & Winfrey, K. L. (2009). Have you come a long way, baby? Hillary Clinton, Sarah Palin, and sexism in 2008 campaign coverage. *Communication Studies, 60(4),* 326–343. doi:10.1080/10510970903109904.

Carroll, S., & Schreiber, R. (1997). Media coverage of women in the 103rd Congress. In P. Norris (Ed.), *Women, media, and politics* (p. 131–148). New York, NY: Oxford University Press.

Caughell, L. (October 2016). When playing the woman card is playing Trump: Assessing the efficacy of framing campaign as historic. *PS: Political Science & Politics (Elections in Focus), 49(4),* 736–742. doi:10.1017/S1049096516001438.

Cawley, J. (2006). Markets and childhood obesity policy. *The Future of Children, 16(1),* 69–88. Retrieved from http://jstor.org.proxy006.nclive.org/stable/3556551.

Centers for Disease Control and Prevention. (1997). *Monthly Vital Statistics Report. Supplement 2. Vol. 45.* Atlanta: National Center for Health Statistics; Report of Final Mortality Statistics, 1995.

Centers for Disease Control and Prevention. (October 22, 2010). Number of Americans with diabetes projected to double or triple by 2050. Retrieved from https://www.cdc.gov/media/pressrel/2010/r101022.html.

Centers for Disease Control and Prevention. (2012). BMI categories. Retrieved from http://www.cdc.gov/healthyweight/assessing/bmi/adult_bmi/index.html.

Chantrill, C. (2014). Government spending in the US. Retrieved from http://usgovernment spending.com.

Chemaly, S. (March 2016). The shocking sexualization of female politicians in porn. *The Establishment*. Retrieved from https://theestablishment.co/the-shocking-sexualization-of-female-politicians-in-porn-c2327f810dd8.

Chow, C. M., & Tan, C. C. (2016). Weight status, negative body talk, and body dissatisfaction: A dyadic analysis of male friends. *Journal of Health Psychology, 21(8)*, 1597–1606. doi:10.1177/1359105314559621.

Chow, C. M., & Tan, C. C. (2018). The role of fat talk in eating pathology and depressive symptoms among mother-daughter dyads. *Body Image, 24*, 36–43. doi.org/10.1016/j.bodyim.2017.11.003.

Close, M. A., Lytle, L. A., Viera, A. J. (2016). Is frequency of fast food and sit-down restaurant eating occasions differentially associated with less healthful eating habits? *Preventive Medicine Reports, 4*, 574–577. doi:10.1016/j.pmedr.2016.10.011.

Cobb, G. (2016). "The Jenner genes definitely helped her": Kardashians, Jenners, and the intersectional politics of thinness. *Critical Studies in Fashion and Beauty, 7(2)*, 173–192. doi:10.1386/csfb.7.2.173_1.

Cohn, L. D., & Adler, N. E. (1992). Female and male perceptions of ideal body shapes: Distorted views among Caucasian college students. *Psychology of Women Quarterly, 16(1)*, 69–79. Retrieved from http://resolver.ebscohost.com.proxy006.nclive.org.

College Board (2017). Average estimated undergraduate budgets, 2016–2017. Retrieved from https://trends.collegeboard.org/college-pricing/figures-tables/average-estimated-under-graduate-budgets-2016-17.

Constantini, E., & Craik, K. H. (1972). Women as politicians: The social background, personality, and political careers of female party leaders. *Journal of Social Issues, 28(2)*, 217–236. Retrieved from http://resolver.ebscohost.com.proxy006.nclive.org.

Cook-Cottone, C.P. (2015). Incorporating positive body image into treatment of eating disorders: A model for attunement and mindful self-care. *Body Image, 14*, 158–167. doi:10.1016/j.bodyim.2015.03.004.

Cook-Cottone, C., Beck, M., & Kane, L. (2008). Manualized-group treatment of eating disorders: Attunement in mind, body, and relationship (AMBR). *Journal of Specialists in Group Work, 33(1)*, 61–83. doi:10.1080/01933920701798570.

Cook-Cottone, C. P., & Vujnovic, R. (2017). Interventions for children and adolescents with eating disorders. In L. Theodores (Ed.), *Handbook of applied interventions for children and adolescents*. New York: Springer Publishing Company.

Cooley, E., Toray, T., Wang, M. C., & Valdez, N. N. (2008). Maternal effects on daughters' eating pathology and body image. *Eating Behaviors, 9(1)*, 52–61. doi:10.1016/j.eatbeh.2007.03.001.

Corning, A. F., & Bucchianeri, M. M. (2016). Is fat talk more believable than self-affirming body talk? *Body Image, 19*, 122–125. doi:10.1016/j.bodyim.2016.09.004.

Corning, A. F., Bucchianeri, M. M., & Pick, C. M. (2014). Thin or overweight women's fat talk: Which is worse for other women's body satisfaction? *Eating Disorders, 22(2)*, 121–135. doi:10.1080/10640266.2013.860850.

Costine, J. (June 27, 2017). Facebook now has 2 billion monthly users … and responsibility. Retrieved from https://techcrunch.com/2017/06/27/facebook-2-billion-users/.

Cotton, C. (2009). Essays—Montaigne. Auckland, New Zealand. The Floating Press.

Coward, L. (2018). Why Trump's fat shaming rants will still do damage after election day. Huffington Post. https://www.huffingtonpost.com/entry/why-trumps-fat-shaming-rants-will-still-do-damage_us_57f2e342e4b0f482f8f0bb55.

Cramer, P., & Steinwert, T. (1998). Thin is good, fat is bad: How early does it begin? *Journal of Applied Developmental Psychology, 19(3)*, 429–451. doi:10.1016/S0193-3973(99)80049-5.

Crandall, C. S. (1988). Social contagion of binge eating. *Journal of Personality and Social Psychology, 55(4)*, 588–598. doi:10.1037/0022-3514.55.4.588.

Crow, S. J., Peterson, C. B., Swanson, S. A., Raymond, N. C., Elke, S. P., Eckert, D., et al. (2009). Increased mortality in bulimia nervosa and other eating disorders. *American Journal of Psychiatry, 166(12)*, 1342–1346. doi:10.1176/appi.ajp.2009.09020247.

Cruwys, T., Leverington, C. T., & Sheldon, A. M. (2016). An experimental investigation of the consequences and social functions of fat talk in friendship groups. *International Journal of Eating Disorders, 49(1)*, 84–91. doi:10.1002/eat/22446.

Cruz Loeza, A., Martz, D. M., & Ballard, M. E. (2018). *Bullying victimization as a predictor of anabolic-androgenic steroid abuse in a nationally representative sample of adolescent males.* Unpublished manuscript.

C-SPAN. (January 23, 2017). Senator Kamala Harris Addresses the Women's March on Washington. https://www.c-span.org/video/?c4651431/senator-kamala-harris-addresses-womens-march-washington.

Currie, J., DellaVigna, S., Moretti, E., & Panthania, S. (2010). The effect of fast-food restaurants on obesity and weight gain. *American Economic Journal: Economic Policy, 2(3)*, 32–63. doi:10.1257/pol.2.3.32.

Darmon, N., & Drewnowski, A. (2008). Does social class predict diet quality? *American Society for Clinical Nutrition, 87(5)*, 1107–1117. Retrieved from http://ajcn.nutrition.org.proxy006.nclive.org.

Darwin, C. (1871). *The descent of man, and selection in relations to sex.* London: Murray.

David, P., & Johnson, M. A. (1998). The role of self in third-person effects about body image. *Journal of Communication, 48(4)*, 37–58. Retrieved from http://eds.a.ebscohost.com.proxy006.nclive.org.

David, P., Morrison, G., Johnson, M. A., & Ross, F. (2002). Body image, race, and fashion models: Social distance and social identification in third-person effects. *Communication Research, 29(3)*, 270–294. Retrieved from http://resolver.ebscohost.com.proxy006.nclive.org.

DeBate, R. D., Gabriel, K. P., Zwald, M., Huberty, J., Zhang, Y. (2010). Changes in psychosocial factors and physical activity frequency among 3rd to 8th grade girls who participated in a developmentally focused youth sport program: a preliminary study. *Journal of School Health, 79(10)*, 474–484. doi:10.2466/PRO.101.3.927–942.

DeBate, R. D., & Thompson, S. H. (2005). Girls on the Run: Improvements in self-esteem, body size satisfaction and eating attitudes/behaviors. *Eating and Weight Disorders, 10(1)*, 5–32. doi:10.1007/BF03353416.

DeBate, R. D., Zhang, Y., & Thompson, S. H. (2007). Changes in commitment to physical activity among 8-to-11-year-old girls participating in a curriculum-based running program. *American Journal of Health Education, 38(5)*, 277–284. Retrieved from http://www.eric.ed.gov/contentdelivery/servlet/ERICServlet?accno=EJ795617.

Denee, M. (June 27, 2017). COOL NEWS! Rebel Wilson launches her own plus size clothing line. *The Curvy Fashionista.* Retrieved from http://thecurvyfashionista.com/2017/06/rebel-wilson-launches-plus-size-clothing-line/.

DeStefano, J. (Unpublished Thesis, 2007). The powerful presence of powerless language: Verbal and nonverbal indicators of hesitation and uncertainty during fat talk Relative to BMI Discrepancies and Peer Influence. Appalachian State University.

Devitt, J. (2002). Framing gender on the campaign trail: Female gubernatorial candidates and the press. *Journalism and Mass Communication Quarterly, 79(2)*, 445–464. Retrieved from http://resolver.ebscohost.com.proxy006.nclive.org.

Dickerson, S. S., & Kemeny, M. E. (2004). Acute stressors and cortisol response: A theoretical integration and synthesis of laboratory research. *Psychological Bulletin, 130(3)*, 335–391. doi:10.1037/0033–2909.130.3.355.

Dittmar, H., Halliwell, E., & Ive, S. (2006). Does Barbie make girls want to be thin? The effect of experimental exposure to images of dolls on the body image of 5- to 8-year-old girls. *Developmental Psychology, 42(6)*, 283–292. doi:10. 1037/0012–1649.42.2.283.

Dockterman, E. (2016). A Barbie for everyone. *Time, 87(4)*, 44–51.

Dolan, K. (2005). Do women candidates play to gender stereotypes? Candidate sex and issues priorities on campaign websites. *Political Research Quarterly, 58(1)*, 31–44. doi: 10.2307/3595593.

Dowd, M. (December 19, 2007). Rush to Judgment. *New York Times: Opinion Pages.* Retrieved

from http://www.nytimes.com/2007/12/19/opinion/19dowd.html?rref=collection%2F
column%2Fmaureen-dowd&action=click&contentCollection=opinion&region=stream
&module=stream_unit&version=search&contentPlacement=2&pgtype=collection.

Dowd, M. (August 31, 2008). Vice in go-go boots? *New York Times, 157(54419)*. Retrieved
from http://go.galegroup.com.proxy006.nclive.org.

Driver, A. M., Martz, D. M., Bazzini, D. G., & Gagnon, S. G. (2012). Media Effects on Body
Image and Overview of Fat Talk. Unpublished honors thesis. Appalachian State University.

Eagly, A. H., & Chrvala, C. (1986). Sex differences in conformity: Status and gender role
interpretations. *Psychology of Women Quarterly, 10(3)*, 203–220. Retrieved from http://
resolver.ebscohost.com.proxy006.nclive.org.

Eagly, A. H., & Karau, S. J. (2002). Role congruity theory of prejudice toward female leaders.
Psychological Review, 109(3), 573–598. doi:10.1037/0033-295X.109.3.573.

Eli, K., Howell, K., Fisher, P. A., & Nowicka, P. (2014). "Those comments last forever": Parents
and grandparents of preschoolers recount how they became aware of their own body
weights as children. *PLOS ONE, 9(11)*, 1–7. doi:10.1371/journal.pone.0111974.

Ellis, J. M., Galloway, A. T., Webb, R. M., & Martz, D. M. (2016). Measuring adult picky eating:
The development of a multidimensional self-report instrument. *Psychological Assessment:
A Journal of Consulting and Clinical Psychology, 29(8)*, 955–966. doi:10.1037/pas0000387.

Engeln, R., & Salk, R. H. (2014). The demographics of fat talk in adult women: Age, body
size and ethnicity. *Journal of Health Psychology, 21(8)*, 1655–1664. doi:10.1177/1359105314
560918.

Engeln, R., Sladek, M. R., & Waldron, H. (2013). Body talk among college men: Content, correlates, and effects. *Body Image, 10(3)*, 300–308. doi:10.1016/j.bodyim.2013.02.001.

Fallon, P., Katzman, M. A., & Wooley, S. C. (1994). *Feminist perspectives on eating disorders.*
New York: Guilford Press.

Fallon, A. E., & Rozin, P. (1985). Sex differences in perceptions of desirable body shape.
Journal of Abnormal Psychology, 94(1), 102– 105. doi:10.1037/0021-843X.94.1.102.

Fardouly, J., Dietrichs, P. C., Vartanian, L. R., & Halliwell, E. (2015). Social comparisons on
social media: The impact of Facebook on young women's body image concerns and
mood. *Body Image, 13*, 38–45. doi:10.1016/j.bodyim.2014.12.002.

Fardouly, J. Pinkus, R. T., & Vartanian, L. R. (2017). The impact of appearance comparisons
made through social media, traditional media, and in person in women's everyday lives.
Body Image, 20, 31–39. doi:10.1016/j.bodyim.2016.11.002.

Feingold, A., & Mazzella, R. (1998). Gender differences in body image are increasing. *Psychological Science, 9*, 190–195. Retrieved from http://eds.b.ebscohost.com.proxy006.
nclive.org.

Fey, T. (2004). Screenplay for *Mean Girls*. Paramount Pictures.

Fiegerman, S. (July 27, 2017). Twitter is now losing users in the U.S. *CNN*. Retrieved from
http://money.cnn.com/2017/07/27/technology/business/twitter-earnings/index.html.

Fiery, M., Martz, D. M., Webb, R. M., & Curtin, L. A. (2016). "She's (and He's) Got it Going
On": An Exploration of Racial Differences in Favorable and Unfavorable Body Talk.
Eating Behaviors, 21, 232–235. doi:/10.1016/j.eatbeh.2016.03.004.

Finn, S. (2016). Fat shaming receives publicity after comments made by presidential candidate
Donald Trump. *UWIRE Text, Academic OneFile*. Retrieved from http://go.galeogroup.
com/ps/i.do?p=AONE&sw=w&u=boon41269&v=2.1&i.d=GALE%7CA473765465&it=
r&asid=7768824d970877a93e454c94768a02df.

Flegal, K. M., Carroll, M. D., Ogden, C. L., & Curtin, L. R. (2010). Prevalence and trends in
obesity among US adults, 1999–2008. *Journal of the American Medical Association,
202(3)*, 235–241. doi:10.1001/jama.2009.2014.

Fleischhacker, S. E., Evenson, K. R., Rodriguez, D. A., & Ammerman, A. S. (2011). A systematic review of fast food access studies. *Obesity Reviews, 12(5)*, 460–471. doi:10.1111/j.1467–
789X.2010.0075x.

Fortin, C. (2014). *Fat talk—The Recognized Epidemic*. YouTube. Retrieved from https://www.
youtube.com/watch?v=SzBO_LtXKd8.

Fortini, A. (April 13, 2008). The feminist reawakening: Hillary Rodham Clinton and the fourth
wave. *New York, 41(14)*, 40–46. Retrieved from http://nymag.com/news/features/46011/.

Fouts, G., & Burggraf, K. (1999). Television situation comedies: Female body images and verbal reinforcements. *Sex Roles, 40,* 473–481. Retrieved from https://link-springer-com.proxy006.nclive.org.

Fouts, G., & Burggraf, K. (2000). Television situational comedies: Female weight, male negative comments, and audience reactions. *Sex Roles, 42,* 925–933.

Franzoi, S. L. (1995). The body-as-object versus the body-as-process: Gender differences and gender considerations. *Sex Roles 33(5/6)*: 417–437. Retrieved from https://link-springer-com.proxy006.nclive.org.

Frechette, J. (2012). Beauty and body image: Beauty myths. *Encyclopedia of gender in the media.* Thousand Oaks, CA: SAGE Publications, Inc.

Frisen, A., & Homlqvist, K. (2010). What characterizes early adolescents with a positive body image? A qualitative investigation of Swedish girls and boys. *Body Image, 7,* 205–212. doi:10.1016/j.bodyim.2010.04.001.

Gabriel, K. K. P., DeBate, R. D., High, R. R., & Racine, E. F. (2011). Girls on the Run: A quasi-experimental evaluation of a developmentally focused youth sport program. *Journal of Physical Activity and Health, 8(2)*, 285–294. Retrieved from http://eds.b.ebscohost.com.proxy006.nclive.org.

Gapinski, K. D., Brownell, K. D., & LaFrance, M. (2003). Body objectification and "fat talk": Effects of emotion, motivation, and cognitive performance. *Sex Roles: A Journal of Research, 48,* 377–388.

Garner, D. M., Garfinkel, P. E., Schwartz, D., & Thompson, M. (1980). Cultural expectations of thinness in women. *Psychological Reports, 47(2)*, 483– 491. doi:10.2466/pr0.1980.47.2.483.

Garnette, B. R., Buelow, R., Franko, D. L., Becker, C., Rodgers, R. F., & Austin, S. B. (2014). The importance of campaign salience as a predictor of attitude and behavior change: A pilot evaluation of social marketing campaign fat talk free week. *Health Communication, 29(10)*, 984–995. doi:10.1080/10410236.2013.827613.

Ghaznavi, J., & Taylor, L. D. (2015). Bones, body parts, and sex appeal: An analysis of #thinspiration images on popular social media. *Body Image, 14,* 54–61. doi:10.1016/j.bodyim.2015.03.006.

Gilbert, P., Clarke, M., Kempel, S., Miles, J. N. V., & Irons, C. (2004). Criticizing and reassuring oneself: An exploration of forms style and reasons in female students. *British Journal of Clinical Psychology, 43(1)*, 31–50. doi:10.1348/014466504772812959.

Gillison, F. B., Lorenc, A. B., Sleddens, E. F. C., Williams, S. L., & Atkinson, L. (2016). Can it be harmful for parents to talk to their child about their weight? A meta-analysis. *Preventive Medicine, 93,*135–146. doi:10.1016/j.ypmed.2016.10.010.

Ginis, K. A. M., Strong, H. A., Arent, S. M., Bray, S. R., & Bassett-Gunter, R. L. (2014). The effects of aerobic-versus strength-based training on women with pre-existing body image concerns. *Body Image, 11(3)*, 219–227. doi:10.1016/j.bodyim.2014.02.004.

Givhan, R. (July 20, 2007). Hillary Rodham Clinton's tentative dip into new neckline territory. *The Washington Post.* Retrieved from http://www.washingtonpost.com/wp-dyn/content/article/2007/07/19/AR2007071902668.html.

Goldmacher, S., & Schreckinger, B. (November 9, 2016). Trump pulls off biggest upset in U.S. history. *Politico.* Retrieved from http://www.politico.com/story/2016/11/election-results-2016-clinton-trump-231070.

Goss, K., & Allan, S. (2014). The development and application of compassion-focused therapy for eating disorders (CFT-E). *British Journal of Clinical Psychology, 53(1)*, 62–77. doi:10.1111/bjc.12039.

Goudarzi, S. (March 14, 2007). Female "fat talk" socially mandatory, study finds. *NBC News.* Retrieved from http://www.nbcnews.com/id/17600911/ns/health-womens_health/t/female-fat-talk-socially-mandatory-study-finds/#.WWkXYdPytsM.

Green, M. C., Brock, T. C., & Kaufman, G. F. (2004). Understanding media enjoyment: The role of transportation into narrative worlds. *Communication Theory, 14(4)*, 311–327. doi:10.1111/j.1468-2885.2004.tb00317.x.

Greer, K. S., Campione-Barr, N., & Lindell, A. K. (2015). Body talk: Siblings' use of positive and negative body self-disclosure and associations with sibling relationship quality and body-esteem. *Journal of Youth and Adolescence, 44(8)*, 1567–1579. doi: 10.1007/s10964-014-0180-1.

Grindy, B., Karaer, A., Riehle, H. (2007). *2008 Restaurant industry forecast*. National Restaurant Association. Retrieved from www.restaurant.org/News-Rsearch/Research/Forecast-2016.

Grogan, S., Williams, Z., & Conner, M. (1996). The effects of viewing same-gender photographic models on body-esteem. *Psychology of Women Quarterly, 20(4)*, 569–575. Retrieved from http://resolver.ebscohost.com/openurl?.

Hahn, R., Teutsch, S., Rothenberg, R., & Marks, J. (1990). Excess deaths from nine chronic diseases in the United States, 1986. *Journal of the American Medical Association. 264(20)*, 2654–2659.

Hakerkamp, N., & Kramer, N. C. (2011). Social comparison 2.0: Examining the effects of online profiles on social-networking sites. *Cyberpsychology, Behavior, and Social Networking, 14(5)*, 309–314. doi:10.1089/cyber.2010.0120.

Halliwell, E. (2013). The impact of thin idealized media images of body satisfaction: Does body appreciation protect women from negative effects? *Body Image,10*, 509–514. doi:10.1016/j.bodyim.2013.07.004.

Halliwell, E., & Diedrichs, P. C. (May 13, 2013). Brief report: Testing a dissonance body image intervention among young girls. *Health Psychology, 32(2)*, 201–204. doi:10.1037/a0032585.

Handler, C. (2017). *Chelsea*. Netflix. Retrieved from https://www.netflix.com/title/80073486.

Hanisch, C. (2009). The personal is political: The women's liberation movement classic with a new explanatory introduction. Retrieved from www.carolhanisch.org/CHwritings/PIP.html.

Hartocollis, A. (September 30, 2013). City unveils campaign to improve girls' self-esteem. *New York Times, NY Region*. Retrieved from http://www.nytimes.com/2013/10/01/nyregion/city-unveils-a-campaign-to-improve-girls-self-esteem.html.

Hausenblas, H. A., & Fallon, E. (2006). Exercise and body image: A meta-analysis. *Psychology and Health, 21(1)*, 33–47. doi:10.1080/ 14768320500105270.

Hayes, D., Lawless, J. J., & Baitinger, G. (2014). Who cares what they wear? Media, gender, and the influence of candidate appearance. *Social Science Quarterly, 95(5)*, 1194–1212. doi:10.1111/ssqu.12113.

Heimer, K. (March 17, 2007). Hillary Rodham Clinton and the media: From intelligent and fair to appallingly sexist and pointless. *National Organization for Women*. Retrieved from http://www.now.org/issues/media1070315hillary_media.html.

Hendrickse, J., Arpan, L. M., Clayton, R. B., & Ridgway, J. L. (2017). Instagram and college women's body image: Investigating the roles of appearance-related comparisons and intrasexual competition. *Computers in Human Behavior, 74*, 92–100. doi:1016/j.chb.2017.04.027.

Henley, J. (2017). "You're in such good shape": Trump criticized for "creepy" comment to Brigitte Macron. The Guardian. https://www.theguardian.com/us-news/2017/jul/14/youre-in-such-good-shape-trump-criticised-for-creepy-comment-on-brigitte-macron.

Hofmann, S. G., Asnaani, A., Vonk, I. J. J., Sawyer, A. T., & Fang, A. (2012). The efficacy of cognitive behavioral therapy: A review of meta-analyses. *Cognitive Therapy Research, 36*, 427–440. doi:10.1007/s10608-013-9595-3.

Homan, K. J., & Tylka, T. L. (2014). Appearance-based exercise motivation moderates the relationship between exercise frequency and positive body image. *Body Image, 11*, 101–108. doi:10.1016/j.bodyim.2014.01.003.

Horby, N., & Strayed, C. (2004). *Wild*. Retrieved from http://www.imdb.com/title/tt2305051/.

Hosman, L. A., & Siltanen, S. A. (2006). Powerful and powerless language forms: Their consequences for impression formation, attributions of control of self and control of others, cognitive responses, and message memory. *Journal of Language and Social Psychology, 25* (1), 33–46. doi: 10.1177/0261927X05284477.

Hospers, H. J., & Jansen, A. (2005). Why homosexuality is a risk factor for eating disorders in males. *Journal of Social and Clinical Psychology, 24(8)*, 1188–1201. doi:10.1521/jscp.2005.24.8.1188.

Hudson, J. I., Hiripi, E., Pope, H. G., & Kessler, R. C. (2007). The prevalence and correlates of eating disorders in the national comorbidity survey replication. *Biological Psychiatry,68(7)*, 714–723.

IMDB 2016. "Frozen Awards." *IMDB*. Retrieved from http://www.imdb.com/title/tt2294629/awards.

Insko, C. A. (1983). Conformity as a function of the consistency of positive self-evaluation with being liked and being right. *Journal of Experimental Social Psychology, 19(4)*, 341–358. doi:10.1016/0022–1031(83)90027–6.

Insko, C. A. (1985). Conformity and group size: The concern with being right and the concern with being liked. *Personality and Social Psychology Bulletin, 11*, 41–50. doi: 10.1177/0146167285111004.

Inter-Parliamentary Union. (2006). Women in politics: 60 years in retrospect. Retrieved from http://www.ipu.org/pdf/publications/wmninfokit06_en.pdf.

Israel, D. (2008). *Beauty mark: Body image & the race for perfection*. Northampton, MA: Media Education Foundation.

Issitt, M. (2016). Princesses as role models for girls: Overview. *Princesses as role models for girls*. Great Neck Publishing. EBSCO CASIAS, Inc.

Jacoby, L., & Cash, T. F. (1994). In pursuit of the perfect appearance: Discrepancies among self-ideal percepts of multiple physical attributes. *Journal of Applied Social Psychology, 24(5)*, 379–396.

Jamieson, K. H. (1995). *Beyond the double bind: Women and leadership*. New York: Oxford University Press.

Jankowski, G. S., Diedrichs, P. C., & Halliwell, E. (2014). Can appearance conversations explain differences between gay and heterosexual men's body dissatisfaction? *Psychology of Men and Masculinity, 15(1)*, 68–77. doi:10.1037/a0031796.

Jellinek, R. D., Myers, T. A., & Keller, K. L. (2016). The impact of doll style of dress and familiarity on body dissatisfaction in 6- to 8-year-old girls. *Body Image, 18*, 78–85. doi:10.1016/j.bodyim.2016.05.003.

Jones, M. D., Crowther, J. H., & Ciesla, J. A. (2014). A naturalistic study of fat talk and its behavioral and affective consequences. *Body Image, 11*, 337–345. doi:10.1016/j.bodyim.2014.05.007.

Kahn, K.F. (1994). The distorted mirror: Press coverage of women candidates for statewide office. *Journal of Politics, 56(1)*, 154–173. Retrieved from http://www.jstor.org/stable/2132350.

Karazsia, B. T., Murnen, S. K., & Tylka, T. L. (2017). Is body dissatisfaction changing across time? *Psychological Bulletin, 143(3)*, 293–320. doi:10.1037/bul0000081.supp.

Kashubeck-West, S., & Tagger, L. (2012). Feminist perspectives on body image and eating disorders in women. In E. N. Williams & C. B. Enns (Eds), *The Oxford Handbook of Feminist Multicultural Counseling Psychology*. New York: Oxford University Press. doi:10.1093/oxfordhb/9780199744220.013.0021.

Kelly, A. C., Carter, J. C., & Borairi, A. (2014). Are improvements in shame and self-compassion early in eating disorders treatment associated with better patient outcomes? *International Journal of Eating Disorders, 47(1)*, 54–64. doi:10.1002/eat.22196.

Kelly, A. C., & Carter, J. C. (2015). Self-compassion training for binge eating disorders: A pilot randomized controlled trial. *Psychology and Psychotherapy: Theory, Research, and Practice, 88(3)*, 285–303. doi: 10.1111/papt.12044.

Kelly, A. C., Miller, K. E., & Stephen, E. (2016). The benefits of being self-compassionate on days when interactions with body-focused others are frequent. *Body Image, 19*, 195–203. doi:10.1016/j.bodyim.2016.10.005.

Kelly, A. C., & Tasca, G. A. (2016). Within-persons predictors of change during eating disorders treatment: An examination of self-compassion, self-criticism, shame, and eating disorders symptoms. *International Journal of Eating Disorders, 49(7)*, 716–722. doi: 10.1002/eat.22527.

Kerr, N.L. (2002). When is a minority a minority? Active versus passive minority advocacy and social influence. *European Journal of Social Psychology, 32(4)*, 471–483. doi:10.1002.ejsp.103.

Kelly, N.R., Cotter, E.W., Tanofsy-Kraff, M., & Mazzeo, S.E. (2015). Racial variations in binge eating, body image concerns, and compulsive exercise among men. *Psychology of Men and Masculinity, 16(3)*, 326–336. doi:10.1037/a0038384.

Kilbourne, J. (1999). *Deadly persuasion: Why women and girls must fight the addictive power of advertising*. New York, New York: The Free Press.

Kilbourne, J. (2018). Retrieved from http://www.jeankilbourne.com/.

Kim, J. W., & Chock, T. M. (2015). Body image 2.0: Associations between social grooming on Facebook and body image concerns. *Computers in Human Behaviors, 48,* 331–339. doi:10.1016/j.chb.2015.01.009.

Kimbrough, A. M., Guadagno, R. E., Muscanell, N. L., & Dill, J. (2013). Gender differences in mediated communication: Women connect more than do men. *Computers in Human Behavior, 29(3),* 896–900. doi:10.1016/ j.chb.2012.12.005.

Kraut, R., Kiesler, S., Boneva, B. Cummings, J., Helgeson, V., & Crawford, A. (2002). Internet paradox revisited. *Journal of Social Issues, 58(1),* 49–74.

Kraut, R. E., Patterson, M., Lundmark, V., Kiesler, S., Mukhopadhyay, T., & Scherlis, W. (1998). Internet paradox: A social technology that reduces social involvement and psychological wellbeing? *American Psychologist, 53(9),* 1017–1032. doi:10.1037/0003–066X.53.9.1017.

Kumar, S., Ghildayal, N. S., & Shah, R. N. (2011). Examining quality and efficiency of the US healthcare system. *International Journal of Health Care Quality Assurance, 24(5),* 366– 388. doi: 10.1108/09526861111139197.

Langlois, J. H., Kalakanis, L., Rubenstein, A. J., Larson, A., Hallam, M., & Smoot, M. (2000). Maxims or myths of beauty? A meta-analytic and theoretical review. *Psychological Bulletin, 26(3),* 390–423.

Langlois, J. H., Ritter, J. M., Roggman, L. A., & Vaugh, L. S. (1991). Facial diversity and infant preferences for attractive faces. *Developmental Psychology, 27(1),* 79–84.

Langlois, J. H., & Roggman, L. A. (1990). Attractive faces are only average. *Psychological Science, 1(2),* 115–121. Retrieved from http://www.jstor.org/stable/40062595.

Lankska, D. J., Lanska, M. J., Hartz, A. J., & Rimm, A. A. (1985). Factors influencing anatomic location of fat tissue in 52,953 women. *International Journal of Obesity, 9(1),* 29–38.

Larson, N. I., Perry, C. L., Story, M., & Neumark-Sztainer, D. (2006). Food preparation by young adults is associated with better diet quality. *Journal of the American Dietetic Association, 106(12),* 2001–2007. doi:10.1016/j.jada.2006.09.008.

Latner, J. D., Knight, T., & Illingworth, K. (2011). Body image and self-esteem among Asian, Pacific Islander, and white college students in Hawaii and Australia. *Eating Disorders, 19(4),* 233–242. doi:10.1080/10640266.2011.584813.

Lawless, J. (2009). Why more women don't hold office. *AFL-CIO.* Retrieved from http://www. aflcio.org/mediacenter/speakout/jennifer_lawless.cfm?RenderFor Print=1.

Lawton, J.F. (1990). *Pretty Woman.* Retrieved from http://www.imdb.com/title/tt0100405/.

Leenaars, L. S., Dane, A. V., & Marini, A. A. (2008). Evolutionary perspective on indirect victimization in adolescence: The role of attractiveness, dating and sexual behavior. *Aggressive Behavior, 24,* 404–415. doi: 10.1002/ab.20252.

Leopold, T. (2016). Why we can't stop body-shaming. *CNN Wire.* Retrieved from http://go. galeogroup.com/ps/i.do?p=AONE&sw=w&u=boon41269&v=2.1&id=GALE%7CA44 9560808&it=r&asid=605a509c4df335399e3468d78560bc32. Accessed 19 May 2017.

Leung, M. Y. M., Carlsson, N. P., Colditz, G. A., & Chang, S. H. (2017). The burden of obesity on diabetes in the United States: Medical expenditure panel survey, 2008–2012. *Value in Health, 20(1),* 77–84. doi:10.1016/j.jval.2016.08.735.

Levine, M. P., & Chapman, K. (2011). Media influences on body image. In T. F. Cash & L. Smolak (Eds.), *Body image: A handbook of science, practice, and prevention.* New York: Guilford Press.

Li, N. P., Bailey, J. M., Kenrick, D. T., & Linsemeier, J. A. W. (2002). The necessities and luxuries of mate preferences: Testing the tradeoffs. *Journal of Personality and Social Psychology, 82,* 947–955. doi:10.1080/10640266.2011.584813.

Lin, B. H., Guthrie, J., & Frazao, E. (1999). Quality of children's diets at and away from home: 1994–1996. *Food Review, 18(2),* 45–50.

Lin, L., & Soby, M. (2016). Appearance comparisons styles and eating disordered symptoms in women. *Eating Behaviors, 23,* 7–12. doi:10.1016/j.eatbeh.2016.06.006.

Lin, L., & Soby, M. (2017). Is listening to fat talk the same as participating in fat talk? *Eating Disorders, 25(2),* 165–172. doi:10.1080/10640266.2016.1255106.

Lind, A., & Brzuzy, S. (2008). *Battleground: Women, gender, and sexuality.* Westport, CT: Greenwood Publishing Group.

Luttrell, Gina. 2014. 7 Moments That Made "Frozen" the Most Progressive Disney Movie Ever. *Mic.* Retrieved from https://mic.com/articles/79455/7-moments-that-made-frozen -the -most-progressive-disney-movie-ever#.fyWjffs0B.

Lydecker, J. A., Riley, K. E., & Grilo, C. M. (2018). Associations of parents' self, child, and other "fat talk" with child eating behaviors and weight. *International Journal of Eating Disorders, 51,* 527–534. doi: 10.1002./eat.22858.

Lynch, M. (2011). Blogging for beauty? A critical analysis of Operation Beautiful. *Women's Studies International Forum, 34(6),* 582–592. doi:10.1016/j.wsif.2011.08.006.

Maas, M. K., Shearer, C. L., Gillen, M. M., & Lefkowitz, E. S. (2015). Sex rules: Emerging adults' perceptions of gender's impact on sexuality. *Sexuality and Culture, 19(4),* 617–636. doi:10.1007/s12119–015–9281–6.

MacDonald, D. E., Dimitropoulos, G., Royal, S., Polanco, A., & Dionne, M. M. (2015). The Family Fat Talk Questionnaire: Development and psychometric properties of a measure of fat talk behaviors within the family context. *Body Image, 12,* 44–52. doi:10.1016/ j.bodyim.2014.10.001.

Maher, B. (February 4, 2011). Episode 201. *Real Time with Bill Maher.* HBO Series. Retrieved from http://www.hbo.com/real-time-with-bill-maher/episodes/0/201-episode/synopsis/ quotes.html.

Major, B., Hunger, J. M., Bunyan, D. P., & Miller, C. T. (2014). The ironic effects of weight stigma. *Journal of Experimental Social Psychology, 51,* 74–80. doi:10.1016/j.esp.2013.11.009.

Malone, C. (June 9, 2016). From 1937 to Hillary Rodham Clinton, how Americans have felt about a woman president. *FiveThirtyEight.* Retrieved from https://fivethirtyeight.com/ features/from-1937-to-hillary-clintonhow-americans-have-felt-about-a-female-president.

Malone, J. (2011). Why are we so obsessed with other people's bodies? Blame body snarking, where your appearance becomes everybody's business. *General Reference Center GOLD.* Retrieved from http://go.galegroup.com/ps/i.do?.

Maltby, J., Giles, D. C., Barber, L., & McCutcheon, L. E. (2005). Intense-personal celebrity worship and body image: Evidence of a link among female adolescents. *British Journal of Health Psychology, 10(1),* 17–32. doi: 10.1348/135910704X15257.

Mann, T., Nolen-Hoeksema, S., Huanh, K., Burgard, D., Wright, A., & Hanson, K. (1997). Are two interventions worse than none? Joint primary and secondary prevention of eating disorders in college females. *Health Psychology, 16(3),* 215–225. doi:10.1037/0278– 6133.16.3.215.

Maor, M., & Cwikel, J. (2016). Mothers' strategies to strengthen their daughters' body image. *Feminism & Psychology, 26(1),* 11–29. doi:10.1177/0959353515592899.

Maphis, L. E., Martz, D. M., Bergman, S. S., & Webb, R. M. (2013). Body size dissatisfaction and avoidance behavior: How gender, age, ethnicity, and relative clothing size predict what some won't try. *Body Image, 10,* 361–368. doi:10.106/j.bodyim.2013.02.003.

Marie Claire. (2016). The top 10 most-followed celebrities on Instagram in 2016. Retrieved from http://www.marieclaire.com/celebrity/a23863/most-followed-celebrities-on- instagram-in-2016/.

Marti, B., Tuomilehto, J., Soloman, V., Kartovaara, J., Korhonen, H. J., & Pietinen (1991). Body fat distribution in a Finnish population: Environmental determinants and pre- dictive power for cardiovascular risk factor levels. *Journal of Epidemiology and Com- munity Health, 45(2),* 131–137. Retrieved from http://www.jstor.org/stable/25567156.

Martz, D., Curtin, L., & Bazzini, D. (2012). Fat talk and body image. *Encyclopedia of body image and human appearance* (pp. 120–127). San Diego: Academic Press.

Martz, D. M., Petroff, A. B., Curtin, L. A., & Bazzini, D. G. (2009). Gender differences in fat talk among American adults: Results from the psychology of size survey. *Sex Roles, 61(1/2),* 34–41. doi: 10.1007/s11199–009–9587–7.

Martz, D. M., & Rogers, C. B. (November-December 2016). Understanding and treating women's body image and eating disorders. *North Carolina Medical Journal, 77(6),* 426– 429. doi:18043/ncm.77.6.426.

Mathison, M., & Spielberg, S. (1982). *E.T., The Extra-Terrestrial.* Los Angeles: Universal Stu- dios, Inc.

Mattel. (2016). Fastfacts about Barbie. Retrieved from http://www.barbiemedia.com/ about- barbie/fast-facts.html.

Mazziotta, J. (May 24, 2016). Amy Shumer shuts down the body shaming "Trolls": "I think I look strong and healthy." *People bodies.* Retrieved from http://people.com/bodies/amy- schumer-shuts-down-the-body-shaming-trolls/.

McAdams, R. H. (1997). The origin, development, and regulation of norms. *Michigan Law Review, 96(2),* 338–433. doi: 10.2307/1290070.

McArdle, K. A., & Hill, M. S. (2009). Understanding body dissatisfaction in gay and hetero-sexual men: The roles of self-esteem, media, and peer influence. *Men and Masculinities, 11(5),* 511–532. doi:10.1177/1097184X07303728.

McCarroll, H. R. (2000). Congenital anomalies: A 25-year overview. *The Journal of Hand Surgery, 25A(6),* 1007–1037. doi:10.1053/jhsu.2000.6457.

McCreary, D. R., & Sasse, D. K. (2000). An exploration of the drive for muscularity in ado-lescent boys and girls. *Journal of American College Health, 48(6),* 297–304.

McGinnis, J. M., & Foege, W. H. (1993). Actual causes of death in the United States. *Journal of the American Medical Association, 270(18),* 2207–2212.

McMaughan, D. K., Huber, J. C., Forjuoh, S. N., Vuong, A. M., Helduser, J., Ory, M. G., & Bolin, J. N. (January-March 2016). Physician recommendation of diabetes clinical pro-tocols. *Hospital Topics, 94(1),* 15–21. doi: 10.1080/00185868.2016.1142313.

McPhail, D. (2009). What to do with the "Tubby Hubby"? "Obesity," the Crisis of Masculinity, and the Nuclear Family in Early Cold War Canada. *Antipode, 41(5):* 1021–1050. doi: 10.1111/j.1467–8330.2009.00708.x.

Merriam-Webster (2017). Definition of a norm. Retrieved from https://www.merriam-webster.com/dictionary/norm.

Mikell, C. M., & Martz, D.M. (2016). Women's Fat Talk Can Kill the Mood for Men. *Eating Behaviors, 21,* 211–213. doi:10.1016/j.eatbeh.2016.03.007.

Miles, C. Martz, D. M., Webb, R. M., Bazzini, A., & Morsch, M. (2018). Fat talk and romantic relationships: Does fat talk affect relationship satisfaction and sexual satisfaction? Unpublished Master's Thesis, Appalachian State University.

Millard, J. (2009). Performing beauty: Dove's Real Beauty campaign. *Symbolic Interaction, 32(2),* 146–168. doi: 10.1525/si.2009.32.2.146.

Miller, D. T., & McFarland, C. (1991). When social comparison goes awry: The case of plu-ralistic ignorance. In J. Suls & T. Wills (Eds), *Social comparison: Contemporary theory and research* (pp. 28–313). Hillsdale, NJ: Lawrence Erlbaum.

Mills, J., & Fuller-Tyszkiewicz, M. (2017). Fat talk and body image disturbance: A systematic review and meta-analysis. *Psychology of Women Quarterly, 41(1),* 114–129. doi:10.1177/0361684316675317.

Mills, J., & Fuller-Tyszkiewicz, M. (2018). Nature and consequences of positively-intended fat talk in daily life. *Body Image, 26,* 38–49. doi:10.1016/j.bodyim.2018.05.004.

Molinaro, N. (2014). Tri Delta fights to end fat talk. *The Miami Student.* Retrieved from http://go.galeogroup.com/ps/i.do?p=AONE&sw=w&u=boon41269&v=2.1&id=GALE%7CA400292843&it=r&asid=bfa86f1e102ca58cd3df00df4ac17c30.

Moore, E. S., Wilkie, W. L., & Desrochers, D. M. (2017). All in the family? Parental roles in the epidemic of childhood obesity. *Journal of Consumer Research, 43(5),* 824–859. doi:10.1093/jcr/ucw059.

Morrison, M. A., Morrison, T. G., & Sager, C. L. (2004). Does body dissatisfaction differ between gay man and lesbian women and heterosexual men and women? A meta-analytic review. *Body Image, 1,* 127–138. doi:10.1016/j.bodyim.2004.01.002.

Morsch, M., Martz, D. M., Miles, C., & Bazzini. (2018). What did she just say: The effect of varying levels of women's fat talk on their likeability. Unpublished honors thesis: Appa-lachian State University.

Moscovici, S. (1976). *Social influence and social change.* Academic Press: London.

Moscovici, S. (1980). Toward a theory of conversion behavior. In L. Berkowitz (Ed.), *Advances in experimental social psychology* (Vol. 13, pp. 209–239). New York: Academic Press.

Moscovici, S. (1985). Social influence and conformity. In G. Lindsey & E. Aronson (Eds.), *The handbook of social psychology* (Vol. 2, 3rd ed., pp. 347–412). New York: Random House.

Muennig, P. (2008). The body politic: The relationship between stigma and obesity-associated disease. *BMI Public Health, 8(1),* 128–138. doi:10.1186/1471–2458–8–128.

Muscanell, N. L., & Guadagno, R. E. (2012). Make new friends or keep the old: Gender and personality differences in social networking use. *Computers in Human Behavior, 28(1),* 107–112. doi:10.1016/j.chb.2011.08.016.

Myers, D. G. (2002). *Social Psychology* (7th ed.). Boston, MA: McGraw-Hill.

National Eating Disorders Association [NEDA], 2018. https://www.nationaleatingdisorders.org/.

NCHS (National Center for Health Statistics). Health, United States (1998). *Socioeconomic Status and Health Chartbook.* Hyattsville, MD: U.S. Dept. of Health and Human Services.

Nedeau, J. (November 10, 2008). Election reflection #5: Did sexism prevail in 2008? Retrieved from http://women'srights.chang.org=blog=view=election reflection5 did sexism prevail in 2008.

Neff, K. D. (2003). Self-compassion: An alternative conceptualization of a healthy attitude toward oneself. *Self and Identity, 2(2),* 85–101. doi:10.1080/15298860309032Neff,.

Neumark-Sztainer, D., Bauer, K. W., Friend, S., Hannan, P. J., Stat, H. M., Story, M., & Berge, J. M. (2010). Family weight talk and dieting: How much do they matter for body dissatisfaction and disordered eating behaviors in adolescent girls? *Journal of Adolescent Health, 47(3),* 270–276. doi:10.1016/j.jadohealth.2010.02.001.

Nichter, M. (2000). *Fat talk: What girls and their parents say about dieting.* Cambridge, MA: Harvard University Press.

Nichter, M., & Vuckovic, N. (1994). Fat talk. In N. Sault (Ed.), *Many mirrors: Body image and social relations* (pp. 109–131). New Brunswick, NJ: Rutgers University Press.

Norman, S., Natarajan, V. S., & Sen, K. C. (2015). Cultural differences in promotion of products in the fast food industry: A case of the U.S. and Sweden Dyad. *Journal of Higher Education Theory & Practice, 15(5),* 45–54.

Noxon, M. (2017). *To the Bone.* AMBI Group, Sparkhouse Media. Retrieved from http://www.imdb.com/title/tt5541240/.

O'Barr, W. M. (1982). *Linguistic evidence: Language, power, and strategy in the courtroom.* New York: Academic Press.

O'Dea, J. A. (1995). Body image and nutritional status among adolescents and adults—A review of the literature. *Australian Journal of Nutrition and Dietetics, 52(2),* 56–68. Retrieved from http://eds.a.ebscohost.com.

Ogden, C. L., Carroll, M. D., Curtin, L. R., McDowell, M. A., Tabak, C. J., & Flegal, K. M. (2006). Prevalence of overweight and obesity in the United States, 1999–2004. *Journal of the American Medical Association, 295(1),* 1549–1555.

Olivardia, R., Pope, H. G., Borowiecki, & Cohane, G. H. (2004). Biceps and body image: The relationship between muscularity and self-esteem, depression, and eating disorder symptoms. *Psychology of Men & Masculinity, 5(2),* 112–120. doi:10.1037/1524–9220.5.2.112.

Orbach, S. (1982). *Fat is a Feminist Issue.* New York: Berkley Books.

Organization for Economic Cooperation and Development: OECD health statistics-frequently requested data (2014). *OECD health statistics 2014 online database.* Retrieved from http://www.oecd.org/els/ health-systems/oecd-health-statistics-2014-frequently-requested-data.htm.

Ornstein, N. J., & Mann, T. E. (July 2016). The republicans waged a 3-decade war on government. They got Trump. *Vox,* Retrieved from https://www.vox.com/2016/7/18/12210500/diagnosed-dysfunction-republican-party.

Ousley, L., Cordero, E. D., & White, S. (2008). Fat talk among college students: How undergraduates communicate regarding food and body weight, shape, & appearance. *Eating Disorders, 16(1),* 73–84. doi:10.1080/10640260701773546.

Owen, R., & Spencer, R. M. C. (2013). Body ideals in women after viewing images of typical and healthy weight models. *Body Image, 10,* 489–494. doi:10.1016/j.bodyim.2013.04.005.

Owens, L., Shute, R., & Slee, P. (2000). I'm in and you're out: Explanations for teenage girls' indirect aggression. *Psychology, Evolution, and Gender, 2,* 1–8.

Oxford Dictionary of Quotations. (2004). Duchess of Windsor [Wallis Simpson]. Ed. Elizabeth Knowles. Oxford University Press.

Palmeira, L., Pinto-Gouveia, J., & Cunha, M. (2017). Exploring the efficacy of an acceptance, mindfulness, and compassion-based group intervention for women struggling with their weight (Kg-Free): A randomized controlled trial. *Appetite, 112,* 112–116. doi:10.1016/j.appet.2017.01.027.

Park, S. Y., Yun, G. W., McSweeney, J. H., & Gunther, A. C. (2007). Do third-person perceptions of media influence contribute to pluralistic ignorance on the norm of ideal female thinness? *Sex Roles, 57(7/8),* 569–578. doi: 10.1007/s11199–007–9284–3.

Parker, S., Nichter, M., Vucovic, N., Sims, C., & Ritenbaugh, C. (1995). Body image and weight concerns among African American and White adolescent females: Differences that make a difference. *Human Organization, 54(2)*, 103–114. doi:10.17730/humo.54.2.06 h663745q650450.

Payne, L., Martz, D., Tompkins, K. B., Petroff, A., & Farrow, C. (2010). Gender Comparisons of fat talk in the United Kingdom and the United States. *Sex Roles: A Journal of Research, 65(7/8)*, 557–565. doi:10.1007/s1119-101-9881-4.

Pellegrini, A. D., & Long, J. D. (2003). A sexual selection theory longitudinal analysis of sexual segregation and integration in early adolescence. *Journal of Experimental Child Psychology, 85*, 257–278.

Perloff, R. M. (2014). Social media effects on young women's body image concerns: Theoretical perspectives and an agenda for research. *Sex Roles, 71(11/12)*, 363–377. doi:10.1007/s11199-014-0384-6.

Petersen, J. L., & Hyde, J. S. (2010). A meta-analytic review of research on gender differences in sexuality, 1993–2007. *Psychological Bulletin, 136*, 21–38.

Planned Parenthood. (2014). 2013–2014 Annual Report. Retrieved from https://www.plannedparenthood.org/files/6714/1996/2641/2013-2014_Annual_Report_FINAL_WEB_VERSION.pdf.

Planned Parenthood. (2017). Planned Parenthood at a glance. Retrieved from https://www.plannedparenthood.org/about-us/who-we-are/planned-parenthood-at-a-glance.

Pope, H. G., Phillips, K. A., & Olivardia, R. (2000). *The Adonis complex: The secret crisis of male body obsession*. New York: Free Press.

Prentice, A. M., & Jebb, S. A. (2003). Fast foods, energy density and obesity: A possible mechanistic link. *Obesity Research, 4(4)*, 187–194. doi: 10.1046/j.1467–789X.2003.00117.x.

Prentice, D.A. (2007). Pluralistic Ignorance. In R. F. Baumeister & K. D. Vohs (Eds), *Encyclopedia of social psychology*, Thousand Oaks: Sage Publications, Inc.

Prentice, D. A., & Miller, D. T. (1993). Pluralistic ignorance and alcohol use on campus: Some consequences of misperceiving the social norm. *Journal of Personality and Social Psychology, 64(2)*, 243–256. doi:10.1037/0022-3514.64.2.243.

Pugh, T., & Aronstein, S. (Eds). (2012). *The Disney middle ages: A fairy tale and fantasy past*. New York: Palgrave Macmillan.

Puhl, R. M., & Heuer, C. A. (2009). The stigma of obesity: A review and update. *Obesity: A Research Journal, 17(5)*, 941–964. doi:10.1038/oby.2008.636.

Puhl, R. M., & Heuer, C. A. (2010). Obesity stigma: Important considerations for public health. *American Journal of Public Health, 100(6)*, 1019–1028. doi:10.2105/AJPH.2009.15 9491.

Reel, J., Greenleaf, C., Baker, W. K., Aragon, S., Bishop, D., Cachaper, C., Handwerk, P., Lociero, J., Rathburn, L., Reid, W. K., & Hattie, J. (2007). Relations of body concerns and exercise behavior: A meta-analysis. *Psychological Reports, 101(3)*, 927–942. doi:10.2466/pr0.101.3.927–942.

Ricciardelli, L. A., McCabe, M. P., Williams, R. J., & Thompson, J. K. (2007). The role of ethnicity and culture in body image and disordered eating among males. *Clinical Psychology Review, 27(5)*, 582–606. doi:10.1016/j.cpr.2007.01.016.

Rice, K., Prichard, I., Tiggemann, M., & Slater, A. (2016). Exposure to Barbie: Effects on thin-ideal internalisation, body esteem, and body dissatisfaction among young girls. *Body Image, 19*, 142–149. doi:10.1016/j.bodyim.2016.09.005.

Robinson, G., & Saint-Jean, A. (1995). The portrayal of women politicians in the media. In F. P. Gingras (Ed.), *Gendered politicians in contemporary Canada* (pp. 112–155). Toronto, Canada: Oxford University Press.

Rocheleau, C. A., Martz, D. M., Walker, K., Curtin, L. A., & Bazzini, D. G. (Unpublished Manuscript). Social impressions of fat talk: Less than ideal.

Rochman, B. (October 13, 2010). Do I look fat? Don't ask. A campaign to ban "Fat Talk." *Time*. Retrieved from http://content.time.com/time/nation/article/0,8599,2025345,00.html.

Rogers, C. B., Martz, D. M., Webb, R. M., & Galloway, A. T. (2017). Everyone else is doing it (I think): The power of perception in fat talk. *Body Image, 20*, 116–119. doi:10.1016/j.bodyim.2017.01.004.

Rooney, K. (July 18, 2017). Reebok trolls Donald Trump over Brigitte Macron comment. *Hnhh, Entertainment.* Retrieved from http://www.hotnewhiphop.com/reebok-trolls-donald-trump-over-brigitte-macron-comment-news.35191.html.

Rosenheck, R. (2008). Fast food consumption and increase caloric intake: A systematic review of a trajectory towards weight gain and obesity risk. *Obesity Reviews, 9(6),* 535–547. doi: 10.1111/j.1467–789X.2008.00477x.

Ross, L., Greene, D., & House, P. (1977). The false consensus effect: An egocentric bias in social perception and attribution processes. *Journal of Experimental Social Psychology, 13(3),* 279–301. doi:10.1016/0022–1031(77)90049-X.

Ross, R., Blair, S., de Lannoy, L., Despres, J. P., & Lavie, C. J. (2015). Changing the endpoints for determining effective obesity management. *Progress in Cardiovascular Diseases, 57(4),* 330–336. doi:10.1016.j.pcad.2014.10.002.

Royal, S., MacDonald, D. E., & Dionne, M. M. (2013). Development and validation of the fat talk questionnaire. *Body Image, 10(1),* 62–69. doi:10.1016/j.bodyim.2012.10.003.

Rozin, P., & Fallon, A. E. (1988). Body image, attitudes to weight and misperceptions of figure preferences of the opposite sex: A comparison of men and women in two generations. *Journal of Abnormal Psychology, 97(3),* 342–345.

Rubin, L. R., Nemeroff, C. J., & Russo, N. F. (2004). Exploring feminist women's body consciousness. *Psychology of Women Quarterly, 28(1),* 27–37. doi:10.10361–6843/04.

Rudiger, J., & Winstead, B. (2013). Body talk and body-related co-rumination: Associations with body image, eating attitudes, and psychological adjustment. *Body Image, 10,* 462–471. doi:10.1016/bodyim.2013.07.010.

Rudloff, M. (2016). *(Post)feminist paradoxes: The sensibilities of gender representation in Disney's Frozen.* Cengage Learning: The University of Western Australia, Women's Studies.

Saguy, A. C. (2013). *What's Wrong with Fat?* New York: Oxford University Press.

Salk, R., & Engeln-Maddox, R. (2011). If you're fat, then I'm humungous! Frequency, content, and impact of fat talk among college women. *Psychology of Women Quarterly, 35(1),* 18–28. doi:10.1177/0361684310384107.

Santee, R. T., & Jackson, S. E. (1982). Identity implications of conformity: Sex differences in normative and attributional judgments. *Social Psychology Quarterly, 45(2),* 121–125. Retrieved from http://www.jstor.org/stable/3033935.

Saunders, E. (July 24, 2015). Kylie Jenner plastic surgery timeline—before and after pictures. *Lifestyle.* Retrieved from http://lifestyle.one/heat/celebrity/news/kylie-jenner-plastic-surgery-timeline/.

Schroeder, C. M., & Prentice, D. A. (1998). Exposing pluralistic ignorance to reduce alcohol use among college students. *Journal of Applied Social Psychology, 28(23),* 2150–2180.

Schutzwohl, A. (2006). Judging female figures: A new methodological approach to male attractiveness judgments of female waist-to-hip ratio. *Biological Psychology, 71(2),* 223–229. doi:10/1016/j.biopsycho.2005.04.005.

Schwartz, B. (April 14, 2015). Kelly Clarkson can't be put down: "I'm never going to obsess about my weight." *Redbook.* Retrieved from http://www.redbookmag.com/life/news/a21410/kelly-clarkson/.

Shannon, A., & Mills, J. (2015). Correlates, causes, and consequences of fat talk: A review. *Body Image, 15,* 158–172. doi:10.1016/j.bodyim.2015.09.003.

Sharpe, H., Naumann, U., Treasure, J., & Schmidt, U. (2013). Is fat talking a causal risk factor for body dissatisfaction? A systematic review and meta-analysis. *International Journal of Eating Disorders, 46(7),* 643–652. doi: 10.1002/eat.22151.

Sheppard, N. (October 8, 2008). Indecent wire service pictures of Sarah Palin. *Media Research Center.* Retrieved from http://newsbusters.org/blogs/noel-sheppard/2008/10/08/indecent-wire-service-pictures-sarah-palin.

Sherman, A. M., & Zurbriggen, E. L. (2014). "Boys can be anything": Effect of Barbie play on girls' career cognitions. *Sex Roles, 70(5/6),* 195–208. doi:10.1007/s11199–014–0347-y.

Shlesinger, I. (2015). *Freezing Hot.* New Wave Entertainment Television.

Siever, M. D. (1994). Sexual orientation and gender factors in socioculturally acquired vulnerability to body dissatisfaction and eating disorders. *Journal of Consulting and Clinical Psychology, 62(2),* 252–260.

Sifers, S. K., & Shea, D. N. (2013). Evaluations of Girls on the Run/Girls on Track to enhance self-esteem and well-being. *Journal of Clinical Sport Psychology, 7(1)*, 77–85.

Singh, D., Dixson, B. J., Jessop, T. S., Morgan, B., & Dixson, A. F. (2010). Cross-cultural consensus for waist-hip ration and women's attractiveness. *Evolution and Human Behavior, 31(3)*, 176–181. doi:10/1016/j.evolhumbehav.2009.09.001.

Singh, D., & Singh, D. (2011). Shape and significance of feminine beauty: An evolutionary perspective. *Sex Roles, 64*, 723–731. doi:10.1007/s11199–011–9938-z.

Sladek, M. R., Engeln, R., & Miller, S. A. (2014). Development and validation of the Male Body Talk Scale: A psychometric investigation. *Body Image, 11(3)*, 233–244. doi:10.1016/j.bodyim.2014.02.005.

Slater, M. D. (2007). Reinforcing spirals: The mutual influence of media selectivity and media effects and their impact on individual behavior and social identity. *Communication Theory, 17(3)*, 281–303. doi:10.1111/j.1468–2885.2007.00296.x.

Smolak, L., Levine, M., & Myers, T. A. (2015). Feminist theories of eating disorders. *The wiley handbook of eating disorders.* doi:10.1002/9781118574089. Retrieved from http://onlinelibrary.wiley.com/doi/10.1002/9781118574089.ch19/summary.

Sobal, J., & Maurer, D. (Eds.). (1999). *Interpreting weight: The social management of fatness and thinness.* New York: Walter de Gruyter, Inc.

Socialblade. (2017). Top 100 Instagram users by followers. Retrieved from https://socialblade.com/instagram/top/100/followers.

Spitzer, B. L, Henderson, K. A., & Zivian, M. T. Gender differences in population versus media body sizes: A comparison over four decades. *Sex Roles, 40(7/8)*, 545–565. doi:10.1023/A:1018836029738.

Sprecher, S., Treger, S., & Sakaluk, J. K. (2013). Premarital sexual standards and sociosexuality: Gender, ethnicity, and cohort differences. *Archives of Sexual Behavior, 42(8)*, 1395–1405. doi:10.1007/s10508–013–0145–6.

Spurlock, M. (2004). *Supersize Me.* http://morganspurlock.com/work/super-size-me/.

Staniford, J., Breckon, J. D., & Copeland, R. J. (2012). Treatment of childhood obesity: A systematic review. *Journal of Child and Family Studies, 21(4)*, 545–564. doi:10.1007/s10826–011–9507–7.

Stephens, M. A. P., Franks, M. M., Rook, K. S., Iida, M., Hemphill, R. C., & Salem, J. K. (2013). Spouses' attempts to regulate day-to-day dietary adherence among patients with type 2 diabetes. *Health Psychology, 32*, 1029–1037. doi:10.1037/a0030018.

Stice, E. (2002). Risk and maintenance factors for eating pathology: A meta-analytic review. *Psychological Bulletin, 128(5)*, 825–848. doi:10.1037/0033–2909.128.5.825.

Stice E., Marti C. N., Shaw, H., & Jaconis, M. (2009). An 8-year longitudinal study of the natural history of threshold, subthreshold, and partial eating disorders from a community sample of adolescents. *Journal Abnormal Psychology, 118(3)*, 587–597. doi:10.1037/a0016481.

Stice, E., Maxfield, J., & Wells, T. (2003). Adverse effects of social pressure to be thin on young women: An experimental investigation of the effects of "fat talk." *International Journal of Eating Disorders, 34(1)*, 108–117. doi:10.1002/eat.10171.

Stice, E., Rohde, P., Gau, J., & Shaw, H. (2012). Effect of a dissonance-based prevention program on risk for eating disorder onset in the context of eating disorder risk factors. *Prevention Science, 13(2)*, 129 –139. doi:10.1007/s11121–011–0251–4.

Stice, E., Schupak-Neuberg, E., Shaw, H. E., & Stein, R. I. (1994). Relation of media exposure to eating disorder symptomatology: An examination of mediating mechanisms. *Journal of Abnormal Psychology, 103(4)*, 836–840.

Strandbu, A., & Kvalem, I. L. (2014). Body talk and body ideals among adolescent boys and girls: A mixed-gender focus group study. *Youth and Society, 46(5)*, 623–641. doi:10.1177/0044118X12445177.

Strang, F. (January 2014). Has Kendall Jenner had a nose job? Kim Kardashian's teenage sister slimmed down nose sparks speculation. *Daily Mail.* Retrieved from http://www.dailymail.co.uk/tvshowbiz/article-2541263/Kendall-Jenner-sparks-speculation-steps-thinner-looking-nose-resembling-sister-Kims.html.

Swami, V. (2015). Cultural influences on body size ideals: Unpacking the impact of Western modernization. *European Psychologist, 20(1)*, 44–51. doi:10.1027/1016–9040/a000150.

Swami, V., Frederick, D. A., Aavik, T., Alcalay, L., Allik, J., Anderson, D., ... Zivcic-Becirevic, I. (2010). The attractive female body weight and body dissatisfaction in 26 countries across 10 world regions: Results of the International Body Project I. *Personality and Social Psychology Bulletin, 36,* 309–325. doi: 10.1177/0146167209359702.

Swami, V., & Szmigielska, E. (2013). Body image concerns in professional fashion models: Are they really an at-risk group? *Psychiatry Research, 207(1),* 113–117. doi:10.1016/j.psychres.2012.09.009.

Swami, V., Taylor, R., & Carvalho, C. (2011). Body dissatisfaction assessed by the Photographic Figure Rating Scale is associated with sociocultural, personality, and media influences. *Scandinavian Journal of Psychology, 52,* 57–63. doi: 10.1111/j.1467–9450.2010.00836.x.

Taniguchi, E., & Lee, H. E. (2012). Cross-cultural differences between Japanese and American female college students in the effects of witnessing fat talk on Facebook. *Journal of Intercultural Communication Research, 41(3),* 260–278. doi:10.1080/17475759.2012.728769.

Tannen, D. (1990). *You just don't understand: Women and men in conversation.* New York: Ballantine Books.

Tannen, D. (1994). *Gender and Discourse.* Oxford: Oxford University Press.

Taylor, J., Johnston, J., & Whitehead, K. (2016). A corporation in feminist clothing? Young women discuss the Dove "Real Beauty" campaign. *Critical Sociology, 42(1),* 123–144.

Thornhill, C., Curtin, L., Bazzini, D. G., & Martz, D. M. (January 2016). *The effect of race on perceptions of fat talk among college women.* Poster presented at the Society for Personality and Social Psychology, San Diego, CA.

Tiggemann, M., & Zaccardo, M. (2015). "Exercise to be fit, not skinny": The effect of fitspiration imagery on women's body image. *Body Image, 15,* 61–67. doi:10.1016/j.bodyim.2015.06.003.

Time. (October 13, 2014). The 25 most influential teens of 2014. Retrieved from http://time.com/3486048/most-influential-teens-2014/.

Time. (October 27, 2015). The 30 most influential teens of 2015. Retrieved from http://time.com/4081618/most-influential-teens-2015/.

Tomiyama, A. J., & Mann, T. (May 1, 2013). If fat shaming reduced obesity, there would be no fat people. *Hastings Center Report, 43(3),* 4–5. doi:10.1002/hast.166.

Tompkins, K. B., Martz, D. M., Rocheleau, C. A., & Bazzini, D. G. (2009). Social likeability, conformity, and body talk: Does fat talk have a normative rival in body image conversations? *Body Image, 6,* 292–298. doi:10.1016/j.bodyim.2009.07.005.

Tribole, E., & Resch, E. (2012). *Intuitive eating: A revolutionary program that works.* New York: St. Martins Griffin.

Tucker, K., Martz, D., Curtin, L., & Bazzini, D. (2007). Examining "Fat Talk" experimentally in a female dyad: How are women influenced by another woman's body presentation style? *Body Image: An International Journal of Research, 4(2),* 157–164. doi:10.1016/j.bodyim.2006.12.005.

Tylka, T.L. (2012). Positive psychology perspective on body image. In T.F. Cash (Ed.), *Encyclopedia of body image and human experience* (Vol. 2, pp. 657–663). Sand Diego, CA: Academic Press.

Tzoneva, M., Forney, K. J., & Keel, P. K. (2015). The influence of gender and age on the association between "Fat-talk" and disordered eating: An examination in men and women from their 20s to their 50s. *Eating Disorders, 23(5),* 439–454. doi:10.1080/10640266.2015.1013396.

Urban Dictionary. (2011). Bodysnarking. Retrieved from http://www.urbandictionary.com/define.php?term=bodysnarking.

U.S. Census Bureau. (2013). Retrieved from https://www.census.gov/content/dam/Census/library/publications/2014/demo/p60–249.pdf.

U.S. Census Bureau. (2015). Retrieved from https://www.census.gov/popest/data/national/asrh/2012/2012-nat-res.html.

USDHHS (U.S. Department of Health and Human Services) Healthy People 2010 (2000). *Understanding and improving health.* Washington, D.C.: U.S. Department of Health and Human Services.

Vaillancourt, T., Brendgen, M., Boivin, M., & Tremblay, R. E. (2003). A longitudinal confirmatory analysis of indirect and physical aggression: Evidence of two factors over time? *Child Development, 74,* 1628–1638.

Vasel, K. (January 9, 2017). It costs $233,610 to raise a child. Retrieved from http://money. cnn.com/2017/01/09/pf/cost-of-raising-a-child-2015/index.html.
Virudachalam, A., Long, J. A., Harhay, M. O., Polsky, D. E. & Feudtner, C. (2013). Prevalence and patterns of cooking dinner at home in the USA: National Health and Nutrition Examination Survey (NHANES) 2007–2008. *Public Health Nutrition, 17(5)*, 1022–1030. Doi:10.1017/S1368980013002589.
Vocks, S., Tuschen-Caffier, B., Pietrowsky, R., Rustenbach, S. J., Kersting, A., Herpertz, S. (2010). Meta-analysis of the effectiveness of psychological and pharmacological treatments for binge eating disorder. *International Journal of Eating Disorders, 434*, 205–217. doi: 10.1002/eat.20696.
Walker, M., Thornton, L., Choudury, M. D., Teevan, J., Bulik, C. M., Levinson, C. A., & Zerwas, S. (2015). Facebook use and disordered eating in college-aged women. *Journal of Adolescent Health, 57(2)*, 157–163. doi:10.1016/j.jadohealth.2015.04.026.
Walsh, R. (2011). Lifestyle and mental health. *American Psychologist, 66(7)*, 579–592. doi:10.1037/a0021769.
Wann, M. (1998). *Fat? So? Because You Don't Have to Apologize for Your Size*. Berkeley, CA: Ten Speed Press.
Warren, A., Martz, D. M., Curtin, L. A., Bazzini, D., & Gagnon, S. (2013). *Understanding gender patterns in fat talk: A qualitative approach to a gender neutral body talk scale*. Poster presented at the annual meeting of the American Psychological Association. Honolulu, Hawaii.
Wasylkiw, L., & Butler, N. A. (2014). Body talk among undergraduate women: Why conversations about exercise and weight loss differentially predict body appreciation. *Journal of Health Psychology, 19(8)*, 1013–1024. doi: 10.1177/1359105313483155.
Wasylkiw, L., & Williamson, M. (2012). Actual reports and perception of body image concerns in young women and their friends. *Sex Roles, 68*, 239–251. doi.org/10.1007/s11199-012-0227-2.
Watson, H. J., & Bulik, C. M. (2013). Update on the treatment of anorexia nervosa: A review of clinical trials, practice guidelines, and emerging interventions. *Psychological Medicine, 43*, 2477–2500. doi.org/10.1017/S0033291712002620.
Waymark, M. (June 23, 2007). Press release, "Dove Evolution Viral Film Wins Film Grand Prix at Cannes Advertising Awards." Retrieved from www.campaignforrealbeauty.ca/flat2.asp?id=7310.
Webb, J. B., Rogers, C. B., Etzel, L., & Padro, M. P. (2018). "Mom, quit fat talking—I'm trying to eat (mindfully) here!": Evaluating a sociocultural model of family fat talk, positive body image, and mindful eating in college women. *Appetite, 126*, 169–175. doi:10.1016/j.appet.2018.04.003.
Webb, J. B., Warren-Findlow, J., Chou, Y. Y., & Adams, L. (2013). Do you see what I see? An exploration of interethnic ideal body size comparisons among college women. *Body Image, 10*, 369–379. doi:10.1016/j.bodyim.2013.03.005.
Weber, L. (2006). *Profits before people? Ethical standards and the marketing of prescription drugs*. Bloomington, Indiana: Indiana University Press.
Wegner, D. M. (1994). *White bears and other unwanted thoughts: The psychology of mental control*. New York, New York: Guilford Press.
Weinstein, H. (1969). How an agency builds a brand—The Virginia Slims story. Papers from the 1969 A.A.A.A. Region Conventions.
Whitaker, R. (2010). *Anatomy of an epidemic: Magic bullets, psychiatric drugs, and the astonishing rise of mental illness in America*. New York: Broadway Paperbacks.
White, C. (May 26, 2015). "Malls segregate plus-sized women!" Melissa McCarthy slams body shaming culture but admits she has moments of doubt when it comes to her appearance. DailyMailwww. Retrieved from http://www.dailymail.co.uk/tvshowbiz/article-3097935/Melissa-McCarthy-slams-body-shamming-culture-admits-moments-doubt-comes-appearance.html.
White, N. (December 2, 2007). Jennifer Love Hewitt: "A size 2 is not fat!" *People Celebrity*. Retrieved from http://people.com/celebrity/jennifer-love-hewitt-a-size-2-is-not-fat/.
Whittal, M. L., Agras, W. S., & Gould, R. A. (1999). Bulimia nervosa: A meta-analysis of psychosocial and pharmacological treatments. *Behavioral Therapist, 30(1)*, 117–135. doi:10.1016/S0005-7894(99)80049-5.

Wiederman, M. W. (2012). Body image and sexual functioning. In T.F. Cash (Ed.), *Encyclopedia of body image and human appearance* (pp. 148–152). Amsterdam: Elsevier.
Wiseman, C. V., Gray, J. J., Mosimann, J. E., & Ahrens, A. H. (1992). Cultural expectations of thinness in women: An update. *International Journal of Eating Disorders, 11(1)*, 85–89. doi:10.1002/1098–108x.
Wolf, N. (2002). *The Beauty Myth*. New York: HarperCollins Publishers, Inc.
Wood-Barcalow, N. L., Tylka, T. L., & Augustus-Horvath, C. L. (2010). "But I like my body": Positive body image characteristics and a holistic model for young-adult women. *Body Image, 7(2)*, 106–116. doi:10.1016.j.bodyim.2010.01.001.
Worchel, S., Grossman, M., & Coutant, D. (1994). *Minority influence in the group context: How group factors affect when the minority will be influential*. In S. Moscovici, A. Mucchi-Faina, & A. Maass (Eds), *Minority Influence* (pp. 97–114). Nelson Hall: Chicago.
World Health Organization. (2007). Spending on health: A global overview Fact Sheet No. 319. Retrieved from http://who.int/mediacentre/factsheets/fs319/en/print.html.
Yates, A., Edman, J., & Aruguete, M. (2004). Ethnic differences in BMI and body/self-dissatisfaction among Whites, Asian subgroups, Pacific Islanders, and African-Americans. *Journal of Adolescent Health, 34(4)*, 300–307. doi:10.1016/j.jadohealth.2003.07.014.
Yelland, C., & Tiggemann, M. (2003). Muscularity and the gay ideal: Body dissatisfaction and disordered eating in homosexual men. *Eating Behaviors, 4(2)*, 107–116. doi:10.1016/S1471–0153(03)00014-X.

Index